The Grotesque in the Fiction of Charles Dickens and Other 19th-century European Novelists

The Grotesque in the Fiction of Charles Dickens and Other 19th-century European Novelists

Edited by

Isabelle Hervouet-Farrar
and Max Vega-Ritter

Cambridge
Scholars
Publishing

The Grotesque in the Fiction of Charles Dickens and Other 19th-century
European Novelists

Edited by Isabelle Hervouet-Farrar
and Max Vega-Ritter

This book first published 2014

Cambridge Scholars Publishing

Lady Stephenson Library, Newcastle upon Tyne, NE6 2PA, UK

British Library Cataloguing in Publication Data
A catalogue record for this book is available from the British Library

ISBN (10): 1-4438-6756-X
ISBN (13): 978-1-4438-6756-6

TABLE OF CONTENTS

Part III: Resisting and Negotiating Change

ACKNOWLEDGMENTS

I would like first of all to thank the members of the Board of the *CELIS (Centre de Recherches sur les Littératures et la Sociopoétique)* of Blaise-Pascal University (Clermont-Ferrand), especially Pascale Auraix-Jonchière and Françoise Le Borgne, who kindly helped Max Véga-Ritter and myself organise the initial conference on "The Grotesque in Dickens's Fiction and 19th-century European Literature" held in Clermont-Ferrand in November 2012. Thanks to the *CELIS* the contributors to the present volume were able to exchange ideas and insights on the grotesque in a spirit of friendly collaboration. Max Véga-Ritter and I are also deeply grateful to the SFEVE (*Société Française des Etudes Victoriennes et Edouardiennes*) for their support.

Carol Koulikourdi and Amanda Millar of Cambridge Scholars Publishing merit special thanks for their kind help and expert guidance in this project.

I am greatly indebted to all the contributors to the present volume for their rich and insightful input. My deepest gratitude goes to Victor Sage, who, when asked, one very, very cold winter morning, on a railway platform in Paris, immediately agreed to take part in the initial conference. Many thanks also to Michael Hollington for his constant generosity and kindness.

My friends and colleagues at Blaise-Pascal University deserve my thanks, but none more so than Anne Rouhette for her encouragement and patience; and above all Sandhya Patel, to whom I am immensely indebted for kindly agreeing to proof-read the chapters which had to be translated from the French. Her expertise is invaluable, as are her constant kindness and support.

Finally many, many thanks to Andy Farrar, for never failing in patience and understanding.

INTRODUCTION

THE GROTESQUE IN THE NINETEENTH CENTURY

ISABELLE HERVOUET-FARRAR

"Real and apparent contradictions abound in discussions of the grotesque; it is an extremely flexible category" (Harpham 1976, 464). Whoever reads into the bulk of criticism attached to the grotesque will see instability as the first defining characteristic of an aesthetic category which Baudelaire called "this indefinable element of beauty [...] that obscure and mysterious element" (Baudelaire 1956, 132). The purpose of this brief introduction is not to provide an exhaustive survey of the many nuances found in the exegesis of the grotesque, which would require a deep foray into historical, architectural, aesthetic and literary approaches, but to sketch in the theories deemed essential to a correct assessment of the prominence and meaning of the grotesque in the context of 19th-century European fiction. The grotesque was theorized in the 19th century notably by Hugo, Ruskin and Baudelaire, who shed light on its significance within Romanticism and Victorian realism. In the following century, the works of the two most influential critics of the grotesque, Wolfgang Kayser and Mikhail Bakhtin, taken together with the comprehensive analysis offered in the 1980s by Geoffrey Galt Harpham, offer a reasonably clear insight into the fundamentally ambivalent concept.

The grotesque famously borrows its name from the accident of the discovery around 1480 of the remains of Nero's *Domus Aurea* and its elaborate ornaments. Its meaning then gradually expanded from the designation of the decorative grotesque of the Renaissance to what may appear as a vague or all-inclusive category. Critics agree, however, on the central idea that the grotesque achieves the harmonious or hair-raising, but always impossible, fusion of heterogeneous elements. The word has come more prosaically to designate an unexpected mixture of comic and horror or of comic and disgust. Laughter is central, since distortion, even taken to its extreme, is not grotesque without laughter. "For an object to be grotesque, it must arouse three responses. Laughter and astonishment are two; either disgust or horror is the third" (Harpham 1976, 463). Harpham's 1976 definition puts to the fore the idea that the grotesque originates in the viewer's gaze and isn't inherent in the grotesque object, an essential aspect which Baudelaire underlined as early as 1855: "Indian and Chinese idols are unaware that they are ridiculous; it is in us, Christians, that their comicality resides" (Baudelaire 1956, 142). To grasp the impact of the viewer's feeling of estrangement and his (at least initial) impossibility to make sense of the grotesque image, one must also remember that the grotesque emerges in a realistic context: "[The grotesque] threat depends for its effectiveness on the efficacy of the everyday, the partial fulfilment of our usual expectations. We must be believers whose faith has been profoundly shaken but not destroyed; otherwise we lose that fear of life and become resigned to absurdity, fantasy, or death" (Harpham 1976, 462).

Virginia Swain explains that "the history of the grotesque is usually described as falling rather neatly into two distinct moments. […] The early grotesque has a carefree, utopian flavour," whereas "the grotesque that arises after the French Revolution," imbued with Romanticism, becomes the expression of "the artist's struggle to overcome feelings of 'helplessness and horror'" (Swain 2004, 3-4). This historical distinction may be too "neat,"[1] but it appealingly points to the traditional distinction between two modes of the grotesque: "the comic and the burlesque" on the one hand, "the abnormal and the horrible" on the other, to use Victor Hugo's terminology (Hugo 1910, 347). Each mode famously has its 20th-century champion: Mikhail Bakhtin and Wolfgang Kayser.

Kayser bases his 1957 analysis of *The Grotesque in Art and Literature* on the Romantic period and the 20th century. Starting from the observation that in the grotesque "the realm of inanimate things is no longer separated from those of plants, animals, and humans" (Kayser 1966, 21), he describes the grotesque as the inscription of familiar elements in a context in which they cease to be recognizable and become menacing, in a manner reminiscent of what Freud develops with *das Unheimliche*. In quite emphatic terms Kayser describes the grotesque world as radically and frighteningly alien, "nocturnal and inhuman" (157), destroying our faith in our world, "instill[ing] fear of life rather than fear of death" (185),

---

[1] The Dance of Death, an important grotesque motif, dates back to long before the Romantic period, and seems to have little "carefree flavour." Besides, as this volume will show, 19th-century grotesque is not concerned only with "helplessness and horror."

rendering us "unable to orient ourselves in the alienated world" (185). Grotesque art, a source of terror, is finally described as an "attempt to invoke and subdue the demonic aspects of the world" (188), though Kayser fails to clearly identify the "dark" or "ominous forces" (188) exorcised by grotesque art.

If Kayser consistently insists on disharmony and alienation, it is, according to Mikhail Bakhtin, because he is incapable of seeing the bigger picture, because he "offers the theory of the Romantic and modernist forms only" (Bakhtin 1984, 46). In 1965 Bakhtin thus goes further back in time to argue that the grotesque is not a post-Renaissance category. In his study of the popular sources of Rabelais's fiction he shows how "grotesque realism" (the literary grotesque) is rooted in medieval carnival culture and fed by festive, universal and ambivalent laughter. Just as medieval carnivals stage political or social inversion through humorous parodies of serious rituals, grotesque realism is based on "degradation [...], the lowering of all that is high, spiritual, ideal, abstract, [...] a transfer to the material level" (19). Such degradation is seen by folk culture in cyclical terms, as part of a movement of universal regeneration celebrating "moments of death and revival, of change and renewal" (9). The emphasis of grotesque realism is placed on materiality and corporeality, "the body and the bodily life hav[ing] [...] a cosmic [...] character" (19). In folk culture, the grotesque body is "a principle of growth" (26), its "lower stratum" (21) a zone of sheer regenerative force.

Geoffrey Harpham's ground-breaking analysis sees beyond grotesque themes and styles to bring to the fore the idea that the grotesque ignores time to create "images of instantaneous process," or "narrative compressed into image" (Harpham 1982, 11). Harpham considers the two main periods of human history concerned with the grotesque: the grotesque of the Renaissance–"the *grottesche*"–and the "grotto-esque" or cave art. Of the Renaissance *grottesche*, he explains that it is characterised by the creation of human-animal or human-vegetal hybrids. Faced with such crossing of species the viewer is arrested between the possibility that it makes no sense and the idea that it means something he/she does not understand. This state of indecision is the grotesque experience. Of the "grotto-esque," Harpham shows how it presents the same crossing of species and reminds us that anthropologists have described hybridity in cave art as corresponding to a primitive, essentially mythic, vision of the world: the anthropomorphic figures are symbols of human-animal intercourse, or of ritual enactment of such union. The grotesque is thus the experience of perceiving "primitive elements in a modern context" (51) and not quite knowing what to make of such presence. As far as critics of the grotesque are concerned, Harpham divides them between the "mythic-minded" like Baudelaire and Bakhtin, who consider the grotesque as a positive force because they perceive mythic or primitive elements as a source of regeneration, and the "less mythic-minded," i.e. those who consider the grotesque with fear and repulsion, like Kayser (69-76).

The grotesque ignores time, but time does not ignore the grotesque: "Each age redefines the grotesque in terms of what threatens its sense of essential humanity" (Harpham 1976, 463). The diversity of sub-genres and aesthetic categories on which 19th-century grotesque fed (caricature, the macabre, drama, tragicomedy, etc.) bears witness to the century's passion for the grotesque, both as an aesthetic category (considered by Hugo as pivotal in the definition of modern literature) and as a way of investigating reality, of questioning 19th-century political and social (r)evolutions. French art-critic André Chastel explains that the hybridity of Renaissance grotesque, "the antithesis of representation," could only appeal to Romantic writers aspiring to creative freedom (Chastel 1988, 25). In 1827, Victor Hugo's influential "Preface to *Cromwell*" turns into a passionate defence of the grotesque as an artistic category: "And so, let addle-pated pedants […] claim that the deformed, the ugly, the grotesque should never be imitated in art; one replies that the grotesque is comedy, and that comedy apparently makes a part of art" (Hugo 1910, 356). For Hugo, the grotesque is a necessary ingredient of comedy, which he sees as a combination of the sublime and the grotesque, because the grotesque is an essential aspect of reality, of "all creation" (350): "everything in creation is not humanly *beautiful*, […] the ugly exists beside the beautiful, the unshapely beside the graceful, the grotesque on the reverse of the sublime, evil with good, darkness with light" (345). If for Hugo the grotesque testifies to man's imperfect nature, "the human beast" (350), it is not, as in Ruskin, a sign of man's imperfect vision, which if removed would leave only the sublime. Hugo's grotesque exists next to the sublime and is necessary to man's apprehension of it, as "a halting-place, a mean term, a starting-point whence one rises toward the beautiful with a fresher and keener perception" (349). Hugo may describe the grotesque as inferior to the beautiful or the sublime—in his view it remains, from an artistic point of view, "the richest source that nature can offer art" (348).

In 1853, in Part III, Chapter 3 of *Stones of Venice*, Ruskin "examine[s] into the nature and essence of the Grotesque" (Ruskin 2009, 114) and establishes two important distinctions. The first is between "sportive" (or "playful") grotesque and "terrible grotesque." Ruskin thus writes: "The grotesque is, in almost all cases, composed of two elements, one ludicrous, the other fearful; [...] as one or other of these elements prevails, the grotesque falls into two branches, sportive grotesque and terrible grotesque" (127). Both modes of the grotesque can be "noble" or "ignoble,"–the second distinction established by Ruskin. Ignoble grotesque is an illegitimate act of artistic creation, "work as false as it is monstrous, a mass of blunt malice and obscene ignorance" (150). Ruskin rejects the grotesque's inventive licence and is indignant at the apparent pointlessness of Renaissance ornamental grotesque in which he can discern no moral or spiritual truths. Ruskin thus logically sees Raphael's work as "the fruit of [a] great [mind] degraded to base objects" (144). For Ruskin, ornamentation must be "rational" (145).

His insistence on noble grotesque shows however that Ruskin has a positive vision of many forms of the grotesque. Even sportive grotesque, the product of "the minds of inferior workmen" (132), can be noble as "the fruits of a rejoicing energy in uncultivated minds" (134). Terrible grotesque, "this [...] more interesting branch of imaginative work" (137), originates in fear, "the fear which arises out of the contemplation of great powers in destructive operation, and generally from the perception of the presence of death" (138). Fear of the divine is experienced by the artist or workman of noble grotesque; terrible grotesque, when noble, is thus contiguous to the sublime. If Ruskin agrees with Hugo that grotesque art remains the sign of man's imperfect vision and fallen nature, he doesn't share Hugo's conception of the grotesque as necessary to man's perception of the sublime. For Ruskin, the grotesque is always an imperfect artistic expression susceptible, as "the mind of the workman becomes informed with better knowledge, and capable of more earnest exertion" (145), of "pass[ing] into perfect sublime" (146).

In "On the Essence of Laughter" (1857), like Hugo, Baudelaire adopts a deeply Romantic approach to the grotesque.[2] Like Hugo and Ruskin, he sees the grotesque as the sign of man's fallen condition, since laughter is always the expression of "the Satanic in man" (Baudelaire 1956, 137). Baudelaire's analysis breaks new ground however in that he sees man's fallen nature in religious but also mythical terms. The grotesque is the primitive expression of an archaic past: "the laughter caused by the grotesque has about it something profound, primitive and axiomatic, [...] [close] to the innocent life and to absolute joy" (144). From such a premise, Baudelaire distinguishes between absolute comic–the grotesque– and significative comic. "[Significative] comic is an imitation mixed with

---

[2] Baudelaire also expresses his love for European masters of the grotesque like Hogarth, Cruikshank or Goya in "Some Foreign Caricaturists" (see Baudelaire 1956-2).

a certain creative faculty" (143), whereas the grotesque, that "intoxication of laughter [...] both terrible and irresistible" (148), is "a creation mixed with a certain imitative faculty–imitative, that is, of elements pre-existing in nature" (143) and the expression of the superiority "of man over nature" (143). The grotesque, Baudelaire seems to lament, is not produced by French artists because it is not suited to French mindsets: "In France, the land of lucid thought and demonstration, where the natural and direct aim of art is utility, we generally find the significative type" (145-6). The grotesque is however seen as a true European production:

> Germany, sunk in her dreams, will afford us excellent specimens of the absolute comic. There all is weighty, profound and excessive. To find true comic savagery, however, you have to cross the Channel and visit the foggy realms of spleen. Happy, noisy, carefree Italy abounds in the innocent variety. [...] The Spaniards [...] are quick to arrive at the cruel stage, and their most grotesque fantasies often contain a dark element. (146)

It is time for a quick visit to "the foggy realms of spleen" to say a few words about the grotesque of Dickens's fiction, in the wake of Michael Hollington's wide-ranging analysis (Hollington 1984). If Dickens was wary of high Romanticism,[3] be it English or European, he famously wished to explore "the Romantic side of familiar things"[4] and there found the grotesque. His "streaky bacon" conception of fiction, as expressed in Chapter 17 of *Oliver Twist*,[5] has a great deal in common with Hugo's vision of the Romantic drama: "[...] the romantic drama [...] would lead the audience constantly from sobriety to laughter, from mirthful excitement to heart-breaking emotion [...]. For the drama is the grotesque in conjunction with the sublime, the soul within the body; it is tragedy beneath comedy" (Hugo 1910, 383). Even leaving Hugo's definition aside, Dickens's art includes, or offers examples of, all the facets of the grotesque mentioned by 19th- and 20th-century theorists. Dickens's grotesque is alternately funny and violent, carefree and sinister. On the sunny side, and because "energy and joy are the father and mother of the grotesque," as G. K. Chesterton once wrote (Chesterton 2014, Chapter 6) Dickens shares Baudelaire's love of pantomime and indulges in sheer farce. On the

---

[3] See John 2001.
[4] A phrase found in his 1853 Preface to *Bleak House*.
[5] "It is the custom on the stage, in all good murderous melodramas, to present the tragic and the comic scenes, in as regular alternation, as the layers of red and white in a side of streaky bacon" (Dickens 1980, 168).

sombre side, he also shares Baudelaire's fascination with the dislocation, incongruity or ugliness of human bodies and constantly displays his awareness of the corporeality of the grotesque. If Bakhtin saw the grotesque body as a source of regeneration but seems to have failed to perceive its horror, fragmentation and dismemberment are often brought to the fore by Dickens, in whose fiction the hybrid, fragmented grotesque body is obsessively represented as a source of fascination, not untinged with repulsion and horror (for example Carker's teeth) or fun (the ubiquitous leg[6]).

Dickens's grotesque is rooted in the exploration of "the Romantic side of familiar things," and thus serves the representation of a new reality, bearing witness to his conviction that in the wake of the disruptions brought about by the advent of an industrial society, "'real life' is more grotesque and fantastical than anything the artistic imagination can produce" (Hollington 1984, ii). The incongruous distortion which characterizes the grotesque becomes an essential element of Dickens's faithful depiction of reality, and the contradiction is only apparent: Harpham reminds us that "by the end of the nineteenth century, it was more common than not to speak of the 'naturalness' of the grotesque."[7] The grotesque is not necessarily pure fantasy but serves for example to denounce the devastation caused by the industrial age: thus the "strange engines" of Chapter 45 of *The Old Curiosity Shop*, "like tortured creatures [...] wild and [...] untamed [...], [screech] and [turn] round and round again" (Dickens 1985, 424). In Dickens's fiction, 19th-century reality becomes "grotesque and wild but not impossible" as he explains in the 1848 Preface to the novel (42).

"To think of Dickens in relation to the grotesque is almost inevitably to stray freely and frequently across national boundaries" (Hollington 1984, 7). This book thus proposes to address Dickens's use of the complex aesthetic category in relation with other 19th-century European writers of the grotesque. This crossing of geographical boundaries aims at providing a close look into the reasons behind the extensive use of such a favoured mode of expression. Rather than providing the reader with a mere survey, the chapters here use intertextuality and comparative or cultural analysis to shed light on Dickens's influences (both given and received) as well as to compare and contrast his use of the grotesque with that of other key

---

[6] See Chapter Twelve of present volume.
[7] This quote is from Harpham's preface to the 2006 edition of his 1982 book (Aurora: The Davies Group Publishers, xxv).

European writers like Victor Hugo and Charles Baudelaire, Nikolai Gogol, William Makepeace Thackeray and Thomas Hardy.

The first section is centred on the first half of the century and looks at the fundamental texts and techniques that shaped 19th-century novelists' conception of the grotesque, notably Dickens's. French specialist of the literary grotesque Dominique Peyrache-Leborgne insists on the visual dimension of the grotesque and the technical developments which made possible the emergence of the "iconotext," the grotesque combination of text and image explored to the full in Nodier's *L'Histoire du roi de Bohême et de ses sept châteaux* (1830), and in *Oliver Twist*. In Chapter 2 Sylvie Jeanneret also considers the visual facets of the grotesque. She analyses the spectacular staging of bodies in Victor Hugo's fiction and highlights its political dimension. Anne Rouhette then situates Dickens's love of Smollett in the context of their shared predilection for grotesque effects through the examples of the human-raven hybrid and the figure of the idiot. In Chapter 4 Dickens specialist Michael Hollington documents the impact that Dickens's 1844-5 trip to Italy had on his creation of grotesque characters in the *Christmas Books* and *Dombey and Son*, and suggests that Dickens's obsession with giants can be partly traced back to his visit of the *Sala dei Giganti* in Mantua's *Palazzo del Te*.

The second section looks into the grotesque as a strategy of representation of 19th-century reality. It focuses on how writers resorted to the grotesque as a strategy aiming at domesticating change, yoking together unconnected or antagonistic emotional, social and political drives and aspirations in order to verbalise and make sense of a fast-changing world. Thus Florence Clerc explains how Gogol used grotesque aesthetics to represent Russian reality as discordant and ambivalent, poised between carnivalesque and sombre distortion. The analysis of Gogol's grotesque expressivity, she argues, enables one to grasp his kinship with Dickens. In Chapter 6 Jacqueline Fromonot's close textual analysis of *The Book of Snobs* shows how Thackeray "truly builds an aesthetics and a poetics of the grotesque" in order to lampoon and denounce the false values of that particular section of British society. The birth of the modern metropolis, a key 19th-century grotesque motif, is then considered by both Bérangère Chaumont and Isabel Vila-Cabanes. Bérangère Chaumont examines how Nerval's perambulations in the Parisian night served as a pretext for putting literary realism to the test; Isabel Vila-Cabanes studies the many descriptions made by Dickens's and Baudelaire's *flâneurs* of the grotesque freaks populating the "uncanny metropolis." Both chapters insist on the fact that at textual level, only grotesque aesthetics were deemed suitable for rendering the paradoxes of modern urban experience. In Chapter 9

Max Véga-Ritter delineates the characteristics of Dickens's collective and individual grotesque monsters from *The Old Curiosity Shop* to *A Tale of Two Cities*. Finally Thierry Goater analyses Hardy's use of the grotesque in *The Mayor of Casterbridge*, whose hybridity, he argues, is also generic, to show how the regenerative power of the grotesque enables the artist to "renew a perception dulled by habit" and unveil the monstrosity of the modern world.

The third section explores darker facets of the Romantic and Victorian grotesque as symbolic expression of resistance to change. The analysis ranges from the difficult confrontation with scientific discoveries–notably Darwin's theory of evolution–to the question of gender. In an essay on *The Mystery of Edwin Drood,* I have examined grotesque metamorphosis resulting from the unsettling permanence of the past in a modern context, due notably to the characters' rejection of progress. Fiction-writer and specialist of the Gothic Victor Sage explores Dickens's persistent fondness for the "Leg" and other body parts which crop up in his work, notably in *Our Mutual Friend*. Victor Sage situates Dickens's passion for paleontological tropes in the context of his allegiance to his friend Professor Owen, the famous expert in comparative anatomy. Also drawing on this allegiance, Delphine Cadwallader then contrasts Dickens's response to Darwin's theory of evolution with Wilkie Collins's. The two following chapters examine grotesque metamorphosis from the angle of gender. The common assumption that the female characters of Dickens's fiction who do not conform to Victorian stereotypes are to be read as grotesque is the central oversimplification corrected by Marianne Camus in Chapter 14. Gilbert Pham-Thanh then looks towards the early 20th century to explore grotesque masculinity in Max Beerbohm's *Zuleika Dobson* and to argue that in this novel, which belongs to the Oxford Novel tradition, grotesque deformity marks the disempowerment of patriarchy at diegetic and discursive levels. As a conclusion to this third section, Florence Bigo-Renault considers the renewed interest in the grotesque in very recent TV adaptations of the novels of the Dickens canon. Such renewed interest attests to the regenerative power of the grotesque–this distinctive feature of Dickens's work and of 19th-century European fiction.

References

Bakhtin, Mikhail. (1965) 1984. *Rabelais and His World*. Translated by Hélène Iswolsky. Bloomington: Indiana University Press.

Baudelaire, Charles. (1857) 1956. "On the Essence of Laughter." In *The Mirror of Art, Critical Studies by Charles Baudelaire*. Translated by Jonathan Mayne, 131-54. New York: Doubleday Anchor Books.

—. (1857) 1956. "A Few Foreign Caricaturists." In *The Mirror of Art, Critical Studies by Charles Baudelaire*, edited and translated by Jonathan Mayne, 179-90. New York: Doubleday & Co. [1956-2]

Chastel, André. 1988. *La Grottesque*. Paris: Editions Le Promeneur.

Chesterton, Gilbert Keith. (1903) 2014. *Robert Browning*. The Project Gutenberg eBook.
http://www.gutenberg.org/files/13342/13342-h/13342-h.htm

Dickens, Charles. (1837-9) 1980. *Oliver Twist*. Harmondsworth: Penguin Books.

—. (1841) 1985. *The Old Curiosity Shop*. Harmondsworth: Penguin Books.

Harpham, Geoffrey Galt. 1976. "The Grotesque, First Principles." *The Journal of Aesthetics and Art Criticism*, Vol. 34, No. 4: 461-8.
Stable URL: http://www.jstor.org/stable/430580. Accessed: 01/08/2012

—. 1982. *On the Grotesque: Strategies of Contradiction in Art and Literature*. Princeton: Princeton University Press.

Hollington, Michael. 1984. *Dickens and the Grotesque*. Beckenham (Kent): Croom Helm.

Hugo, Victor. (1827) 1910. "Preface to *Cromwell*." Translated by J.R. Effinger. In *Prefaces and Prologues to Famous Books*, edited by Eliot, Charles W., 337-87. New-York: P.F. Collier & Son.

John, Juliet. 2001. *Dickens's Villains: Melodrama, Character, Popular Culture*. Oxford: Oxford University Press.

Kayser, Wolfgang. (1957) 1966. *The Grotesque in Art and Literature*. Translated by Ulrich Weisstein. New-York: McGraw-Hill.

Ruskin, John. (1853) 2009. *Stones of Venice, Vol. III: The Fall*. The Project Gutenberg eBook.
http://gutenberg.readingroo.ms/3/0/7/5/30756/30756-h/30756-h.htm

Swain, Virginia. 2004. *Grotesque Figures: Baudelaire, Rousseau, and the Aesthetics of Modernity*. Baltimore: The Johns Hopkins University Press.

PART I

INFLUENCES AND EARLY FORMS

CHAPTER ONE

L'HISTOIRE DU ROI DE BOHÊME AND OLIVER TWIST UNDER CRUIKSHANK'S PATRONAGE: THE DYNAMICS OF TEXT AND IMAGE AT THE CORE OF THE GROTESQUE IN THE NOVEL OF THE 1830s

DOMINIQUE PEYRACHE-LEBORGNE

In his book on Romantic vignettes, the art historian and Baudelaire's friend Champfleury wrote in 1883: "There is no other period in history, it seems to me, when pencil and the engraver's burin formed one body with literature so closely as they did during Romanticism"[1] (Champfleury 1883, v). In *Le Métier d'illustrateur*, Philippe Kaenel confirms that "the genesis of commercial and popular illustration coincided with the history of Romanticism" (Kaenel 1996, 39). The novel of the beginning of the 1830s is indeed linked to the rapid development of illustration, thanks to etchings and on-wood engravings. From the 1820s, the publication of novels in magazines also favoured the development of illustration. The engravings illustrating novels were displayed in shop windows to attract potential readers whenever a new installment was published. There were thus commercial reasons behind the development of the illustrated novel. What this paper wishes to examine however is the intrinsic link–beyond the strictly chronological concomitance–between the emergence of the grotesque as the dominant aesthetic category of European Romanticism and the growing recourse to novelistic illustration and to iconotexts–or bi-generic works. This close alliance of text and image brings to the fore the specificity of the literary grotesque, highlighting the differences with other genres like the comic–namely its essential visual quality. In France, the publication of Nodier's *Histoire du roi de Bohême et de ses sept châteaux*

---

[1] All translations from the French in this chapter are mine unless specified otherwise in the references.

(1830) marked the beginning of such interaction of image and text, the novel acting as an iconotext conceived as such from the very beginning by its author.[2] Nodier's novel is the result of the novelist's close and amicable collaboration with the illustrator, Tony Johannot,[3] and then with the engraver Porret. The result was a new and unique category of work in French production, a montage in which fifty vignettes engage in an ironic, disruptive and complex dialogue with the text. During the same period in England, there was already a solid tradition of literary illustration established by a group of caricaturists who devoted some of their time and talent to the illustration of novels. The most famous among them was George Cruikshank (1792-1878), who produced engravings for novels by Cervantes, Smollett, Fielding, Sterne and Goldsmith. He illustrated Dickens's *Sketches by Boz,* published as a two-volume set in 1836; then *Oliver Twist* (1838) which Dickens wanted from the start to be a bi-generic work. In France, Cruikshank was well-known by 1830 and had inspired Monnier and Daumier. Nodier claimed to have drawn the inspiration for the eccentric and satiric orientation of his novel from Cruikshank. Thus, in spite of their differences, these two examples of iconotexts, the Romantic and the Victorian, *L'Histoire du roi de Bohême* and *Oliver Twist*, were both placed–though to a different degree–under Cruikshank's patronage. The two works suggest a diametrically opposed conception of the novel, but they share the same vision of illustration as an integral part of the grotesque.

L'Histoire du roi de Bohême was both "one of the first important illustrated books" (Boisacq-Generet 1994, 270) of French Romanticism and one of the first novels to explicitly combine Romanticism and the tradition of the eccentric narrative. Such an approach runs of course parallel to Hugo's first theoretical and poetic writings on the grotesque ("The Preface to *Cromwell*" in 1827, *The Hunchback of Notre-Dame* in

---

[2] In his work on illustrations in French novels in the 18th century, Christophe Martin explains that "the illustration of a literary work was organized by printers-*cum*-booksellers: they usually selected the artist and the segments to illustrate. Apart from a few exceptions (Rousseau, Restif), the authors had no say in the matter." Because of the high costs of illustrations, "booksellers usually concentrated their attention on works already considered as classics" (Martin 2005, 4).

[3] A prolific vignette-artist, Johannot was one of the main illustrators of French Romanticism, esp. between 1826 and 1850. He illustrated, among others, the works of W. Scott, Balzac, A. Dumas, Goethe, Hoffmann, Hugo, Jules Janin, Lamartine, Eugène Sue, George Sand and A. de Vigny (Cf. Marie 1925).

1831), but is not informed by the Hugolian alliance of the grotesque and the sublime. *L'Histoire du roi de Bohême,* based on an anecdote briefly mentioned in *Tristram Shandy* and not at all referred to in Nodier's novel, was actually written to put to the test the combination of the eccentric and the grotesque in a literary text. It also explored the limits of writing and of the association of text and illustration.

The originality of the work lies first in the radical deconstruction of the novel. Every aspect of *L'Histoire du roi de Bohême* works as a metatextual game and as a matter of literary auto-derision. The loosely-connected chapters often only have in common their titles in "*–tion*" (such as "Convention," "Demonstration," "Objection," but also "Dentition," "Equitation," "Mystification" or "Distraction"). The narrator–a new literary Don Quixote–is accompanied by two companions for his novelistic adventures, one called "Breloque" and the other "Don Pic de Fanferluchio," two paper characters whose impossible names[4] reveal that all literary enterprise and academic knowledge are both imposing and derisory.

It is therefore a light-hearted novel without a plot or a hero which playfully does away with diegesis and sometimes results in pages in which illustrations replace the text. The originality of the grotesque attempt therefore also lies in the disconcerting effect produced by the intertwining of vignettes and words. Tony Johannot's drawings deliberately interfere with a discursive fabric which is itself overtly disjointed. Such imbrication of two modes of representation was possible thanks to the new wood-engraving technique invented in England by Thomas Bewick and Charles Thompson. This technique allowed greater correspondence between text and image[5] whereas throughout the 18th century and at the beginning of the 19th, the wood-cut technique of Bewick's predecessors meant that text and image had to be placed on two separate pages.

Nodier and Tony Johannot were therefore able to opt out of the simple system of illustration and to write four-handedly a work in which images could turn into text and text–or rather words–could become images. Such imbrication of the two media came in a variety of forms, original ones but also traditional ones like historiated initials, arabesque frames or tailpieces. As to the new practices, they introduced new ways in which vignettes could interact with text, by illustrating, not the adventure, but

---

[4] "Breloque" means "bracelet charm;" the name "Don Pic de Fanferluchio" sounds Italian and evokes the "acme (Pic) of frills and flounces" (in French "franfreluches").
[5] Bewick's technique consisted in carving hard wood against the grain, which allowed greater detail and finer engraving than in the past (cf. Mélot 1984).

sometimes only a word or an idea. Further vignettes could be entirely unrelated to the text, or subvert the traditional hierarchy between text and illustration and therefore the concept of illustration itself. In such cases, the image comes first and the text is simply used to clarify meaning. In other examples, images appear where the reader expects words, thereby disrupting the visual and graphic continuity of sentences which are left unfinished. This extreme case is found in the chapter entitled "Convention," in which the image of Don Pic de Fanferluchio, carnivalesque scholar of Romantic culture, is seen entering the text.[6]

Furthermore, among the purely textual effects we can also note the devices used to reinforce the illusion of an *ut pictura poesis*, i.e. the illusion of an almost complete fusion of narrative and iconography. Liliane Louvel in *L'Oeil du texte* distinguishes between several principles of "interpicturality," some in the mode of what she calls "hypopicturality" (the narrativisation of a painting or of a painting-effect in the style of...), others in that of "archipicturality" (the main currents in painting acting on the narrative modes) (Louvel 1998, 151-5). It is precisely at the level of interpicturality that the reference to Cruikshank is crucial since his work serves both as a model ("hypopicturality") creating *mise-en-abyme*, and as an informing principle ("archipicturality"). It would only be slight exaggeration to say that Tony Johannot was the illustrator of *L'Histoire du roi de Bohême* but George Cruikshank its secret inspirer. This comes as no surprise in the light of Nodier's love of English culture,[7] and how much influence the golden age of English caricature had on 19th-century French culture (from Monnier to Daumier and Gavarni, from Nodier to Baudelaire and Champfleury).[8] Werner Hofmann notes that Daumier as well as Monnier, who was Cruikshank's friend, owed their inspiration in part to English satiric imagery; and that Thackeray, staying in Paris around 1830, noted everywhere how influential English caricature was.[9]

---

[6] To view Johannot's illustrations, go to
http://gallica.bnf.fr/ark:/12148/bpt6k108013v/f3.image
[7] Nodier was inspired by Ann Radcliffe and Walter Scott; he edited Byron's works and published *Promenade de Dieppe aux montagnes d'Ecosse (A Walk from Dieppe to the Mountains of Scotland)* in 1821.
[8] In his *Histoire de la caricature moderne*, devoted almost exclusively to the French tradition, Champfleury evokes the influence of Cruikshank's Punch on Daumier's political cartoons, notably his caricatures of Adolphe Thiers (Champfleury 1865, 45-6).
[9] Werner Hofmann is probably thinking of the chapter "Caricatures and Lithography in Paris" published by Thackeray in 1840 in *The Paris Sketch Book* (Hofmann 1958, 44). Philippe Kaenel underlines the frequency of exchanges between Paris and London: "Eugène Lami, Henry Monnier, William Thackeray,

In Nodier's work, the explicit reference to Cruikshank first creates a form of metatextual interruption in the middle of the narrative when Nodier takes on the theatrical role of a narrator himself, busy reading or looking at an image:

"By Popokambu," I cried, dropping Cuyshank's Punch (*sic*). (Nodier 1979, 219)

Although left unspecified, the allusion to Punch seems to be a reference to the series of engravings that Cruikshank did in 1828 depicting puppet theatre and Punch and Judy. In the character of Punch, we find all the main ingredients of the grotesque, and more specifically of the Romantic grotesque: visual comedy based on the character's deformed body and excessive gesticulation, timeless, decontextualized comedy melding the ancient and the modern, popular, anti-classic and non-academic art, relying on artifices and language opposed to those of scholarly culture, e.g. simple drawing and the rejection of complex allegorical references; finally an overtly meta-literary grotesque since in Nodier, the reference to Punch comes after a relatively long section on the mock-heroic praise of the *commedia dell'arte* character, who is raised to the rank of symbol of modernity and Romantic irony.[10]

Similarly, Cruikshank's taste for popular culture and his early interest in literary illustration enabled him to expand his range of caricatures and to separate his grotesque drawings from any specific socio-political context.[11] Did Nodier know about Cruikshank's series of wood-engravings inspired by popular literary sources, destined to advertise lotteries (*Lottery Puffs and Advertisements*) and in which playful structures based on words

---

Gavarni, Gustave Doré and Edmond Morin saw a great deal of their English neighbours and took part in shared editorial ventures" (Kaenel 1996, 37).

[10] Ironically placed under the double patronage of Cruikshank and of the German theorists of Romanticism (notably Schlegel), Nodier's praise of Punch undermines academic culture and thwarts all attempts at turning Romanticism into serious theoretical literature. The two chapters devoted to Punch are entitled "Insurrection" and "Dissertation," the former parodying the precepts of the Romantic revolution, the latter ironically staging the inherent contradictions of Romanticism itself, which is seen as doomed to contest Classicism while using its rhetorical figures, reducing to pastiche or parody all attempts at producing a new type of serious literature.

[11] Besides the *Punch and Judy* series, between 1810 and 1826 Cruikshank produced numerous engravings illustrating popular English tales or tales by Grimm; as well as little humoristic drawings used for advertisements in which text and image interact.

in –*tion*, as in Nodier,[12] appear? Similarly carnivalesque inversion of the order in which the text should be read is also a characteristic of both. For example, Cruikshank's advert for the lottery reads from bottom to top, whereas Nodier's text can sometimes only be read by turning the page upside down, or by going to and fro between the text and the image next to it. In the chapters on Punch, a drawing by Tony Johannot is very similar to Cruikshank's engravings. Placed on a level with the text, the drawing takes over from the narrative and completes the unfinished sentence. The drawing provides immediate access to reality, which abstract words might not do. In this particular case, the image becomes a text in its own right. In other instances, the text becomes image: hence Punch's box is as though materialized by framing words in large font and capital letters which are hollow and shaded and form a parallelogram. Here words regain their primary status as ideograms–or image-words.

When it is used to expand meaning, the image sometimes also ironically conflicts with the apparent or literal meaning of the text and thus reveals what has been left unsaid or should remain taboo. In this case, the relationship between the two media can be defined as ironic dialogism, the iconotext being the pretext for role-play between novelist and cartoonist, one feigning to respect propriety and to show due deference to monarchy and censorship, the other developing political satire thanks to the resources of graphic caricature. For example in the final chapter ironically entitled "Approbation," the text parodically authorizes the publication of the book that Nodier is writing, *L'Histoire du roi de Bohême*.[13] On the contrary, the image represents an ageing, wrinkled Charles X, holding a gigantic pair of scissors in his hands which represent his immoderate passion for censorship. The reference to Cruikshank as the underlying figure of archipicturality then takes on its full meaning, since it is the entire tradition of graphic caricature which implicitly becomes a system of comic criticism that can be transposed into the language of the anti-novel.

The variety of iconic strategies used in *L'Histoire du roi de Bohême et de ses sept châteaux* therefore considerably reinforces the grotesque effect

---

[12] At the end of his novel Nodier explains that the titles of the chapters (made of words in –*tion*) are inspired by an old French game in which everyone has to provide an answer in –*ion* to the question "What shall we put in my *corbillon* ?" A "*corbillon*" is a small basket.

[13] "I, the undersigned Expert Weigher of Ideas, Official Translator of Equivocal Words, […] Timbuktu's Literary Provost, hereby certify that I have tried to read *L'Histoire du roi de Bohême et de ses sept châteaux*, and that the said novel is neither impious, obscene, seditious nor satiric" (397-8).

of the eccentric novel. For such a bi-generic work, it would be unthinkable to publish the text without the illustrations. Never in the 19th century was the combination of the two media pushed so far. It is difficult to find another work in which images so radically disrupt reading habits as in *L'Histoire du roi de Bohême*, and this in spite of the inventiveness found in iconotexts such as *Voyage où il vous plaira* (with drawings by Tony Johannot, 1842), *Un autre Monde* (1842) and *Scènes de la vie privée et publique des animaux* by illustrator Jean-Jacques Grandville (1840-2); or, in England, *Vanity Fair* (1847-8)[14] and *A Book of Nonsense* by Edward Lear (an instance of the incongruous, published in 1846). Did Sterne's influence wane more rapidly in England than in France and Germany? The novelistic and illustrative strategies chosen by Dickens and his publisher may seem relatively conventional when compared to Nodier's experiments, since the traditional wood-cut technique chosen rendered compulsory the separation of text and illustration.

A novel such as *Oliver Twist* nevertheless attests even today to what the development of the literary grotesque owes to the art of illustration and the influence of caricaturists. The collaboration between Dickens and Cruikshank, which started with *Sketches by Boz*, shows the importance of such interpicturality. As a title for his *Sketches*, Dickens had initially considered *Sketches by Boz and Cuts by Cruikshank*, or even *Etchings by Boz and Wood-Cuts by Cruikshank*, which explicitly associated writing with drawing and the visual arts (see Monot 1986, 1550). Even if Cruikshank's influence was played down by Dickens when *Oliver Twist* was published, it is clear that the synergy worked both ways: first because sections of the novel were inspired by iconic elements that make up the interpicturality of the novel (see Hill 1981, 55-62), secondly because Cruikshank, who did not always see the final version of the text, was allowed a certain amount of leeway and therefore left his personal mark on the novel's general tone.[15]

The rhetoric of laughter in *Oliver Twist* is heavily influenced by several iconic references which create the inherently grotesque (i.e. concrete and visual) dimension of verbal comedy. As Michael Hollington has shown, grotesque iconicity is here mainly based on three elements: the writing of Hogarthian scenes, the general influence of pantomime, and that

---

[14] Thackeray illustrated *Vanity Fair* himself mixing several techniques (full-page illustrations as well as vignettes). He also chose a somewhat Sternian narrator whom he represented wearing carnivalesque costume and hat.

[15] "Cruikshank drew Fagin, Sikes and Nancy before the story was written at all. The originals were models or drinking acquaintances of Cruikshank." (Jack Lindsay, "At Closer Grips," in Hollington 1995, Vol. II, 175).

of graphic caricature (Hollington 1984, 7-25; 58-65). Hogarth, referred to in the 1841 preface to the third edition and praised for the realism of his London street scenes, appears as the original model shared by the two artists–and the true founding father of English caricature.[16] And as in some of Hogarth's or Cruikshank's engravings, Dickens's world relays an impression of number and crowds which reflects the collective dimension of social satire. It is essentially in the depiction of the multitude of secondary characters that strategies that complement the grotesque are to be found: the caricature of worthies shaping social satire; eccentricity interfering with the sentimental sphere and creating characters both comic and amiable; finally the grotesque of physical and moral deformity provoking neither clear derision nor clear adhesion, but ambivalent reactions whenever the reader encounters Fagin, his accomplices and the murky world of criminality.

The first group of characters brings us closer to Cruikshank's *London Characters*, a series of engravings of 1827-9 in which a potbellied beadle wearing an impressive button-coat and a cocked hat could be understood as Dickens's inspiration for the (in)famous Bumble who plays such a significant part in *Oliver Twist*. Dickens continually draws on recurrent and concrete images as his inspiration for his small world of miserly, middle-class materialists; the ancient carnivalesque tradition–the allegory of thin men and fat ones, so often developed by Brueghel–being thus updated again in modern caricature, both verbal and iconic.[17]

Inspiring the text and inspired by it, Cruikshank's work as an illustrator bears witness to his developed understanding of Dickens's rhetoric of description. In his illustrations, the caricaturist's characters too are systematically contrasted, and are placed within "the realm of contrasts and anomalies" to use Jean Emelina's definition of the comic (Emelina 1991, 43). As in the ancient carnivalesque tradition, faces and profiles fall within the province of expressionist excess with their prominent outlines and twisted expressions. This type of imagery is entirely in keeping with the comic-grotesque described by Bakhtin:

---

[16] Dickens knew Hogarth's works very well and acknowledged his influence when he chose "A Parish Boy's Progress" as the sub-title of his novel. The phrase evokes Bunyan's *Pilgrim's Progress* (1678-84) of course, but also Hogarth's series "A Harlot's Progress," whose last two engravings represent scenes very much like those in Chapter One of *Oliver Twist*.

[17] There are numerous examples of this type of character in the novel: Mr. Fang, Mr. Gamfield, Mr. Bumble, Mrs Mann or Mrs Corney, to name but a few.

Of all the features of the human face, the nose and mouth play the most
important part in the grotesque image of the body. [...] The grotesque is
interested only in protruding eyes [...] [since] it is looking for that which
protrudes from the body, all that seeks to go out beyond the body's
confines. (Bakhtin 1984, 316)

Finally, Cruikshank's particularly dynamic and gesticulating style[18]
perfectly matches Dickens's taste for pantomime. Extravagantly
expressive or writhing faces and bodies are found throughout, in the
narrative and its illustrations, creating a subterranean web of similitudes
between the different spheres of the novel: the comic-grotesque sphere of
the worthies, the sentimental circle of Oliver's friends and adoptive
family, and the sinister world of criminality. After the famous inaugural
scene in which Bumble explains why he chooses to give Oliver the
patronym of "Twist," the reader finds the motif of torsion and contortion
in the descriptions of other characters: Noah Claypole for example, the
other orphan from the workhouse, turned crook, who is both Fagin's dupe
and his accomplice and whose body regularly wriggles like an eel.
Similarly Toby Crackit's sparse hair is "tortured into long corkscrew
curls" (Dickens 1980, 209) and the "little ugly hump-backed man" who
guards the thieves' den "[a] misshapen little demon [...] twist[s] himself,
dexterously, from the doctor's grasp" (286-7). Then there is Fagin who
devises his Machiavellian plans "busying his bony hands in the folds of
his tattered garment" (403). Even Mr. Brownlow, Oliver's benefactor,
greets the boy with an expression going through "a very great variety of
odd contortions" (129). Grimwig, Brownlow's old bachelor friend, first
appears dressed in incongruous clothing, making numerous facial
contortions and burlesque gestures borrowed from pantomime (147).
Finally Mr. Losberne, the philanthropic doctor-*cum*-detective (to meet the
needs of melodrama), answers "with many wry faces" (375) when told
about a risky plan to arrest the thieves and protect Oliver.

In such a context, the most remarkable element is that the dialogue
between text and image enables the bi-generic work to go beyond the
models offered by Hogarthian grotesque realism and to create a new, more
somber–almost fantastic–type of grotesque, which generates a mixture of
contradictory tones and reactions. We find here one specificity of the
grotesque, if compared to satire and caricature: it has a wider range of

---

[18] Cf. Baudelaire, "I would say that the essence of Cruikshank's grotesque is an
extravagant violence of gesture and movement, and a kind of explosion, so to
speak, within the expression. Each one of his little creatures mimes his part in a
frenzy and ferment, like a pantomime character" (Baudelaire 1956, 183).

tones and goes from the comic to the unfamiliar and the uncanny. Satire usually remains univocal or monological, because inextricably linked to clearly-defined moral and social references, but the grotesque can free itself from all realistic reference and remain semantically equivocal, thanks to the range of contrasted emotions it stages and provokes. Mixing the influences of the Gothic novel, of ancient demonology and of modern caricature, Dickens thus peopled his London world with poverty-stricken figures, sinister elderly men and women with grimacing faces. Macabre laughter is thus made spectacular (in the original sense of the word) and becomes the obsessional leitmotif which gives the depiction of madness or abject poverty its scandalous dimension. One of the first key scenes of terrifying grotesque is found in Chapter 5, when Oliver and the undertaker visit a poverty-stricken family in which the mother has starved to death. The scene is highly visual, thus reinforcing the trauma inflicted on young Oliver: the slums are infested with rats, the atmosphere of the rooms is somber and noxious, and the narrative focuses on the grandmother, a hideous old woman with a grimacing face, as she chuckles and mumbles madly.

After Chapter 5, these macabre images resurface and become a leitmotiv. With the old woman in the asylum who is to play a part in Oliver's fate, Dickens takes up again the rhetoric of *ut pictura poesis*, and invokes a graphic, visual universe, though he does not mention any specific artist:

> [...] her face, distorted into a mumbling leer, resembled more the grotesque shaping of some wild pencil, than the work of Nature's hand. (223)

The references to the cartoonist's art, to madness and to the importance of night-time, irresistibly evoke Goya. At that point Dickens seems closer to the fantastic grotesque of the *Caprichos* (1799) than to social caricature. We know however that the combination of the fantastic and the comic grotesque was not unfamiliar to the English satiric tradition: the medieval archetypes of the Dance of Death, of the Devil and of Hell, were used by caricaturists like Rowlandson and also by the Cruikshank brothers.[19] It is

---

[19] "With the Devil, the caricatures inherited also the medieval Death. In 1815-1816, Rowlandson and Combe let the traditional skeleton rove through the world in which they lived, in *The English Dance of Death*. From caricature, the Dance of Death was passed on the book-illustration by such prints as the frontispiece by Robert Cruikshank for Pierce Egan's *Finish to the Adventures of Tom, Jerry and Logic*. [...] Dickens had read *Finish to Tom and Jerry*, and he could scarcely have

unlikely that Dickens then knew of the *Caprichos*, even if towards the end of the 1820s a small group of connoisseurs had become familiar with Goya–but they were mainly French. As Nigel Glendinning notes, Goya's work was introduced in England by rich collectors and aristocrats (the Duke of Wellington and the Earl of Clarendon who was the English ambassador in Spain in 1830).[20] Only in the 1840s and the 1850s does Goya become well-known to French and English intellectuals as producing examples of fantastic grotesque. His name is mentioned in the works of intellectuals and in travel narratives through Spain (for example Musset, Gautier[21] and Baudelaire, Bulwer Lytton's brother, Augustus J.C. Hare[22] and Thackeray[23]).

In 1838 however, like Goya with Madrid and his *Caprichos*, Dickens recreates London as a kind of hell on earth. In the novel, the criminal sphere that revolves around Fagin logically partakes of the blending of the grotesque and the uncanny. Occasionally compared to an actor in a pantomime, both satanic and carnivalesque, Fagin remains, from beginning to end, essentially a nocturnal character and is associated with dark places. He is often described as grinning horribly, his whole face contorted (Chapters 15 and 20) and an "expression of villainy perfectly demoniacal" (189) screws up his face. This terrifying grotesque reaches its peak in the novel's final scenes. In Fagin's imprisonment scene, important modulations of the narrative voice may be identified. An unexpected narrative mode takes over in which free indirect speech expresses introspection and which

---

escaped seeing the Dance of Death in the caricatures of Rowlandson and others. He also owned a set of Holbein's *Dance of Death* bought in 1841. [...] The caricatures of the early 19th century, of Gillray, Rowlandson and the Cruikshanks, are not merely caricatures. They perpetuate and revitalize an older vision of life, and this vision coincides surprisingly with that of Dickens" (John R. Harvey, "Bruegel to Dickens: Graphic Satire and the Novel" in Hollington 1995, Vol. IV, 473-4). F.D. Klingender notes that Goya's fantastic caricature presents similarities with the English tradition, notably Cruikshank (see Klingender 1948).

[20] On Goya's reception in England, see Glendinning and Macartney 2010. Besides, we know now that Goya was influenced by English caricature, notably Gillray, thanks to the part played by the painter's friend, Leandro de Moratin, who had lived in London (see Wolf 1991).

[21] Before his 1845 trip to Spain where he studied Goya's art, Gautier wrote an article in 1838 entitled "Les Caprices de Goya" (*La Presse*, July 5th 1838).

[22] *Wanderings in Spain*, 1873. See Glendinning and Macartney 2010.

[23] In the introduction to his *History of Caricature and Grotesque...*, Thomas Wright explains that Thackeray once told him that he contemplated writing a similar type of book, a chapter of which would be devoted to Spanish caricature and Goya (see Wright 1865).

combines several voices: Fagin's, who is sentenced to death, Oliver's, who feels sorry for him, and the omniscient narrator's. The latter two cannot be distinguished from the imprisoned, distraught old man's:

> It was like sitting in a vault strewn with dead bodies–the cap, the noose, the pinioned arms, the faces that he knew, even beneath that hideous veil–Light, light! (469)

What is then grotesque around and in Fagin is of course much closer to Kayser's definition of the grotesque as fantastic disintegration of existential and moral bearings, than to Bakhtin's as comic and liberating carnivalesque inversion.

How then does Cruikshank organize his work when having to deal with such a range of novelistic tonalities, and what are the dynamics of text and image? Most engravings focus on grotesque scenes rather than on sentimental or serious ones. Out of the twenty-four engravings, only the last one–which represents Rose Maylie and Oliver finally freed from criminal influence–is not grotesque but simply melodramatic. All the others contain remarkably varied grotesque effects. Much use is made of the character of Fagin, since he appears in six engravings which are not conditioned by, but only loosely connected with, mimetic representation or social caricature. The image then functions as a system of signs which must be deciphered, at times loosely linked to the narrative and at times offering a concentration of elements disseminated in Dickens's text.

The first of these six engravings features Fagin cooking sausages as he welcomes Oliver to his den. As Jane R. Cohen has shown, the illustration produces a remarkable effect of dramatic and semantic condensation, since the ordinary "toasting-fork" (105) of the narrative becomes a long trident of devilish connotations, symbolically pointing to an embedded image which is either a small painting or perhaps a window which displays a gibbet and three hanged men (see Cohen 1980). Such concentration of meaning foreshadows the fate awaiting the gang of criminals, who are for the time being busy with everyday life. As is the case with Nodier (though we have here no true iconotext), the image has become a text to decipher because it expresses what the narrative does not say, or does not say *yet*, and makes explicit the underlying fantastic grotesque which appears only progressively in the novel.

In the last engraving featuring the old criminal, Fagin is represented alone and gripped by anguish in his prison. This engraving is a fine example of the combination of caricature comedy and sinister shadows. It again evokes the existential darkness of Goya's etchings and is far less conventional than the engravings depicting prison scenes from turn-of-century Gothic novels (1790-1820; see Lévy 1973). Even if Cruikshank's style is more realistic than fantastic, the image is made remarkable by the violent contrasts between black and white (notably the bright outside world and the dark cell) and by the emphasis on the external signs of Fagin's dementia: the sinister whiteness of his fleshless hand rolled into a fist next to his grimacing mouth and the bulging, hallucinated eyes of a man sentenced to death. Inspired by the text, the caricaturist is drawn towards the horrific and the fantastic, towards the "credible form of the monstrous" which Baudelaire defined as Goya's style (Baudelaire 1956, 185). It is not entirely coincidental, it seems, if Baudelaire celebrates in the same article both Cruikshank's "understanding of the fantastic" (181) and the monstrosity which he sees as "viable, harmonious" in Goya (185).

Thus it seems that Cruikshank and the early Dickens constitute the missing link between Hogarth and Goya. And if the purpose of illustration is to shed light on and make concrete certain narrative elements, then it is best achieved when the image is given a degree of autonomy, when it is not simply subjected to the text, as is shown best in *L'Histoire du roi de Bohême*, whose illustrations constitute a true mode of expression without which the novel would be quite fragmentary and incomplete. The two examples considered here show the key role played by the tradition of graphic caricature, when it was breaking new ground and becoming an integral part of the illustrated novel.[24] The proximity of the two modes of expression also explains why most writers of the grotesque were inspired by visual artists (Hogarth and Cruikshank in the case of Nodier and Dickens, Bruegel, Callot or Goya in the case of others) who helped them give shape and presence to the physiognomic, "universal language"[25] of grotesque caricature, as well as to their own obsessive images.

---

[24] John R. Harvey and Nathalie Vanfasse have shown that graphic caricature continued to be part of Victorian illustration after Cruikshank, notably with Phiz, Dickens's other famous illustrator. The grotesque, however, gradually disappeared in favour of other styles like genre painting (see Harvey in Hollington 1995, Vol. IV and Vanfasse 2007).

[25] The phrase comes from Goya. It was inscribed on a 1797 sketch for one of the *Caprichos* engravings.

References

Bakhtin, Mikhail. (1965) 1984. *Rabelais and His World*. Translated by Helene Iswolsky. Bloomington: Indiana University Press.

Baudelaire, Charles. (1857) 1956. "A Few Foreign Caricaturists." In *The Mirror of Art, Critical Studies by Charles Baudelaire*, edited and translated by Jonathan Mayne, 179-90. New-York: Doubleday & Co.

Boisacq-Generet, Marie-Jeanne. 1994. *Tradition et modernité dans L'Histoire du roi de Bohême et de ses sept châteaux de Charles Nodier*. Paris: Champion.

Champfleury, Jules. (1865) 2010. *Histoire de la caricature moderne*. Coeuvres-et-Valsery: Editions Ressouvenances.

—. 1883. *Les Vignettes romantiques. Histoire la littérature et de l'art, 1825-1840, 150 vignettes*. Paris: Librairie E. Dentu.

Cohen, Jane R. 1980. *Charles Dickens and his Original Illustrators*. Columbus: Ohio State University Press.

Dickens, Charles. (1837-8) 1980. *Oliver Twist*. Harmondsworth: Penguin English Library.

Emelina, Jean. 1991. *Le Comique, essai d'interprétation générale*. Paris: SEDES.

Glendinning, Nigel and Macartney, Hilary, eds. 2011. *Spanish Art in Britain and Ireland, 1750-1920: Studies in Reception*. London: Tamesis Books.

Hill, Nancy K. 1981. *A Reformer's Art: Dickens' Picturesque and Grotesque Imagery*. Athens and London: Ohio University Press.

Hofmann, Werner. 1958. *La Caricature de Vinci à Picasso*. Translated by Anna-Elisabeth Leroy and Edouard Roditi. Paris: Editions Aimery Somogy.

Hollington, Michael. 1984. *Dickens and the Grotesque*. Beckenham (Kent): Croom Helm.

—, ed. 1995. *Charles Dickens: Critical Assessments* (Four Volumes). London: Helm Information.

Kaenel, Philippe. 1996. *Le Métier d'illustrateur, 1830-1880: Rodolphe Töpffer, J.J. Grandville, Gustave Doré*. Paris: Editions Messene.

Kayser, Wolfgang. (1957) 1981. *The Grotesque in Art and Literature*. Translated by Ulrich Weisstein. New-York: Columbia University Press.

Klingender, F.D. 1948. *Goya in the Democratic Tradition*. London: Sidgwick & Jackson.

Lévy, Maurice. 1973. *Images du roman noir*. Paris: Editions Eric Losfled.

Louvel, Liliane. 1998. *L'Oeil du texte : texte et images dans la littérature de langue anglaise.* Toulouse: Presses Universitaires du Mirail.

Marie, Aristide. 1925. *Alfred et Tony Johannot, peintres, graveurs et vignettistes.* Paris: Floury.

Martin, Christophe. 2005. *"Dangereux suppléments." L'illustration du roman en France au dix-huitième siècle.* Louvain & Paris: Editions Peeters.

Mélot, Michel. 1994. *L'Illustration, histoire d'un art.* Genève: Skira.

Monot, Sylvère. 1986. Introduction to *Esquisses de Boz.* In *Esquisses de Boz, Martin Chuzzlewit* by Charles Dickens. Bibliothèque de la Pléiade. Paris: Gallimard.

Nodier, Charles. (1830) 1979. *L'Histoire du roi de Bohême et de ses sept châteaux.* Paris: Editions Plasma.

Peyrache-Leborgne, Dominique. 2012. *Grotesques et arabesques dans le récit romantique. De Jean-Paul à Victor Hugo.* Paris: Champion.

Vanfasse, Nathalie. 2007. *Charles Dickens entre normes et déviance.* Aix-en-Provence: Publications de l'Université de Provence.

Wolf, Reva. 1991. *Goya and the Satirical Print in England and on the Continent, 1730-1850.* Boston: D.R. Godine.

Wright, Thomas. 1865. *A History of Caricature and Grotesque in Literature and Art.* London: Virtue Brothers & Co.

CHAPTER TWO

THE GROTESQUE AND THE "DRAMA
OF THE BODY" IN *NOTRE-DAME DE PARIS*
AND *THE MAN WHO LAUGHS* BY VICTOR HUGO

SYLVIE JEANNERET

In 19th-century France, the grotesque constituted an integral part of
Romanticism, an artistic movement closely associated with the name of
Victor Hugo, without doubt its prominent theorist in the 1830s. Of his
famous "Preface to *Cromwell*," a text considered as the manifest of French
Romanticism, I will retain the discussion of the grotesque as the
theoretical basis of this paper.

As Elisheva Rosen has shown in her book on the grotesque (Rosen
1991), French Romantic writers, especially Hugo, turned the grotesque
into an aesthetic category and a literary concept useful to their approach to
creation. In the "Preface to *Cromwell*," the notion of grotesque becomes
operative in that it is inscribed in Hugo's diachronic vision of the history
of literature. It is defined as "a new type" (Hugo 1910, 346) and opposed
to classicism, which is deemed "conventional" (346) and inert. Hugo uses
bold formulation:

> This type is the grotesque. [...] we have now indicated the significant
> feature, the fundamental difference which, in our opinion, separates
> modern from ancient art, the present form from the defunct form; or, to use
> less definite but more popular terms, *romantic* literature from *classical*
> literature. (346, italics his)

Besides, Hugo defines the grotesque as a dynamic category enabling
him to renew genres like drama and the novel, or at least to legitimate a
literary practise which embraces the bodily, the ugly and the deformed
because they form an integral part of real life. In the "Preface," Hugo
explains: "on the one hand [the grotesque] creates the abnormal and the

horrible, on the other the comic and the burlesque" (347). Because it is "a germ of comedy" (349) contrasting with the sublime, with Hugo the grotesque becomes part of modern creation. Hugo gives the example of Shakespearian drama, "which with the same breath moulds the grotesque and the sublime, the terrible and the absurd, tragedy and comedy" (352) while pointing out "its close creative alliance with the beautiful in the so-called 'romantic' period" (351).

The Romantic claim to new literary forms therefore relies on the assertion of the grotesque as an aesthetic concept, a concept which leads to the perception of creation as a whole, as embracing the beautiful and the ugly, the sublime and the grotesque. Once anchored in Hugo's creation, the aesthetic notion will not be upheld by him in the 1860s. In his *William Shakespeare* for example–an ambitious and comprehensive essay on creative freedom–Hugo does not once mention the grotesque. In 1827 however, it was necessary for Hugo to establish it as an indisputable creative principle:

> [...] the real results from the wholly natural combination of two types, the sublime and the grotesque, which meet in the drama, as they meet in life and in creation. (355)

The grotesque as an aesthetic principle bears witness to Hugo's ability to capture one element and its opposite in a single image (the surface and inner depth of reality, the highest and lowest strata of society, nobleness of heart and degradation of spirit, etc.). This creative principle thus encourages the imbrication of antagonistic poles while making such imbrication spectacular (or visible) either to the amateur of Romantic drama or to the reader of novels. To achieve such an eye-catching effect, Hugo resorts to several devices, some of which I will now consider: the bringing to the fore of the characters' bodies and inner dilemma; and the important part (literally) played by travelling performers and other thespian characters.

As Anne Ubersfeld reminds us in her introduction to the "Preface to *Cromwell*": "the grotesque is the body" (Ubersfeld 2002, 715). The grotesque therefore plays a pivotal role in Hugo's novelistic production since it confers an aesthetic dimension to a typically Hugolian type of characters such as Hans (in *Hans of Iceland*), Quasimodo, Gwynplaine (in *The Man Who Laughs*) and Gilliatt (in *Toilers of the Sea*)–to mention but a few. The spectacular staging of these characters' bodies leaves no one indifferent. Hugo's aim is to provoke an emotional reaction in his readers' minds, but also to stir social awareness. This is not saying much about Hugo, of course, but one must acknowledge that he breaks new ground by conferring to his own creation power explicitly relying on excess. Thus in his novels the human body becomes the stakes of a drama which Hugo defines in the "Preface" by its ability to "illuminate at the same time the interior and the exterior of mankind" (Hugo 1910, 368), i.e. to use the visual to give access to the invisible, often by contrast. This is how I purport to read the spectacular staging of bodies in two novels by Hugo: *Notre-Dame de Paris* (1831) and *The Man Who Laughs* (1869).

The bodies of Quasimodo and Gwynplaine are typical examples of Hugolian grotesque. Neither character laughs–even though a grimacing smile has been forcibly inscribed on their faces. Both characters are considered as monstrous and socially inferior and the reader goes from an aesthetic to a political reading, a central one in the case of *The Man Who Laughs*. Those bodies scarred by ugliness contrast of course with the characters' noble minds which are apparent early in the novels. Besides, the two characters are confronted to their physical and moral opposites: Gwynplaine to the Duchess Josiana, Quasimodo to Phoebus (as well as to Esmeralda, not his moral but his physical opposite).

In *Notre-Dame de Paris*, Quasimodo's monstrous body is on public display in front of the people of Paris and its sight provokes both rejection and magnetic appeal. At the beginning of the narrative, the hunchback is elected "Pope of Fools." When Hugo describes the character, he carefully brings to the fore the people's fascination in front of such physical ugliness: "From it they brought in triumph the blessed Pope of Fools. But it was then that surprise and wonder reached their peak. The grimace was his ordinary face. Or rather, his whole person was grimace" (Hugo 2009, 58). According to the narrator, Quasimodo represents "a strange exception to the eternal rule which says that strength, like beauty, results from harmony" (58). The monstrous harbours its own category of beauty, as François Kerlouégan explains: "Romantic beauty relinquishes harmony in favour of effect–which is why the ugly can be beautiful" (Kerlouégan 2006, 295, my translation). We can even go further and suggest the possibility that in Hugo's mind, beauty does not have more aesthetic, moral or even political worth than ugliness. For him it is interesting to mix or confront these categories which fascinate both the novelist and his readers, who must however appreciate the contrast between them for fear of misapprehending reality.

It is difficult for Quasimodo not to establish a hierarchy however, since the man Esmeralda falls in love with, the aptly-named Phoebus, is as beautiful as a Greek God. That he is also vain and stupid changes nothing. Hugo does not give his deformed character a chance and his destiny can be predicted as early as the first pages. This takes away none of the novel's interest, since such predictability becomes fate: Quasimodo suffers from the beginning to the end of the novel, a victim of man's cruelty. Later in the novel the hunchback's body is whipped and tortured when Quasimodo is put in the stocks after attempting to abduct Esmeralda in order to take her to Claude Frollo. Hugo depicts the scene insisting on the contrast between the mob's wild delight and the hunchback's humiliation, and ends it by reversing the situation completely when the pretty gypsy girl comes to give Quasimodo a drink:

> It would have been a touching spectacle anywhere, this beautiful girl, fresh, pure, charming and at the same time so weak, coming thus piously to the help of so much misery, deformity, and malice. On a pillory the spectacle was sublime. All the people in this crowd were themselves struck by it, and began to clap their hands and shout: "Noël! Noël!" (Hugo 2009, 252-3)

This is a particularly dramatic moment (in the Hugolian sense of the word), one in which the conjunction of sublime and grotesque deeply moves the crowd and when the notions of beauty and ugliness and of good and evil are interconnected and contrasted.

The visual interweaving of the grotesque and the sublime appears most strikingly in another section of the novel: at the end of Book 8, Esmeralda, who has been sentenced to death, is abducted again by Quasimodo. He wishes to save her this time and takes her into the cathedral–then considered as a sanctuary. The abduction takes place in broad daylight and is experienced as a moment of magic by the jubilant crowd. Quasimodo is then perceived, in spite of (or thanks to) his exceptional deformity, as a wondrous being:

> Then the women laughed and cried, the crowd stamped with enthusiasm, for at that moment Quasimodo truly had a beauty of his own. He was beautiful, he, the orphan, the foundling, the reject, he felt august and strong, he looked society in the face, that society from which he had been banished, and in which he was intervening so powerfully, that human justice whose prey he had snatched, all these tigers forced to chew on emptiness, those police agents, those judges, those executioners, all that royal might, which he had just broken, he the lowliest of the low, with the might of God.
>
> Besides it was very affecting, this protection coming from so deformed a creature upon so unhappy a being, a girl condemned to death rescued by Quasimodo. It was two extremes of wretchedness, of nature and of society, meeting and helping each other. (377)

In this excerpt Hugo is obviously trying to bring into contact radical extremes–extreme ugliness and upmost beauty–and to stage the moment of contact in order to render their contrast manifest. The spectacle is all the more striking since Quasimodo is deprived of speech–he can speak but is never given the chance to. In this excerpt the reader is led to read about Quasimodo's unclear thoughts, or rather to *see* them since the hunchback is depicted as a body deprived of words. The aesthetic dimension of the grotesque is supplemented with a political and social dimension, more obvious in the second paragraph, which considers poverty. Poverty-ridden bodies, be they beautiful like Esmeralda's or ugly like Quasimodo's, are united by their political and social status as oppressed bodies, and their visual staging only brings out their wretchedness. This is confirmed in the many scenes of the novel in which Esmeralda finds herself humiliated. Both Quasimodo and Esmeralda are mere bodies deprived of speech, sentenced before they have been allowed to utter a single word in their defense. They are wretched bodies destined to be seen but condemned to silence.

In *The Man Who Laughs*, Gwynplaine, the disfigured performer, tries to give poverty a voice–to make it speak. The 1869 novel is the crowning achievement of Hugo's reflection, started very early in his career, on what could be called the clown's tragic laughter and by extension the miserable man's laughter. Several examples inevitably come to mind, the very first one that of Triboulet, in *Le Roi s'amuse* (*The King's Fool*). The 1832 play was a powerful charge against the abuses of aristocratic power and was soon banned. Other examples include the convicts in *Le Dernier jour d'un condamné* (*The Last Day of a Condemned Man*, 1829), forced to manage a smile in order to put on a good show at the precise moment when they hit abject poverty; or Fantine in *Les Misérables*, forced to have all her teeth pulled out in order to sell them, grinning with her bloodied and toothless mouth before dying of poverty and disease. Hugo's reflection on the tragedy of laughter thus leads to *The Man Who Laughs*, the action of which takes place in 17th-century England and in which the aesthetic and political dimensions of the grotesque are closely linked, notably in the staging of monstrosity.

In this novel, the association of the monstrous and the ideal is quite paroxysmal. Through several strategies of disclosure, Hugo shows the superposition of the visible and invisible strata of reality and gradually leads his novel towards a violent indictment of the nobility. In his very interesting study of Hugo's work, Charles Renouvier points out the distinctive characteristics of *The Man Who Laughs*: "Hugo no longer stages the coarse and isolated monsters of his early novels but whole groups of human peculiarities, natural or artificial, the divers products of fate in an unfair society, which he contrasts when depicting their ways of life. [...] The two extremes of corruption–the *Comprachicos* and the court–serve as a framework to the novel" (Renouvier 2002, 235-6, my translation).

The perversion and cruelty of English aristocrats–who like to laugh at the expense of the wretched–is set against Gwynplaine's naivety and Ursus's benevolence. Gwynplaine, the hero of this *Bildungsroman*, was disfigured as a child by the *Comprachicos*, who transform children into jesters to sell them to noblemen. The whole novel is built around the following paradox: Gwynplaine bears a monstrous grimace on his face but is a good, generous being; whereas the lords and ladies, among them the Duchess Josiana, handsome and splendid, are degenerate and evil. This paradox however–already apparent in the first chapters and intensified when Ursus's little theatrical company arrives in London–is gradually superseded by the staging of bodies, where the grotesque and the beautiful are opposed and contrasted but also combined and united. The aesthetic dimension I will quickly show now gradually paves the way to political considerations.

Three significant sections of the novel are centred round the merging of beauty and the grotesque. The first one is represented by the play that Ursus conceives round the antithesis formed by Gwynplaine and Dea, the young and beautiful blind girl who travels with them. In his short play entitled "Chaos Vanquished," Ursus uses Gwynplaine's ugly features as a contrast to Dea's diaphanous beauty. The narrator comments thus on the impression produced:

> Her white face by the side of the gnome represented what might have been called divine astonishment. [...] This depth of night and this glory of day united, formed in the mind of the spectator a chiaroscuro in which appeared endless perspectives. (Hugo 2012, 177)

The visual dimension of bodies–central to Ursus's drama–finally refers to a metaphysical level of meaning and lifts the spectators' minds to the invisible. The play, which Gwynplaine's contagious laughter turns into a great success, is only seen by the common people. One night however, drawn to it by the perspective of popular pleasure, the Duchess Josiana attends a performance. In the novel, this scene is built round the notion of watching and being watched. All the spectators' eyes converge on the Duchess, but also on Gwynplaine, whose ugliness is thus made more conspicuous. The visual effect is thus diffracted through the conjunction of these two bodies, one splendid and radiant, the other hideous and laughable:

> "Chaos Vanquished" was rather a dream than a piece; it generally produced on the audience the effect of a vision. Now, this effect was reflected on the actors. The house took the performers by surprise, and they were thunderstruck in their turn. It was a rebound of fascination. (212)

Hugo pushes the confrontation of beauty and the grotesque to its extremes and creates a shock in the minds of both the spectators of the show and the readers of his novel. Beyond the aesthetic shock, which leads to and ends in redeeming laughter, there remains the social and political opposition between two worlds, that of the "happy," as the narrator calls them in Part I, and that of the wretched. Gwynplaine faces this irreparable divide between two worlds which nothing can unite: though his title is restored to him towards the end of the novel, he continues to be a monstrous jester. This is true also when Josiana, during a memorable scene, suggests that she and Gwynplaine become lovers, in order to join the two monsters that they are, he outside, she inside:

> "I love monsters, and I love mountebanks. A lover despised, mocked, grotesque, hideous, exposed to laughter on that pillory called a theatre, has for me an extraordinary attraction. [...] Bring the highest and lowest depths together, and you have chaos, and I delight in chaos." (303)

Josiana here gives the definition of drama that one finds in Hugo's "Preface to *Cromwell*," i.e. the combination of two aesthetic categories, the sublime and the grotesque. This conception is shared by Ursus, who reminds his spectators that "Chaos Vanquished [...] 'is in the style of one Shakespeare'" (177). In the "Preface to *Cromwell*," Hugo asserts that "Shakespeare is the drama; and the drama [...] is the distinguishing characteristic of the third epoch of poetry, of the literature of the present day (Hugo 1910, 352).

The drama which unites Josiana and Gwynplaine, the sublime and the grotesque, ends in tragedy: rejected by Josiana and jeered at by the Lords, Gwynplaine loses everything he loves and commits suicide. By realising the fusion of opposites and shedding light on them, the Hugolian grotesque works at unveiling reality, thus showing the duality and hidden monstrosity of human beings. *The Man Who Laughs* conveys a message still valid today, that modern societies have the ability to create monsters. The proof of the novel's modernity is found in a text which is well-known to all the lovers of detective fiction:

It was the portrait of a clown, a young boy done up in court jester's garb from long, long ago. His body was gnarled and hunched; he wore a stuporous ear-to-ear smile that looked like one continuous deep scar.

I stared, transfixed, thinking of Elizabeth Short, DOA at 39th and Norton. The more I stared the more the two blended. (Ellroy 2006, 265-6)

In 1987, James Ellroy published *The Black Dahlia*, in which he painted an unparalleled picture of Los Angeles in the 1950s as a sombre and cruel place. The narrator of the novel hunts down the murderer of Elizabeth Short, a starlet found dead, her body cut in two and dumped in a stretch of wasteland somewhere in L.A. A horrible detail can be seen on the photographs taken of the corpse: the murderer has cut her mouth from ear to ear. In his book, James Ellroy gives specific meaning to this detail, establishing a connection between the act of torture of which Elizabeth Short was the victim and the mutilation inflicted on Gwynplaine by the *Comprachicos*. Ellroy's murderer has read *The Man Who Laughs* and policeman Bucky Bleichert accidentally comes across a painting sold by the murderers' family to their rich neighbour. Bucky makes the connection much later, when he sees the neighbour again and she gives him details about the painting bought by her husband, a valuable painting, "'A Frederick Yannantuono original, [...] inspired by an old classic novel–*The Man Who Laughs* by Victor Hugo'" (339). At that point everything suddenly becomes clear for Bucky. *The Man Who Laughs* leads the policeman to the truth because it gives meaning to the victim's mutilation:

There was a copy of *The Man Who Laughs* in the shack where Betty Short was killed. I was buzzing so hard I could hardly hear what Jane was saying.

"–a group of Spaniards back in the fifteenth and sixteenth centuries. They were called the Comprachicos, and they kidnapped and tortured children, then mutilated them and sold them to the aristocracy so that they could be used as court jesters. Isn't that hideous? The clown in the painting is the main character, Gwynplain. When he was a child he had his mouth slashed ear to ear. Bucky, are you all right?"

MOUTH SLASHED EAR TO EAR.

I shuddered, then forced a smile. "I'm fine. The book just reminded me of something. Old stuff, just a coincidence." (339)

Bucky only has to read the receipt confirming the sale of the painting to discover the murderer's name. Had it not been for the painting, for

Gwynplaine and his mutilation–as Ellroy makes it clear–he would not have tracked down the murderess and her accomplice.[1]

Both Hugo and Ellroy wished to tell the stories of human monsters, asking a question which is not limited to the context of their times: how can man create monsters? The question is not to know how man can give birth to monsters, but actually fashion them. The question haunts both Ellroy and Hugo: how and why does one become Gwynplaine or Quasimodo, or Romana Sprague in *The Black Dahlia*? The grotesque appears very much as a modern-day notion if we consider its political, rather than its aesthetic, dimension. Victor Hugo was the first in France to suggest this political approach to the grotesque by leading us to *see* the superimpositions of beautiful and grotesque bodies and asking us to reflect on the invisibility of the outcast, whom he depicted as ignored or oppressed and tortured bodies.

Perhaps the beginning of the 21st century makes us very susceptible to the sufferings of these outcasts which inhabit the pages of European literature and societies, because so little seems to have changed since Hugo's time. Hugo wrote about a notion which he called grotesque and which he linked to its opposite because he thought that any vision of the world must be plurivocal and not univocal. The necessity of adopting such a vision is still patent today.

References

Ellroy, James. (1987) 2006. *The Black Dahlia*. New-York: Hachette Book Group.

Hugo, Victor. (1827) 1910. "Preface to *Cromwell*." Translated by J.R. Effinger. In *Prefaces and Prologues to Famous Books*, edited by Eliot, Charles W., 337-87. New-York: P.F. Collier & Son.

---

[1] When he wrote the murder scene, Ellroy insisted on the atrocious violence inflicted on the victim. In that he showed that he perfectly understood the violence that Hugo had tried to bring to the fore when he conceived the operation destined to turn Gwynplaine into a monster: "Elizabeth Short tried to run. She knocked her unconscious and made Georgie strip her and gag her and tie her to the mattress. She promised him parts of the girl to keep forever. She took a copy of *The Man Who Laughs* from her purse and read aloud from it, casting occasional glances at the girl spread-eagled. Then she cut her and burned her and batted her and wrote in the notebook she always carried while the girl was passed out from the pain. Georgie watched, and together they shouted the chants of the Comprachicos. And after two full days of it she slashed Elizabeth Short ear to ear like Gwynplain, so she wouldn't hate her after she was dead" (345).

—. (1831) 2009. *Notre-Dame de Paris*. Translated by Alban Krailsheimer. Oxford: Oxford World's Classics.

—. (1869) 2012. *The Man Who Laughs. A Romance of English History*. Unidentified translator. Los Angeles: Indo-European Publishing.

Kerlouégan, François. 2006. *Poétique du corps romantique*. Paris: Champion.

Renouvier, Charles. (1900) 2002. *Victor Hugo le philosophe*. Paris: Maisonneuve et Larose.

Rosen, Elisheva. 1991. *Sur le grotesque. L'ancien et le nouveau dans la réflexion esthétique*. Vincennes: Presses Universitaires de Vincennes.

Ubersfeld, Anne. 2002. Introduction to "Préface de *Cromwell*." In *Œuvres complètes* by Victor Hugo, Coll. Bouquins, Vol. *Critique*, 715-8. Paris: Robert Laffont.

CHAPTER THREE

AN INSTANCE OF THE GROTESQUE
FROM SMOLLETT TO DICKENS:
RODERICK (RANDOM), BARNABY (RUDGE)
AND THE RAVEN

ANNE ROUHETTE

Smollett's influence on Dickens has been frequently commented upon,[1] and goes deeper than one might infer from the passing allusions made by David Copperfield, who, echoing the views of his creator, expresses several times his admiration for Smollett and for *Roderick Random* (1748) in particular. Smollett and Dickens shared a common admiration for Hogarth and for his interest in human physiognomy, as well as a common taste (common to Hogarth too of course) for visual satire[2]– like Smollett, Dickens considered the human face as representative of character and used this for satirical purposes. Smollett's predilection for the grotesque probably explains why his impact on Dickens was weightier than Fielding's; although the latter was another master of satire, his novels do not stray beyond the bounds of caricature to venture into grotesque territory, at least not as much or often as Smollett's do. In fact, Smollett resorts consistently and recurrently to a grotesque mode of writing; grotesque figures abound in his novels and especially his early ones, among which *Roderick Random*. This predilection probably derives in part from his Scottish origins since the Scottish literary tradition repeatedly mingles the ridiculous and the terrible,[3] two elements which, as we shall

---

[1] The similarities between Smollett and Dickens have been explored most extensively by F. D. Wiestra (see Wiestra 1928).

[2] Dickens's interest in physiognomy and its link with the grotesque are developed for instance in Hollington 1984, 14.

[3] See Notestein 1946, 328, and especially Wittig 1958, 48, 71 and 120.

see, play a major role in the grotesque. The following excerpt from *Roderick Random*, which consists in a grotesque description of the loathsome apothecary Crab, may help illustrate Dickens's debt to Smollett:

> This member of the faculty was aged fifty, about five feet high, and ten round the belly; his face was as capacious as a full moon, and much of the complexion of a mulberry: his nose, resembling a powder-horn, was swelled to an enormous size, and studded all over with carbuncles; and his little grey eyes reflected the rays in such an oblique manner that, while he looked a person full in the face, one would have imagined he was admiring the buckle of his shoe. (Smollett 2008, 26)

If this depiction begins as a caricature, with exaggerated physical traits, it soon becomes grotesque by way of the comparison with a mulberry then with a powder-horn as the man turns into a fruit then into a threatening object. A disquieting and vaguely sinister element is thus introduced and reinforced by the deformed nose, which is not only excessively big but resolutely "enormous" and "studded all over with carbuncles," a term whose two meanings, physical and ornamental, interact here humorously largely thanks to the past participle "studded," as Crab's monstrous nose is transformed into a work of art. With this distortion, borne out by the "oblique" manner in which he looks at people, his physical deformation clearly corresponds to the moral deformity of a bad apothecary and domestic tyrant who beats his wife and servants and probably killed one of his footmen–his appearance matches his vicious character. In Jerry Beasley's words, Crab is "a moral grotesque who, as perceived and recreated, becomes a physical grotesque in a convincingly authentic visual representation" (Beasley 1998, 49).

In Smollett's as in Dickens's novels, the descriptions of grotesque characters go beyond the exaggeration of features typical of caricature to incorporate elements (animal, vegetal, supernatural, mechanical, etc.) which are alien to human nature, turning these characters into hybrids which both require and elude definition, and blurring the perception of what is supposed to be known in a process of defamiliarisation. As John Ruskin explains in his famous definition of the grotesque:

> It seems to me that the grotesque is, in almost all cases, composed of two elements, one ludicrous, the other fearful; that, as one or other of these elements prevails, the grotesque falls into two branches, sportive grotesque and terrible grotesque; but that we cannot legitimately consider it under these two aspects, because there are hardly any examples which do not in some degree combine both elements; there are few grotesques so utterly

playful as to be overcast with no shade of fearfulness, and few so fearful as absolutely to exclude all ideas of jest. (Ruskin 2007, 126)

Here Ruskin lays stress on the paradoxical blend of the ridiculous (or comical) and the terrible (or fearful) inherent in the grotesque before examining different types of grotesque according to the "degree" in which either element predominates. It is this question of degree, the essentially terrible shading into the jestful and the jestful into the terrible, that I would now like to consider by way of a specific instance of the grotesque which crops up in both Smollett's and Dickens's work. I wish above all to focus on the way this blend of antagonistic principles is perceived, analysing the responses it calls forth both on a diegetic level, in the characters confronted with it, and on the reader's part. The instance I am referring to is itself a "blend," so to speak—the strange couple formed by the association of an idiot with a tamed raven. In Dickens, the idiot is the eponymous character of *Barnaby Rudge* (1841), who never goes without Grip, his dancing and talking (and talkative) crow whose favourite utterance is "I'm a devil!" Grip's author deliberately gifted him with a reason, or with the semblance of a reason, Barnaby himself is deprived of; as Dickens put it to Forster, he wanted to have Barnaby accompanied by "a pet raven who is immeasurably more knowing than himself."[4] If Dickens explains in the preface he added to the novel in 1849 that he modelled Grip on the two tamed ravens he had owned (he would acquire a third one at a later date and commemorated him in an altered version of the preface in 1858),[5] the association between a raven and an idiot probably sprung from a literary source, indeed, as both F. D. Wiestra and Jerome H. Buckley speculate,[6] from the following passage in Smollett's *Roderick Random* (as it will be analysed in detail, it is necessary to quote here at length):

We arrived at our inn, supped and went to bed; but Strap's distemper continuing, he was obliged to get up in the middle of the night, and taking the candle in his hand, which he had left burning for the purpose, he went down to the house of office; whence in a short time he returned in a great hurry, with his hair standing on end, and a look betokening horror and

---

[4] Dickens 1969, 197. Ruskin, who detested *Barnaby Rudge* and all its characters, thought Grip the only redeeming feature of the novel (cited in Bowen 2003, xxvii-xxviii).
[5] His most beloved raven was called "Grip" and died in 1841. There are many references to Dickens's pet ravens in his letters.
[6] See Wiestra 1928, 74 and Buckley 1992, 30.

astonishment. Without speaking a word, he set down the light and jumped into bed behind me, where he lay and trembled with great violence.—When I asked him what was the matter? he replied, with a broken accent, "God have mercy on us! I have seen the devil."—Though my prejudice was not quite so strong as his, I was not a little alarmed at this exclamation, and much more so, when I heard the sound of bells approaching our chamber, and felt my bedfellow cling close to me, uttering these words, "Christ have mercy upon us! there he comes."—At that instant, a monstrous overgrown raven entered our chamber, with bells at its feet, and made directly towards our bed.—As this creature is reckoned in our country, a common vehicle for the devil and witches to play their pranks in, I verily believed we were haunted; and in a violent fright, shrunk my head under the bed-cloaths.—This terrible apparition leapt upon the bed, and after giving us several severe dabs with its beak through the blankets, hopped away, and vanished. Strap and I recommended ourselves to the protection of heaven with great devotion, and when we no longer heard the noise, ventured to peep up and take breath. But we had not been long freed from this phantom, when another appeared, that had well nigh deprived us both of our senses. We perceived an old man enter the room, with a long white beard that reached to his middle; there was a certain wild peculiarity in his eyes and countenance, that did not savour of this world: and his dress consisted of a brown stuff coat, buttoned behind, and at the wrists, and an odd-fashioned cap of the same stuff upon his head. I was so amazed that I had not power to move my eyes from such a ghastly object, but lay motionless, and saw him come streight up to me: when he got to the bed, he wrung his hands, and cried, with a voice that did not seem to belong to a human creature, "Where is Ralph?" I made no reply; upon which, he repeated in an accent still more preternatural; "Where is Ralpho?"—He had no sooner pronounced these words, than I heard the sound of the bells at a distance; which the apparition having listened to, tript away, and left me almost petrified with fear. It was a good while before I could recover myself so far as to speak: and when at length I turned about to Strap, I found him in a fit, which, however, did not last long.—When he came to himself, I asked his opinion of what had happened; and he assured me, that the first must certainly be the soul of some person damned, which appeared by the chains about its legs (for his fears had magnified the creature to the bigness of a horse, and the sound of small morris bells to the clanking of massy chains)—As for the old man, he took it to be the spirit of somebody murdered long ago in this place, which had power granted it to torment the assassin in the shape of a raven, and that Ralpho was the name of the said murderer.—Although I had not much faith in his interpretation, I was too much troubled to enjoy any sleep; and in all my future adventures, never passed a night so ill.—In the morning, Strap imparted the whole affair to Joey, who after an immoderate fit of laughter, explained the matter, by telling him that the old man was the landlord's father, who had turned idiot some years ago, and diverted himself with a tame raven, which, it seems, had hopped away from his apartment in the night, and induced him to follow it to our chamber, where he had inquired after it, under the name of Ralpho. (Smollett 2008, 60-2)

There is an almost pre-Radcliffean Gothic quality to this extract, in the sense that an incident perceived as belonging to the supernatural ultimately receives a rational explanation. A few introductory sentences launch the episode, set in the middle of the night, by the flicker of a candle; the fearful event is heralded with Strap's return, with all the outward signs of terror. It is given a supernatural quality ("I have seen the devil"), confirmed by the ringing of bells–at this stage, the reader cannot guess that Roderick is referring to morris bells and not to the more solemn bells used in religious rituals, particularly funerals, and thus possibly endowed with sinister connotations, such as the bell which "invites" Macbeth to kill Duncan.[7] Strap's panic affects Roderick and the scene is set for the terrifying apparition. Enter the raven. Of course, his size horribly exceeds the norm ("monstrous overgrown"), and as if guided by his own will, he heads straight to the bed, to attack Roderick and Strap, or so it seems. He is called "creature," "apparition" and "phantom," in a progression towards a greater degree of unreality which as a result tends to efface his animal nature and gives him a supernatural, more precisely devilish dimension which Roderick no longer questions ("I verily believed we were haunted"), partly because of his Scottish origins. The human-made bells the bird is associated with blur all the more Roderick's (and the reader's) perception of it; the raven is nevertheless not personified since the possessive used remains "its" and not "his" ("its feet," "its beak"). Although the apparition is said to be "terrible" and arouses Roderick's and Strap's "violent fright," several elements convey a different impression to the reader: Strap's jumping into bed with "his hair standing on end" and cowering behind Roderick, in a clichéd representation of terror; the reference to "pranks;" the strange behaviour of this supposedly fearful apparition, underlined by the pleasant alliterative patterns ("several severe," "beak through the blankets"); and the definitely un-Gothic quality of a scene in which a raven hops around while two grown men hide underneath the blankets, child-like, before "peep[ing] up." The terrible and

---

[7] "I go, and it is done; the bell invites me/ Hear it not, Duncan; for it is a knell/ That summons thee to heaven or to hell" (William Shakespeare, *Macbeth* (1606), II, 1, 62-4).

fearful are greatly qualified for the reader as this first episode clearly comes across as comical.[8]

But the atmosphere soon changes as a human apparition succeeds the bird's. To a large extent, this episode repeats the first one, which contributes to the impression of unease, as though the old man were imitating the raven. The same terms ("creature," "apparition"), phrases ("hopped away," "tripped away") or patterns recur in the two instances: "a raven entered our chamber…[and] made directly towards our bed" parallels "an old man enter[ed] … the room… I …saw him come streight up to me." Like the bird, the old man possesses a hybrid dimension, both animal ("wild") and inanimate ("a ghastly object") but above all supernatural ("that did not savour of this world," "a voice that did not seem to belong to a human being," "accent still more preternatural"). But the effect produced on the characters and on the reader varies from the first apparition to the second. Strap seems to disappear, as if by magic, as the apparition comes "streight up to *me* [i.e. Roderick, emphasis added]" and the personal pronouns "I" and "me" abruptly replace "we" and "us"– Roderick's sudden and inexplicable isolation emphasises the frightening character of this passage.[9] Furthermore, hiding behind blankets becomes impossible since Roderick, "almost petrified with fear," is incapable of making the slightest movement or uttering a single sound: "I was so amazed that I had not power to move my eyes from such a ghastly object, but lay motionless," in the thralls of what Ann Radcliffe would later define as horror.[10] The long white beard, revealing the man's old age, contrasts with the coat he has "buttoned behind," as a child might, while the repetition of his request "Where is Ralph," with the diminutive form "Ralpho" which could sound somewhat childish, may be ridiculous but is far from comical and on the contrary, reinforces the disturbing impression created by the scene. This man, between childhood and old age, nature and the supernatural, seems utterly dependent on the raven whose behaviour he

---

[8] Cruikshank's illustration of this scene in an 1831 edition of *Roderick Random* shows the night-capped heroes clinging to their bed-sheets in a neat little bedroom with checkered curtains, hardly a frightening sight.

[9] Roderick's faithful sidekick Strap is a largely comic character sometimes verging on the ridiculous; he makes Roderick's hardships more bearable, either by actually helping him, or by adding a humorous touch. The novel is at its darkest when he is not by Roderick's side, as on board the Thunder for instance.

[10] Radcliffe famously differentiated between terror and horror, writing: "Terror and Horror are so far opposite that the first expands the soul, and awakens the faculties to a high degree of life; the other contracts, freezes and nearly annihilates them" (see Radcliffe 1826).

reproduces; the sound of the bells, which ushered in the raven, now signals the old man's departure, imparting a cyclical dimension to the passage. This grotesque creature is fearful to Roderick and puzzlingly sinister for the reader who cannot assign him a clear and stable definition.

His disappearance is followed by two codas. First, Strap provides Roderick and the reader with an elaborate interpretation based on supernatural premises (the raven and the old man are both unearthly creatures), an interpretation which Roderick rejects–although in his terror, Strap enhanced the deformity of what was already distorted, magnifying the bird to horse-size and mistaking the ringing of bells for the clanking of chains, Roderick correctly identified both the large raven and the morris bells. If Strap's fertile imagination may raise a smile, Roderick notes that "in all [his] future adventures, [he] never passed a night so ill," which retrospectively sounds surprising in a novel containing the terrible chapters on board the Thunder, in which Roderick falls dangerously ill or is tied up to a mast in the middle of a deadly battle at sea, or in jail, where the hero nearly becomes insane. This sentence, which stresses the psychological impact of those apparitions and specifically the impossibility of defining them precisely and coming up with a convincing explanation, arguably urges the reader to look beyond a merely comical interpretation of the passage as a whole and to consider it in a more disturbing, or at least in a less straightforward light. In the morning, a second interpretation (the second coda) is given by Joey, the driver of the coach in which Roderick and Strap journey to London. He bursts out laughing, as everything is ridiculous to him, both the episode in itself and Strap and Roderick's reactions. Then he explains away the whole mystery in a few short lines: the heroes met with what can now be firmly defined as an idiot and his tamed bird. No relief, no amusement (or shame) however is mentioned by Roderick, nothing is said of the impact of Joey's revelations on the heroes, while the interpolated clause "it seems" might even cast a slight doubt over this explanation. The unease created by this encounter with the grotesque does not appear to be entirely dissipated by the return to daylight, to order and definition. To conclude briefly on this excerpt and return to Ruskin's branches of the grotesque, we may say that the sportive mode predominates with the monstrous raven, while the old idiot's ridiculous traits do not prevent him from falling into the category of the terrible grotesque, which is partly due precisely to his link with the raven, to the fact that he imitates his bird–a repetitive, almost mechanical nature made clear by the two nearly identical sentences he pronounces ("repeated") and by the fact that he follows his raven and reproduces his behaviour, and not the other way round: he is called away by the ringing of a bell like a servant obeying his master's call.

Such is also the way in which Barnaby presents his own relationship with Grip in Dickens's novel. Grip is the master, and Barnaby the servant:

> "Call him!" echoed Barnaby, sitting upright upon the floor, and staring vacantly at Gabriel, as he thrust his hair back from his face. "But who can make him come! He calls me, and makes me go where he will. He goes on before, and I follow. He's the master, and I'm the man. Is that the truth, Grip?" (Dickens 2003, 61)

"I'm the man" has two meanings: if the context (Grip is "the master") makes it clear that it is to be understood as "man servant,"[11] its first sense of "human being" cannot be rejected and Barnaby's insistence on his human condition becomes slightly disturbing, hinting as it does that his human identity needs to be reasserted because it is fundamentally unstable or ill-defined. The blurring of the limit between man and animal recurs several times in the novel, notably when Barnaby describes Grip as his "brother" (473). Since Barnaby and Grip are important characters in a work comprising 700 pages or so, my purpose is not to study one particular passage but rather to distinguish a few recurrent traits in the depiction of each and of their relationship, which in fact relies more on complementarity than on domination.

Indeed, Grip apparently possesses the sense which Barnaby lacks ("The bird has all the wit," 61, explains the novel's true hero, the locksmith Gabriel Varden), filling a gap left by what is explicitly presented by the narrative voice as the "absence of a soul" (35), a void confirmed by the repetition of the adjective "vacant" or the adverb "vacantly" to describe the young man throughout the novel (58, 61, 209, etc.). Barnaby is incomplete, not entirely a man, while Grip is more than a bird, a being whose very nature Varden seems to question: "The locksmith shook his head—perhaps in some doubt of the creature's being really nothing but a bird" (62). Terms like "reflective" or "reflect" are repeatedly associated with the raven (e.g. "the raven was in a highly reflective state," 216), which underlines Grip's presumed thought process and at the same time reveals one aspect of his relationship with Barnaby as man and bird reflect each other in a mirror-image, again making the frontiers between man and animal porous. Gifted with language, Grip appears to understand

---

[11] This idea is taken up a few lines further down, with phrases such as "the bird appeared disposed to come of himself" and "condescending to be held out at arm's length" (61).

what he is told and to answer accurately: "'Is that the truth, Grip?' The raven gave a short, comfortable, confidential kind of croak;—a most expressive croak, which seemed to say, 'You needn't let these fellows into our secrets. We understand each other. It's all right'" (61). The expressive croak aptly answers Barnaby here and elsewhere. Grip might even be able to read, as when he takes a stroll in a cemetery, "appearing to read the tombstones with a very critical taste" (216). Grip calls forth an uncomfortable reaction from the angelically-named Gabriel Varden, who sees him as an evil creature and declares: "'If there's any wickedness going on, that raven's in it, I'll be sworn'" (63). Gabriel's impression, shared by several critics,[12] is caused by certain elements in the story and confirmed by some narrative techniques, which may cast a doubt on Grip's real nature. For instance, like Smollett's bird, Grip is oversized, "a large raven" (60). His hybrid character is frequently brought out when he is compared to a rooster, to a dog (because of the barking sound he makes) and most of all to a man, for instance: "[Grip] went to Barnaby—not in a hop, or walk, or run, but in a pace like that of a very particular gentleman with exceedingly tight boots on, trying to walk fast over loose pebbles," (61) or "walking up and down when he had dined, with an air of elderly complacency which was strongly suggestive of his having his hands under his coat-tails" (216).[13] Grip is regularly personified thanks to the pronoun "he" or the possessive "his" and the narrative voice endows him with human feelings or attributes, "critical taste," "complacency" or condescension for instance in the passages quoted above.

Most of all perhaps, as evoked previously, the preternaturally long-lived Grip[14] presents himself as a fiendish creature, repeatedly asserting "I'm a devil," usually three times in a row, incantation-like. He does so for instance when, most fittingly, he visits a cemetery: "Sometimes, after a long inspection of an epitaph, he would strop his beak upon the grave to

---

[12] James K. Gottshall thus describes Grip as "a clear symbol of evil ironically loved by the innocent boy," which "stands as a kind of externalized demon in possession of Barnaby" (Gottshall 1961, 141). Such an extreme interpretation, both of Grip as a "symbol of evil" and of Barnaby as an "innocent boy," is convincingly challenged by other critics, as will be seen further down in the present chapter; a more nuanced view is put forward by John Bowen, who sees Grip as "one aspect of the ghostly and uncanny forces" which cannot be "easily exorcised" (Bowen 2003, xxvii).

[13] Grip does not "hop," as ravens do–and as Smollett's does.

[14] Described as "a mere infant for a raven, when Barnaby was grey," he is presumed to have "very probably gone on talking to the present time" (688) in the very last sentence of a novel published in 1841 but set in 1780.

which it referred, and cry in his hoarse tones, 'I'm a devil, I'm a devil, I'm a devil!'" (216). Similarly, he seems to draw a "magic circle" (520) around Barnaby and his father in jail and is described as "look[ing] like the embodied spirit of evil" (212). Black, carrion-eating ravens with their "hoarse" cries (the adjective is repeated many times to describe Grip's voice), have "long been regarded as creatures of mystery and ill omen, presagers of doom and death," as Jerome H. Buckley puts it (Buckley 1992, 29); they also mediate the opposition between life and death, as Grip does when he enjoys his walk around the cemetery and urges his audience "Never say die" (Dickens 2003, 61, 96, 152, 153, etc.). For anthropologists like Claude Lévi-Strauss (Lévi-Strauss 1963, 224), the crow, hovering between nature and the supernatural, the human and the inhuman, stands for a figure of the trickster, an a-moral creature which can be comical as well as sinister and is often considered as grotesque, by Geoffrey Harpham for instance (Harpham 1982, 53). This hybrid figure eludes ready definition and acts as a go-between, linking different worlds, notably the divine and the human, a role which mirrors Barnaby's mediation as a messenger between the novel's thwarted lovers as well as between its sworn enemies.

The effect this grotesque bird produces on Gabriel Varden is not altogether positive as the locksmith is "divided between admiration of the bird and a kind of fear of him" (Dickens 2003, 60). Grip's hybrid character and his strange relationship with Barnaby, as described above, might lead the reader to share Varden's suspicion and conclude that the raven belongs to the terrible grotesque, a demonic creature leading Barnaby, who would be as it were his victim, into a nocturnal world; the fact that the pair appears mostly by night in the first part of the novel would confirm this, as well as the description of Barnaby's soul as "benighted" (51). The raven's fiendish nature as perceived by Varden would thus reflect on Barnaby, turning the two of them into representatives of the forces which elude the understanding and remain unfathomable to human beings, nocturnal, perhaps demonic forces which, like Grip, are here tamed. This reading of Barnaby and especially of Grip, based mostly on Varden's reactions and propounded in particular by James Gottshall, comes very close to Wolfgang Kayser's conception of the grotesque as "an attempt to invoke and submit the demonic aspects of the world" (Kayser 1981, 185). It might be argued however that the reader reacts differently to Grip from Varden and perceives the raven in an essentially comic light, as Gordon Spence points out (Spence 1986, 16). Indeed, Grip's interventions often contribute to ease the tension in some highly emotionally-charged passages, as when Barnaby probes into the secret his mother desperately tries to conceal:

"I have always seen you—I didn't let you know it, but I have—on the evening of that day grow very sad. I have seen you cry when Grip and I were most glad; and look frightened with no reason; and I have touched your hand, and felt that it was cold—as it is now. Once, mother (on a birthday that was, also), Grip and I thought of this after we went upstairs to bed, and when it was midnight, striking one o'clock, we came down to your door to see if you were well. You were on your knees. I forget what it was you said. Grip, what was it we heard her say that night?"

"I'm a devil" rejoined the raven promptly. (Dickens 2003, 150-1)

Grip's catch-phrase "I'm a devil" here provides comic relief, and is elsewhere used or referred to comically by the narrative voice, who thus comments that the bird "asserted his brimstone birth and parentage with great distinctness" (61). Furthermore, the personification alluded to above operates through comparisons or modalised utterances such as "appeared," "seemed," or "looked like," revealing that Grip's recurrent characterization as a hybrid or ill-defined creature is ultimately to be interpreted as playful; this is confirmed by the definitely clear-cut definition he once receives as "a creature of mere brute instinct" (390). This definition, which dispels any shade of ambiguity, occurs in a passage where Grip and Barnaby, likewise clearly defined as an "idiot" on the same page, are confronted with a landed proprietor, a stupid, illiterate, and violent magistrate said to be a "man," and even a "gentleman," who will be responsible for the death sentence passed on Barnaby and appears as much more truly terrifying than either Barnaby or his raven.

Unlike the phrase "a creature of mere brute instinct" though, the definition given to Barnaby ("an idiot") still retains a part of ambiguity as it refers to a hybrid character caught between two worlds, whose nature, that of an adult who will always remain a child, as his mother well knows,[15] is uncertain. This appears plainly in the description he is given at his first entrance into the novel in a passage where, and it must be noted, Grip is *not* present:

As he stood, at that moment, half shrinking back and half bending forward, both his face and figure were full in the strong glare of the link, and as distinctly revealed as though it had been broad day. He was about three-and-twenty years old, and though rather spare, of a fair height and strong make. His hair, of which he had a great profusion, was red, and hanging in

---

[15] "...perhaps the comfort springs that he is ever a relying, loving child to me— never growing old or cold at heart, but needing my care and duty in his manly strength as in his cradle-time—help him, in his darkened walk through this sad world, or he is doomed, and my poor heart is broke" (154).

disorder about his face and shoulders, gave to his restless looks an expression quite unearthly—enhanced by the paleness of his complexion, and the glassy lustre of his large protruding eyes. Startling as his aspect was, the features were good, and there was something even plaintive in his wan and haggard aspect. But, the absence of the soul is far more terrible in a living man than in a dead one; and in this unfortunate being its noblest powers were wanting.

His dress was of green, clumsily trimmed here and there—apparently by his own hands—with gaudy lace; brightest where the cloth was most worn and soiled, and poorest where it was at the best. A pair of tawdry ruffles dangled at his wrists, while his throat was nearly bare. He had ornamented his hat with a cluster of peacock's feathers, but they were limp and broken, and now trailed negligently down his back. Girt to his side was the steel hilt of an old sword without blade or scabbard; and some parti-coloured ends of ribands and poor glass toys completed the ornamental portion of his attire. The fluttered and confused disposition of all the motley scraps that formed his dress, bespoke, in a scarcely less degree than his eager and unsettled manner, the disorder of his mind, and by a grotesque contrast set off and heightened the more impressive wildness of his face. (35)

Wolfgang Kayser considers madness as a paradigm of the grotesque, insisting on the estrangement from human nature which it represents while seeing it as belonging to what Ruskin would term the "terrible grotesque": "it is as if an impersonal form or alien and inhuman spirit had entered the soul. The encounter with madness is one of the basic experiences of the grotesque which life forces upon us" (Kayser 1981, 186). As we saw, this was very much the effect produced by the old man in the excerpt from Smollett's novel, while Barnaby's description, explicitly evoking a "grotesque contrast," is not comical and conveys first of all an idea of disorder (the word is repeated twice). Barnaby's expression is "quite unearthly" while the "paleness of his complexion" evokes a ghost. The "wildness of his face," reminiscent of the "wild peculiarity" of the old man's "eyes and countenance" in *Roderick Random*, is heightened by the peacock's feathers he uses as ornaments for his hat, thus displaying his ornithological kinship with Grip–his animal dimension, which does not require Grip's presence to be effective, will be developed later on in the novel when Barnaby wanders off with dogs (and Grip) as his sole companions. No wonder then that Barnaby's closest associate, Hugh, is an ostler nicknamed the "centaur," who sleeps in a stable and is happiest when around horses and dogs. Barnaby's outfit is made up of diverse elements curiously put together and "parti-coloured," while "motley" conjures up the image of a fool or jester, to whose habit the term is traditionally applied–in this case, of a fool whose aspect may be ridiculous but whose demeanour is not amusing. Barnaby thus belongs to a type of grotesque partly ridiculous and slightly fearful; the young man's position itself, "half shrinking back and half bending forward," seems to obey two contradictory impulses while the reaction he arouses in Gabriel Varden is also ambiguous. Although Gabriel feels both pity and tenderness for Barnaby, a tenderness entirely absent from Smollett's extract,[16] he mistrusts him, speaking for instance as low as possible to avoid being overheard by him (Dickens 2003, 58), and here the reader may well be led to share Gabriel's mixed sentiments towards an idiot who bears physically the trace of the crime committed by his father, as though he were marked by evil. A young man fascinated by gold who abandons his mother to take part in the Gordon riots alongside very shady characters, Barnaby "is not only a victim of evil, but also a participator in it," writes Gordon Spence (Spence 1986, 17), making him a far more elusive and thus destabilizing character than his raven. So while the traditionally ominous raven belongs to the sportive grotesque in both *Roderick Random* and *Barnaby Rudge*, at least as perceived by the reader, the balance is more complex when we consider the *human* grotesque figure of the idiot, where the fearful predominates in Smollett and a slight unease remains perceptible in Dickens, caused by Barnaby's ambiguous character. "Unease" is however not quite the same thing as the fear or repulsion caused by evil, which in these two novels is the mark of clearly-defined, non-grotesque, supposedly reasonable "men" like Oakhum in *Roderick Random* or Dickens's magistrate and sir John Chester, whereas "poor Barnaby" (Dickens 2003, 43-44, 412, 417, 480, etc.), whatever his errors, does not cease to be the object of Varden's compassion–and of his author's.

References

Beasley, Jerry. 1998. *Tobias Smollett, Novelist*. Athens: The University of Georgia Press.

Bowen, John. 2003. Introduction to *Barnaby Rudge* by Charles Dickens. xiii-xxxi. London: Penguin.

---

[16] This points to an essential difference between Dickens and Smollett, as Dickens perceived it at least when he seemed to regret that Smollett's was "a way without tenderness" in a letter to Frank Stone (2 November 1854). He alludes here particularly to *Roderick Random* and *Peregrine Pickle*.

Buckley, Jerome H. 1992. "'Quoth the Raven': The Role of Grip in *Barnaby Rudge.*" *Dickens Studies Annual: Essays on Victorian Fiction* 21: 27-35.

Dickens, Charles. (1841) 2003. *Barnaby Rudge.* London: Penguin.

—. 1969. *The Letters of Charles Dickens, Volume II, 1840-1.* Edited by Madeline House and Graham Storey. Oxford: Clarendon Press.

Gottshall, James K. 1961. "Devils Abroad: The Unity and Significance of *Barnaby Rudge.*" *Nineteenth-Century Fiction* 16: 133-46.

Harpham, Geoffrey. 1982. *On the Grotesque: Strategies of Contradiction in Art and Literature.* Princeton: Princeton University Press.

Hollington, Michael. 1984. *Dickens and the Grotesque.* Beckenham (Kent): Croom Helm.

Kayser, Wolfgang. (1957) 1981. *The Grotesque in Art and Literature.* Translated by Ulrich Weisstein. New York: Columbia University Press.

Lévi-Strauss, Claude. (1958) 1963. *Structural Anthropology.* Translated by Claire Jacobson and Brooke Grundfest Schoepf. New-York: Doubleday Anchor Books.

Notestein, Wallace. 1946. *The Scot in History.* New Haven: Yale University Press.

Radcliffe, Ann. 1826. "On the Supernatural in Poetry." *New Monthly Magazine.* Vol. 16, n° 1.

Ruskin, John. (1886) 2007. *Stones of Venice. Volume III: The Fall.* New York: Cosimo.

Smollett, Tobias. (1748) 1999, 2008. *Roderick Random.* With an Introduction by Paul-Gabriel Boucé. Oxford: Oxford University Press.

Spence, Gordon. 1986. Introduction to *Barnaby Rudge* by Charles Dickens, xi-xlii. London: Penguin.

Wiestra, F. D. 1928. *Smollett and Dickens.* Amsterdam: De Bor.

Wittig, Kurt. 1958. *The Scottish Tradition in Literature.* Edinburgh: Oliver and Boyd.

CHAPTER FOUR

OF GIANTS AND GROTESQUES: THE DICKENSIAN GROTESQUE AND THE RETURN FROM ITALY

MICHAEL HOLLINGTON

Although, by Dickensian standards, *Pictures from Italy* is a very short book, it uses the word "grotesque" more frequently than any other written by him. It's as though he knew, or sensed, that "grotesque" was an Italian term (coined in the Renaissance, with the archaeological discovery of Nero's *Domus Aurea*, mistakenly believed at first to be a set of caves or "*grotta*," hence the word "*grottesche*" applied to the new hybrid human/animal/floral/monstrous decorative patterns, half-sinister, half-playful, to be found there). And he uses the word with some accuracy in relevant contexts, that is to say, largely in connection with buildings, paintings and other works of art.

Even *en route* in France Dickens is on the look-out for signs of the grotesque foreign other. He passes through French towns where he observes on the city walls "little towers at the angles, like grotesque faces, as if the walls had put a mask on, and were staring down into the moat" (Dickens 1987, 264). Hybridity reigns in this classic Dickensian simile, which personifies these walled towns via the intermediate inanimate mask, as in English pantomime and Italian *commedia dell'arte*–important reference points for thinking about the Dickensian grotesque. He is already in fact anticipating Italian architecture here, for there he will note in similar fashion "ancient buildings, of a sombre brown, embellished with innumerable grotesque monsters and dreamy-looking creatures carved in marble and red stone" (318). But in Parma we have moved from fanciful "as if" to rather more precise, if imaginatively heightened, descriptive writing of conventional grotesque ornamentation of a kind that seems to correspond pretty closely to that of the *Domus Aurea* classic original decorative friezes.

Again in France, this time in Lyon, Dickens uses the word "grotesque" as a term of art criticism when he comments on the votive offerings in the chapels of the cathedral: "in a grotesque squareness of outline, an impossibility of perspective, they are not unlike the woodcuts in old books" (273). In Genoa he again applies it to painting, though now in an obviously satiric context that emphasises through oxymoron the role of humour in grotesque art as well as hybridity and paradoxicality, as he describes "a most grotesque and hideously comic old soul: for ever blistering in the red sun, and melting in the mimic fire, for the gratification and improvement (and the contributions) of the poor Genoese" (299).

But the most distinctive confrontation with grotesque art in *Pictures from Italy* occurs in Mantua, in the *Sala dei Giganti* of the Mannerist artist Giulio Romano at the *Palazzo del Te*. "Inconceivably ugly and grotesque," is how Dickens describes the frescoes (343), and the tone is on the surface at least thoroughly disapproving. But isn't there a modicum of the familiar Dickensian "attraction of repulsion" here, in such choices as the use of the word "marvellous" to exclaim "that it is marvellous how any man can have imagined such creatures," or in the energy of the evocation in vivid participles of the giants' struggle against God, "staggering," "falling," "being overwhelmed," "upheaving," "striving," etc.? I shall argue that Dickens was in fact fascinated by this work, and that giants–although an essential part of Dickens's inheritance from fairy tale and popular culture from the very beginning–occur more frequently than one might otherwise expect in the works that follow the return from Italy. I shall also suggest more generally that there is perhaps thereafter a new element in the Dickensian grotesque, that I shall call the "composite grotesque."

To get at this latter it is necessary to move away from examining specific instances of the word "grotesque" in an artistic context to looking at Dickens's intense experience of everyday human grotesques on the streets of Italy. If Dickens the London *flâneur* came across grotesque sights at every turn, in Genoa or Naples or Rome these could be replicated several times over. What had Leonardo's famous *Grotesque Heads* been, if not the reflection of the bizarre, disturbing faces and bodies that the artist saw about him in Renaissance Italian cities (Zöllner 2000, 42)? Things had perhaps not changed all that much by the time Dickens went there–he certainly thought they had been stuck in a rut for centuries. And so there were perhaps plenty of grotesque faces and bodies to be seen on city streets in Italy. At any rate, I shall now look at two passages of many that can be used to suggest an intense exposure to pre-modern displays of physical monstrosity in public places in 19th-century Italy, and to propose again that in some shape or form they haunted Dickens's imagination long thereafter.

As with the Giants, both these passages concern groups or crowds of grotesques–in this case actual, living nightmares–but both of them in fact juxtapose and interconnect what can be called very crudely, the grotesque in art with the grotesque in life. The first, in purely visual terms, is perhaps the subtler and more arresting: it is the description of a crowd of beggars in the town of Fondi on the way to Naples, who came

> [...] flocking about us, fighting and jostling one another, and demanding, incessantly, charity for the love of God, charity for the love of the Blessed Virgin, charity for the love of all the Saints. A group of miserable children, almost naked, screaming forth the same petition, discover that they can see themselves reflected in the varnish of the carriage, and begin to dance and make grimaces, that they may have the pleasure of seeing their antics repeated in the mirror. A crippled idiot, in the act of striking one of them who drowns his clamorous demand for charity, observes his angry counterpart in the panel, stops short, and thrusting out his tongue, begins to wag his head and chatter. (Dickens 1987, 410-1)

The passage may have its ultimate origin in Dickens's imagination in a memory of ubiquitous advertisements for Warren's Blacking, where he had worked as a child, which show a man shaving in front of the brilliant shine on the boots supposedly created by the product, or a cock recoiling in shock from its image reflected in another boot mirror. What I am chiefly interested in here, though, is how the mirror effect of the varnish on the coach multiplies the grotesque images, giving us hosts of children dancing, or duplicated crippled idiots.

The other passage is yet more illuminating in this respect, for here the separate fragments of grotesque bodies, as seen in the *Sala dei Giganti*, are reassembled in the writing into a yet more hideous inorganic amalgam. Dickens conflates what he has seen on the walls of the upper church in Parma with what he sees amongst real live human beggars in the subterranean one,

> [...] supported by marble pillars behind each of which there seemed to be at least one beggar in ambush: to say nothing of the tombs and secluded altars. From every one of these lurking-places, such crowds of phantom-looking men and women with twisted limbs, or chattering jaws, or paralytic gestures, or idiotic heads, or some other sad infirmity, came hobbling out to beg, that if the ruined frescoes in the cathedral above, had been suddenly animated, and had retired to this lower church, they could

hardly have made a greater confusion, or exhibited a more confounding
display of arms and legs. (319)

The image of this jumble of bodies–or indeed, elsewhere in Dickens,
of things–as a nightmarish grotesque heap of inorganic matter was, I
believe, to take hold of Dickens's imagination throughout the rest of his
career. Followed through, it might lead us to such places as Krook's in
Bleak House or Mr. Venus's in *Our Mutual Friend*. But I repeat that my
aim today is something much more limited and general. It is simply to
show how the experience of the grotesque in Italy lingered on in Dickens's
mind, and is at times directly reflected in the main works that Dickens
wrote in the three years following his return from Italy in July 1845–that is
to say, in the three Christmas books of 1845, 1846 and 1848 (*The Cricket
on the Hearth*, *The Battle of Life*, and *The Haunted Man*), and above all in
Dickens's first mature masterpiece *Dombey and Son*. These works can be
treated as a group that can be circumscribed by saying that if the word
"grotesque" is more prominent in *Pictures from Italy* than anywhere else,
it is *Dombey and Son*, amongst the novels, that runs it closest. Let me add
parenthetically that although I am obviously not claiming that Italy was an
essential catalyst for Dickens's grotesque imagination–prominent, of
course, since his earliest writings–his experience of grotesque art, popular
culture, and the daily theatre of street life in that country in the mid-1840s
was I believe a consciousness-raiser that seems to have spurred him on to
produce a greater range of grotesque effects in his writing than he had
attempted hitherto.

So I want to look first very briefly into the grotesque in the three
Christmas Books. In *The Cricket on the Hearth*, the only book written in
1845, just as *The Chimes* had been the only book written in 1844 in this
period of sabbatical, Dickens focuses on a grotesque toy factory.
Returning to London from Italy, he had been dismayed by what he found
there: "London is as flat as it can be," he wrote in August 1845, "there is
nothing to talk about but Railroad shares. And as I am not a Capitalist, I
don't find anything very interesting in that" (Dickens 1977, 361). Railway
mania was to become a major focus in *Dombey and Son* in 1846, of
course, but for the moment, instead of railroad track, Dickens focuses on
another commodity: toys. Tackleton, the grotesque Pantaloon of this
novella–the main plot of which hinges on the thwarting of his project of
ensnaring in marriage a young morsel of female flesh–deals in assembly
lines of duplicated human and animals, monsters and of course giants, and
these get piled up in heaps and jumbles as in the Italian grotesques. He is a
kind of Giulio Romano of the toy world, revelling in creating
"unaccountable nightmares," and teaching his apprentices how to create

things that are "inconceivably ugly and grotesque" to frighten the children who are the customers of his merchandise. We learn that:

> In intensifying the portraiture of Giants, he had sunk quite a little capital; and, though no painter himself, he could indicate, for the instruction of his artists, with a piece of chalk, a certain furtive leer for the countenances of those monsters, which was safe to destroy the peace of mind of any young gentleman between the ages of six and eleven, for the whole Christmas or Midsummer Vacation. (Dickens 2006, 180)

As with Major Bagstock in *Dombey and Son*, the grotesque in Tackleton shades over into the diabolical. Like Joey B., he peppers his speech with references to the "old gentleman," as the devil is appositely named in this January/May story. Admiring another young female item of potential consumption, Dot, he mutters to himself, *sotto voce*, that she is "handsomer every day! Better too, if possible! And younger ... that's the Devil of it!" (179). His totem is the raven, and Dickens is clearly remembering his own pet Grip when he sketches his physical appearance, and also seems to refer with the prominent word "essence" to the "humours" psychology operative in the play he was appearing in at the same time as writing this book, Ben Jonson's *Every Man in His Humour*:

> He didn't look much like a bridegroom, as he stood in the Carrier's kitchen, with a twist in his dry face, and a screw in his body, [...] and his whole sarcastic ill-conditioned self peering out of one little corner of one little eye, like the concentrated essence of any number of ravens. (181)

But the most interesting thing for me about the grotesque in *The Cricket on the Hearth* is the working up of the experience of jumbled fragments of bodies in Italy into an image in London of an entire system. The word "grotesque," indeed, makes its one appearance in this work at a very salient moment, referring to the mounds of "spare part" human effigies lying around in Caleb Plummer's room, commenting on their allegorical significance, and denying that there is anything caricatural about perceiving this:

> As it would have been hard to count the dozens upon dozens of grotesque figures that were ever ready to commit all sorts of absurdities on the turning of a handle, so it would have been no easy task to mention any human folly, vice, or weakness, that had not its type, immediate or remote, in Caleb Plummer's room. And not in an exaggerated form, for very little handles will move men and women to as strange performances, as any Toy was ever made to undertake. (190)

The extent to which this system routinely and mechanically takes over anyone who gets mixed up in it is illustrated in the handling of Caleb Plummer himself. Essentially a sympathetic figure–the victim of Tackleton rather than his assistant or agent–he nevertheless betrays the extent to which he has absorbed and internalised that reification of others into commodities that distinguishes the capitalist entrepreneur for whom he works. When Peerybingle comes home with another "old gentleman" (Edward) this is how Caleb Plummer sizes him up as a potential toy or novelty item for household use:

> "A beautiful figure for a nut-cracker; quite a new model. With a screw-jaw opening down into his waistcoat, he'd be lovely […] or for a firebox either, […] what a model! Unscrew his head to put the matches in; turn him heels up'ards for the light; and what a firebox for a gentleman's mantel-shelf, just as he stands." (184)

The irony of course is that the person whom he thus mentally translates into an object is his own son in disguise, returned from overseas, and like Harmon in *Our Mutual Friend*, wishing to make incognito assessment of the continuing fidelity of his former sweetheart now about to be married to the monstrous Tackleton.

There are no giants in the 1846 Christmas Book *The Battle of Life* (written abroad again, this time in Switzerland: Dickens had wanted to go straight back to Genoa and the *Palazzo Peschiere*, but his wife had flatly refused on account of his "mesmerising" experiments with Mrs. De la Rue), but there is one figure worth commenting on in the context of the idea of the "composite grotesque." This is Clemency Newcome, whose essence is summed up in another of those oxymorons characteristic of Dickensian grotesques as "dislocated tidiness." She is presented as an amalgam, in her own body, of multiple bits of other people:

> She was about thirty years old, and had a sufficiently plump and cheerful face, though it was twisted up into an odd expression of tightness that made it comical. But, the extraordinary homeliness of her gait and manner, would have superseded any face in the world. To say that she had two left legs, and somebody else's arms, and that all four limbs seemed to be out of joint, and to start from perfectly wrong places when they were set in motion, is to offer the mildest outline of the reality. (253)

And again–although separate body parts with a will of their own is a staple of early Dickens as much as of late–it is possible to speculate that the experience of stringed puppets in Italy, together with that of crowds of cripples, had a hand in bringing the conception to consciousness.

The comedy of Clemency, like that of the nurse Tilly Slowboy in *The Cricket on the Hearth*, thus resides in her clumsiness. She has unruly elbows that are forever collecting bruises and scabs as she bumps into objects and persons alike. But the crucial point that Dickens is trying to make about her–again perhaps reflecting his gradual acceptance that the ugly exterior of things seen in Italy did not reflect the essential nature of the country and its people–is that she may be grotesquely "dislocated" but she is essentially "tidy," in a moral sense implying more than just the fact that her husband-to-be can relish the sight of himself, like the idiot in Fondi, in the reflection of his own appearance offered by the spotlessly clean copper pans in her kitchen. Again the story functions as ironic allegory, for he, "little" Britain, in his patronising belittlement of her supposed mental backwardness, serves obviously enough as a reflection of the indifference of "Great" Britain to the virtues and courage of its common people. Clemency is the heroine of this story at its crucial moment, her key unlocking the door that allows Marion to escape and thereby sacrifice herself so that her sister can marry Alfred Heathfield.

I shall also look at one image only from *The Haunted Man*, the fifth and last of the Christmas Books, appearing in 1848 after the completion of *Dombey and Son*. The story clearly reflects that novel, as we shall see, but it also relates recognisably to *Pictures from Italy*: first, in its emphasis on "shadows," proclaimed as the essential medium of the travel book ("This Book is a series of faint reflections–mere shadows on the water," Dickens 1987, 260), and second, in its quasi-obligatory reference to a fairy-tale giant. In the course of the long virtuoso evocation of Redlaw's lonely world at twilight in winter with which the story commences, consisting of a string of anaphoric sentences each beginning with "when," there is a passage that focuses on the grotesque transformations of everyday objects in the half-light of his rooms, and climaxes in gigantism:

> When twilight everywhere released the shadows, prisoned up all day, that now closed in and gathered like mustering swarms of ghosts. When they stood lowering, in corners of rooms, and frowned out from behind half-opened doors. When they had full possession of unoccupied apartments. When they danced upon the floors, and walls, and ceilings of inhabited chambers, while the fire was low, and withdrew like ebbing waters when it sprang into a blaze. When they fantastically mocked the shapes of household objects, making the nurse an ogress, the rocking-horse a monster, the wondering child, half-scared and half-amused, a stranger to itself, the very tongs upon the hearth, a straddling giant with his arms a-kimbo, evidently smelling the blood of Englishmen, and wanting to grind people's bones to make his bread. (Dickens 2006, 328)

Here, in the striking phrase "the wondering child, half-scared and half-amused, a stranger to itself," we can see I think the greater psychological depth in the deployment of the grotesque that Dickens has achieved in the meantime in *Dombey and Son*. Paul Dombey is surrounded by grotesques–Glubb, Feeder, Pipchin, etc.–but there is an ominous undertone to his being drawn to them. Here, in the case of Pipchin, the word is used in a context that has less to do with art than with an attempt to convey the profound ontological insecurity that his fascination with the grotesque betrays: "He was not fond of her; he was not afraid of her; but in those old, old moods of his, she seemed to have a grotesque attraction for him" (Dickens 1960, 103). Earlier in the same chapter, in a related passage, Paul had been seen

> [...] sitting brooding in his miniature arm-chair, when he looked (and talked) like one of those terrible little Beings in the Fairy tales, who, at a hundred and fifty or two hundred years of age, fantastically represent the children for whom they have been substituted. (91)

That Paul Dombey might not be Paul Dombey at all but a changeling in his shape is a powerful way of bolstering the suggestion, here and elsewhere, of the tenuousness of his hold on life.

Here he is clearly "a stranger to himself," as he is in another passage where the term "grotesque" accompanies psychological probing. Here Paul is about to leave the surroundings of Doctor Blimber's school (for the last time, as it turns out), and wanders into some of the rooms to bid them, as it were, farewell. As he does so he imagines a mirror image of himself:

> He had to think–would any other child (old-fashioned, like himself) stray there at any time, to whom the same grotesque distortions of pattern and furniture would manifest themselves; and would anybody tell that boy of little Dombey, who had been there once? (193-4)

Imagining this double who is not Paul Dombey, Paul seems tacitly in the process of losing his own grip on life.

The link with giants can be achieved by means of a third passage in which the term "grotesque" figures prominently, this time in connection with another child, Paul's sister Florence. In Chapter 34 we are introduced to a striking instance of what Francesco Orlando calls the "threadbare grotesque": "a heap of rags, a heap of bones, a wretched bed, two or three mutilated chairs or stools, etc.," together with a fire and an old woman "with a gigantic and distorted image of herself thrown half upon the wall behind her, half upon the ceiling above ... [looking] as if she were watching at some witch's altar for a favourable token." That giant shadow (reflecting *Pictures from Italy* of course once more) corresponds it seems to Florence's memory of her terrifying childhood encounter with the person it reflects:

> If Florence could have stood within the room and looked upon the original of the shadow thrown upon the wall and roof, as it cowered thus over the fire, a glance might have sufficed to recall the figure of Good Mrs. Brown; notwithstanding that her childish recollection of that terrible old woman was as grotesque and exaggerated a presentment of the truth, perhaps, as the shadow on the wall. (484)

But even if Florence is spared the reliving of that terror, the image of magnification contained in the idea of the grotesque giant shadow of Mrs Brown has deep structural significance in this book. Staggs's Garden is a primary instance, another essential Giulio Romano nightmare that combines giant forms and chaos to make a colossal jumble. It is, like the *Sala dei Giganti*, as "unintelligible as any dream," where "there were a hundred thousand shapes and substances of incompleteness, wildly mingled out of their places," with "fragments of unfinished walls and arches," and, towering over everything, "giant forms of cranes, and tripods straddling above nothing" (63).

Britain as a whole, it seems, has become one vast hall of giants threatening to tear down its walls. A later, related instance of the monstrous size and scale of industrial exploitation overtaking the countryside of England in the name of "the conquest of nature" is the waste land caused by urban development around the house of Mr. Carker the junior in Chapter 33. It is an area that

> [   ] is neither of the town nor country. The former, like the giant in his travelling boots, has made stride and passed it, and has set his brick-and-mortar heel a long way in advance; but the intermediate space between the giant's feet, as yet, is only blighted country, and not town. (472)

Later still, the focus of all this feverish enterprise, the steam railway engine itself, takes centre stage as Carker the manager endures a night of terror as it passes by outside his bedroom:

> He still lay listening; and when he felt the trembling and vibration, got up and went to the window, to watch (as he could from its position) the dull light changing to the two red eyes, and the fierce fire dropping glowing coals, and the rush of the giant as it fled past, and the track of glare and smoke across the valley. (777)

Everywhere there is giant construction, even in the home. Florence does in fact experience a version of the Giulio Romano nightmare at the time of her father's remarriage, when the house she has known as home is pulled apart in the name of "improvements." There is direct reference to the *Palazzo del Te* here, which of course functions as ironic foreboding of the fall of the house of Dombey:

> [...] a whole Olympus of plumbers and glaziers was reclining in various attitudes on the skylight [...]. She went up swiftly to that other bedroom, where the little bed was; and a dark giant of a man with a pipe in his mouth, and with his head tied up in a pocket-handkerchief, was staring in at the window. (405)

The home figures prominently elsewhere in connection with giants, and here again they stand as allegorical figures of the enormous shadows cast upon domestic hearths by hidden secrets. Harriet Carker seated alone at home, anxious about her brother in the hours before the arrival of Alice Brown the prostitute, who is to die there, can experience no respite from her fearful imaginings of what may happen to him:

> The room resumed its shadowy terrors, the moment she left it; and she had no more power to divest herself of those vague impressions of dread, than if they had been stone giants, rooted in the solid earth. (750-1)

Most significantly of all, Edith Dombey sits alone in front of the blasted domestic hearth, brooding on the huge and momentous consequences of her estrangement from her husband that are to come:

> Far into the night she sat alone, by the sinking blaze. In dark and threatening beauty, watching the murky shadows looming on the wall, as if her thoughts were tangible, and cast them there. Whatever shapes of outrage and affront, and black foreshadowings of things that might happen, flickered, indistinct and giant-like, before her, one resented figure marshalled them against her. And that figure was her husband. (603)

Dombey himself, it appears, is the giant who brings down his own household.

And yet, to conclude by remembering Mr. Sleary in *Hard Times*– "people mutht be amuthed," (Dickens 1966, 293)–there are giants to laugh at in *Dombey and Son* as well: Joey B, for instance, who eats himself silly at the Royal Hotel in Leamington Spa, and then "rose next morning [...] like a giant refreshed [...] [and] conducted himself, at breakfast, like a giant refreshing" (Dickens 1960, 284), or those that haunt the immortal

Toots after he engages his boxing tutor The Game Chicken: "there were husks in his corn, that even Game Chickens couldn't peck up; gloomy giants in his leisure, that even Game Chickens couldn't knock down" (314). For Dickens's essential case is that the banishing of giants and dwarves and all forms of the marvellous and fanciful in fairy tale and legend from the landscape of Victorian England, in the name of rationality, progress, and economic advancement, then as now, boomerangs back upon itself, producing monstrous distortions of the imagination in the form of refracted consequential nightmares. At Dr. Blimber's school, Paul's schoolfellow Tozer has his life blighted by a Gradgrindian uncle who shadows forth the offence to childhood that will cause Paul's death:

> […] if this uncle took him to the play, or, on a similar pretence of kindness, carried him to see a Giant, or a Dwarf, or a Conjuror, or anything, Tozer knew he had read up some classical allusion to the subject beforehand, and was thrown into a state of mortal apprehension. (181)

At the wedding of Mr Dombey and Edith the pew-opener forcibly expels a pair of grotesques who might have brought a blessing to their marriage: "Truly, Mrs. Miff has cause to pounce on an unlucky dwarf child, with a giant baby, who peeps in at the porch, and drive her forth with indignation!" (439). The result of course is cataclysmic disaster for both husband and wife.

References

Dacos, Nicole. 1969. *La découverte de la* Domus Aurea *et la formation des grotesques à la Renaissance*. London: Warburg Institute.

Dickens, Charles. (1846) 1987. "Pictures from Italy." In *American Notes and Pictures from Italy*. With an Introduction by Sacheverell Sitwell. London: Oxford University Press.

—. (1843-6) 2006. *A Christmas Carol and Other Christmas Books*. Edited by Robert Douglas-Fairhurst. Oxford: Oxford University Press.

—. (1848) 1960. *Dombey and Son*. With an Introduction by H.W. Garrod. London: Oxford University Press.

—. (1854) 1966. *Hard Times*. With an Introduction by Dingle Foot. London: Oxford University Press.

—. 1977. *Letters* (Volume Four). Edited by Kathleen Tillotson. Oxford: Clarendon Press.

Kayser, Wolfgang. (1957) 1966. *The Grotesque in Art and Literature*. New York: McGraw Hill.

Orlando, Francesco. 2006. *Obsolete Objects in the Literary Imagination*. Translated by Gabriel Pihas and Daniel Seidel. New Haven CT: Yale University Press.
Zöllner, Frank. 2000. *Leonardo*. Cologne: Taschen.

PART II

EXPRESSING 19TH-CENTURY REALITY: REASON VS. UNREASON

CHAPTER FIVE

GROTESQUE EXTRAVAGANCE IN THE FICTIONAL WORLDS OF CHARLES DICKENS AND NIKOLAI GOGOL FROM THE PERSPECTIVES OF "FANTASTIC REALISM" AND THE EUROPEAN GROTESQUE TRADITION

FLORENCE CLERC

Dickens is probably the most popular English novelist. Nikolai Gogol (1809-1852) was his contemporary and is considered as the father of the Russian novel. Beyond the prominent part they both played in the literature of their respective countries and if one considers the European novel as a whole, strong similarities appear between many aspects of their work. These have been identified but rarely explored in detail.[1] Thus, without playing down the differences in the respective social and cultural contexts,[2] numerous affinities become apparent, most of which revolve

---

[1] Gogol's contemporaries (Vissarion Belinski, Nikolay Chernyshevsky for example) established a connection in the 1840s when Dickens's novels were first published in Russian. As early as 1886, Eugène-Melchior de Voguë considered that "the Russian naturalist school" formed in the 1840s, whose precursor Gogol was, "reminded one of English naturalism and owed a great deal to Dickens," especially in its moral inspiration which differentiated it from French naturalism (Voguë 2010, 65, my translation). Georges Nivat suggests that reading Dickens led Gogol to understand that the metropolis (St. Petersburg in his case) was the common denominator of his fiction (see Nivat 1982). See also Slipchenko 1966; Fanger 1998; Futrell 1956 and Bryner 1963.

[2] Gogol's Russia was feudal and still largely agricultural. Further, he never showed any interest in social reform or the public sphere, as Dickens so consistently did. Culturally speaking, Dickens the novelist was heir to a solid national tradition

around the nature of their comic genius and more specifically their use of the grotesque aesthetics in their representation of reality, notably in the construction of characters and those characters' specific interaction with their milieu.

Nikolai Gogol was already a famous writer when in 1842 he published *Dead Souls*, the masterpiece which founded the Russian novel. At the beginning of the 1830s, *Evenings on a Farm near Dikanka* had been inspired by the legends and traditions of Gogol's native Ukraine. The fantastic and the lyrical were blended with conventional realism in these tales which brought him the fame he had hoped to find in the capital, Saint Petersburg, as well as the friendship of illustrious writers like Pushkin. Gogol then, in the Ukrainian vein, published *Mirgorod*, a collection of stories in which he added to the humour so characteristic of his writings a myriad of nuances ranging from irony to tenderness, while concocting in "Taras Bulba" a narrative both epic and delightful, to tell the story of the Zaporozhian Cossacks' battle against the Polish army. In 1835 three short stories were published in the collection entitled *Arabesques*: "The Portrait," "Nevski Prospekt" and "Diary of a Madman." After later reworking, they formed with "The Calash" (sometimes called "The Carriage"), "The Nose" and "The Overcoat" the collection *Petersburg Tales.*[3] The stories were greatly influenced by Hoffmann's tales, which were very popular in Russia at that time and which Gogol particularly admired. They are set in the metropolis of the North, depicted here as a sombre, often frozen, almost always foggy, urban landscape. The characters are mostly minor public officials, all aristocrats since it is their "*chin*" (social rank) which gives them access to the various positions in the highly hierarchical organization of Czarist administration. These functionaries are often as poor as, if not poorer than, the labourers they walk past in the streets. Gogol, a member of the Russian gentry, who had brought letters of recommendation with him on first arriving in the capital, had been one of those officials and had probably experienced the life he describes in the tales: a lowly clerk's dull existence characterised by the daily laborious routine and the return at night to dismal furnished lodgings. In the confined world of the hero of "Diary of a Madman" or of "The Overcoat,"[4] hope suddenly takes the pitiful shape of a prospective

---

whereas Russia's literature depended mainly on a handful of poets and Romantic writers (Pushkin, Lermontov and others). Gogol gave Russia its first great novel. The horizon of expectation was therefore different.

[3] At the time the *Moscow Observer* rejected the excellent "The Nose," described as "filth."

[4] Probably the best of these short stories, published in 1840.

promotion, of romance with a superior's daughter, or the purchase of a colourful uniform. Thus in *Petersburg Tales* Gogol represents both the mediocrity and pathos of ordinary lives trapped in cruel, comical games of petty social ambition. Gogol resorts to a series of stylistic devices which construct a type of grotesque expressivity[5] similar to what is found in Dickens's depiction of London life in the 1830s in *Sketches by Boz*. In Gogol's short stories however, disappointment, humiliation or simply the unexpected are sources of deep disturbance which, by occasionally leading the characters to madness, push the narrative to the brink of the fantastic.[6]

Circa 1835, Pushkin suggested to Gogol the basic idea for *Dead Souls*. Driven by creative fervour but always lacking inspiration when it came to finding a theme for his works, Gogol also asked Pushkin for an idea for a play. The ensuing play was *The Revisor* (or *The Inspector-General*),

---

[5] Gogol's aesthetics was studied in the first decades of the 20th century by critics of the Russian formalist school. According to Viktor Shklovsky and Boris Eichenbaum, the analysis of Gogol's creation shows that it is based on grotesque expressivity, of which Gogol is a master. Gogol's grotesque, so present in the *Petersburg Tales*, relies on contrast, on violent and sudden oppositions, on the quick succession of tragic and comic details which precipitate the reader from one emotional state to another. Through such fusion of heterogeneous elements, reality is represented as distorted or discordant. The analysis of Gogol's humour led Boris Eichenbaum to define the grotesque: "The style of the grotesque demands, in the first place, that the described situation or event be contained in a world small to the point of the fantastic, [...] completely cut off from the large reality, from the real fullness of spiritual life, and in the second place, that this be done not with a didactic or satirical intent, but with the aim of giving scope for playing with reality, for breaking up and freely displacing its elements, so that the usual correlations and connections (psychological and logical) turn out, in this newly constructed world, to be unreal, and each trifle can grow to colossal dimensions." (Eichenbaum, 1963, 395). This "cutting-off" of the object from its environment corresponds to what Viktor Shklovsky calls "defamiliarization" or "estrangement" and produces the grotesque (see Shklovsky 1998). Gogol's aesthetics, based on the fusion of opposites, corresponds to an essentially ambivalent vision of the world, which Bakhtin describes as the origin of the "carnivalesque" degradation of reality in popular culture (see Bakhtin 1984).

[6] The proximity between the grotesque and the fantastic is evident in the short stories. The intrusion of a fantastic element within every-day reality is not different, in Gogol's fiction, from the alienation of the mundane created by the grotesque. For example, in "The Overcoat," Akaky Akakievich's fixation with his coat, in which he harbours his frustrated ambition, and which Gogol depicts extensively and comically, is closely linked to, and as unlikely as, the fantastic ending of the story. On Gogol's "fantastic Realism" and its links with the grotesque, see Picon-Vallin, 1980.

adapted from a true story: a quid-pro-quo leads corrupt small-town officials to entertain a young man they have mistaken for an inspector working incognito. The play avoided censorship thanks to the Czar's intervention and created a scandal while being received enthusiastically by young writers and progressive critics. But such success worried Gogol, who feared he had been misunderstood.[7] He then embarked on several journeys through Europe to Germany, Switzerland, France and Italy, during which he continued work on *Dead Souls*. He was in Paris in February 1837 when he learned that Pushkin had been killed in a duel and the news affected him deeply. But he had had time to show the great poet the first chapters of his novel, which had met with approval, and Gogol could write to a friend: "It is my duty to see the work through to the end, which he made me write and which he inspired, and for which reason has become for me a sacred legacy."[8]

The manuscript was ready in the early months of 1842, but the censorship committee in Moscow banned it, a fact worthy of Gogol's fiction. The story, once again inspired by a true anecdote, revolves around the adventures of a petty crook, Chichikov, who travels through Russia to buy "dead souls," i.e. title deeds relating to serfs who have died since the last official census, hence remaining on record and for whom serf-owners still have to pay tax. Country squires are often eager to sell these "souls" for a pittance to avoid paying tax, and Chichikov hopes to be able to apply for a low-interest loan to buy a large estate using the fictitious serfs as collateral. The head of the censorship committee was particularly indignant at the novel's title, on the grounds that the soul is immortal. When informed that the "souls" in question were actually serfs, he was even more incensed, believing the novel to be a pamphlet against serfdom. Other committee members took offence at the price per soul (two and a half roubles) and objected that foreigners would be shocked and reluctant to come to Russia. The publication was finally authorized after minor corrections and the title of the work was changed to *The Adventures of Chichikov or Dead Souls*, the addition supposed to soften the impact of the original title through the foregrounding of fictionality.

---

[7] The play was received as a simple farce by some, as political satire by others and Gogol felt that the moral dimension he thought he had conferred on it had not been duly appreciated. A century later, stage-director and avant-garde theorist V. Meyerhold staged *The Revisor* as a grotesque play, after stating that "the grotesque [is] the common denominator of all theatrical forms" (in Picon-Vallin 2004, 55, my translation).

[8] Letter to Vasily Zhukovsky, 6-18th April 1837 (Gogol 1966, 52, my translation from the French).

At the beginning of Chapter One the hero has little about him of the adventurer when he arrives in an ordinary provincial town. In the carriage sits "a gentleman who [is] neither a beauty nor yet very plain [...] neither too stout nor too thin: it was impossible to say that he was old, neither could he be called very young," whose "arrival produce[s] no commotion whatever in the town" (Gogol 2010, 5). The narrator then introduces two muzhiks and an elegant young man who stare at the equipage before disappearing from the story without a trace. Then comes the servant from the inn, "so lively and restless that it was even impossible to see what sort of a face he had," and finally the inn itself is described:

> [...] like all taverns in provincial towns, where, for two roubles a day, travellers receive a sleeping-room with beetles which peep out of every corner like plums, and a door into the adjoining apartment, which is always blocked up with a chest of drawers: in that room a neighbour is always lodged, who is a silent and quiet, but very curious, man, who takes an interest in finding out every particular relating to the stranger. (4)

As the man is inspecting his room his luggage is brought in, which marks the appearance of the first of the many heteroclite objects which haunt the fictional universe: "a trunk of white leather [...], a dressing-case of mahogany with inlaid decorations of veined birch, a boot-jack, and a roast chicken wrapped up in blue paper" (5). These objects constitute an initial, mysterious insight into the character of Chichikov, one the reader will have to be satisfied with since he is given no other detailed description of the hero, either physical or moral. This is probably why the mysterious roast chicken travelling with Chichikov (and which will not end up in the kitchen) and its blue paper remain in the reader's mind for so long. Then follows the description of the parlour:

> Every traveller knows what these common parlours are like: the same walls, painted in oil-colours, darkened above by pipe-smoke, and covered below with marks by the backs of various travellers, and still more by local tradespeople, for merchants came thither on market-days by sixes and sevens to drink their usual two glasses of tea; the same smoke-begrimed ceiling; the same smoky chandelier with its multitude of pendent glass drops, which leaped and jingled every time the waiter ran across the worn oil-cloth, boldly flourishing the tray, upon which stood as many teacups as there are birds on the seashore; the same oil-paintings on all the walls; in a word, everything was exactly the same as what is found everywhere: the only difference was, that one of the pictures represented a nymph with such an enormous bust as the reader has, in all probability, never beheld. Such freaks of nature, however, occur in various historical pictures,

whence, at what time, and by whom, brought to us in Russia is unknown, but sometimes by our grandees, and art-lovers who have purchased them in Italy on the advice of the couriers who conducted them. (5-6)

Such excerpts are typical of Gogol's tendency to single out the incongruous from the ordinary, particularly by conferring on inert objects a life which tends to become exuberant, and thus uncanny.[9] According to Mikhail Bakhtin, the recurrence of images linked to "the material bodily principle" (Bakhtin 1984, 19) originates in the culture of folk humour, closely linked to parodic and subversive carnivalesque rites. Such culture is identifiable in artistic production during the Middle-Ages and the Renaissance, among which one finds Rabelais' work. The type of imagery corresponds to what Bakhtin calls "grotesque realism" (18) and the literary forms derived from that tradition favour corporeal and material representations of the world, "the body and bodily life hav[ing] [...] a cosmic and at the same time an all-people's character" (19). The key principle of grotesque realism is "degradation, that is, the lowering of all that is high, spiritual, ideal, abstract; it is a transfer to the material level, to the sphere of earth and body in their indissoluble unity" (19-20). Ambivalence is therefore a fundamental characteristic of the grotesque, as is the visualization of the process of change, of the "phenomenon in transformation" (24). "In [the grotesque] image," Bakhtin adds, "we find both poles of transformation, the old and the new, the dying and the procreating, the beginning and the end of the metamorphosis" (24).

According to Bakhtin, Gogol's work, "the most significant example of comic literature of the modern period" (Bakhtin 1985, 28), contains aspects of popular comedy which probably originated in his intimate knowledge of grotesque realism, a vital dimension in the "popular culture of feast-days and fairs" (28) of his native land, Ukraine.[10] In Gogol, Bakhtin pinpoints numerous allusions to "the nether regions of both the world and the human body" (31), even in the "distinctive style of the crier's invitation" (32) or "the ambivalent, laudatory-debunking name"

---

[9] Such a tendency is of course also typically Dickensian. To stick to domestic matters, one only has to think of the incipit of "The Cricket on the Hearth" with its intractable kettle and frightening Dutch clock.

[10] Bakhtin analyses Gogol's use of grotesque realism independently from the question of Rabelais' possible influence on the Russian novelist. Such influence, however, may have been transmitted through Sterne, whom Gogol admired. Sterne is considered by Bakhtin as another heir of the carnivalesque tradition: "in all these aspects of Gogol's style and imagery the influence of Sterne (and, through him, of Rabelais) mingled with direct influence of folk comedy" (Bakhtin 1985, 32).

(33) given both to characters and places. Bakhtin considers that in *Dead Souls* Gogol expresses the "popular notions of the link between life and death" (38) and turns the novel into "carnival play with death and the boundaries between life and death" (38).

Bakhtin notes however that Gogol's perception of the carnivalesque "in most cases [...] acquire[s] a romantic colouring through his writing" (33). Even if the Russian critic acknowledges that the Romantics revived the popular tradition of the grotesque, he considers that with Romantic grotesque, laughter loses most of "its positive regenerating power" (Bakhtin 1984, 38). The grotesque becomes somber and private, "an individual carnival" (37). This explains why Bakhtin considers Kayser's analysis of the grotesque as necessarily inadequate, since Kayser bases his definition essentially on Romantic works, in which the "festive madness" of the Renaissance acquires "a somber, tragic aspect of individual isolation" (39). However, the dark and chilling perception of an estranged world, which is a key element in Kayser's definition, seems essential to Gogol's–as well as Dickens's–fiction.

The serialization of *The Old Curiosity Shop* began more or less two years before *Dead Souls* was published. From the beginning of this early novel, Dickens surrounds Little Nell, his heroine, with both comical and uncanny[11] objects and characters, thus described in his 1848 preface:

> In writing the book, I had always in my fancy to surround the lonely figure of the child with grotesque and wild, but not impossible, companions and to gather about her innocent face and pure intentions, associates as strange and uncongenial as the grim objects that are about her bed when her history is first foreshadowed. (Dickens 1985-2, 42)

There is no evidence of Dickens's direct influence on Gogol's style. Gogol's understanding of English was poor, and Dickens's fiction was translated into Russian only at the beginning of the 1840s (*Nicholas Nickleby* in 1840, *Oliver Twist* in 1841; a few excerpts from *The Pickwick Papers* and *Sketches by Boz* had been translated in 1838). Gogol had discovered most of the English writers he knew through Russian or French translations; and that rather haphazardly. We know that he read and re-read Walter Scott, that he admired Shakespeare (whom he had first read thanks to Pushkin), and Fielding too, for what Gogol saw as his epic

---

[11] One thinks of the array of miscellaneous objects found in the shop, or of Nell's grand-father, whose "haggard aspect [...] was wonderfully suited to the place" (Dickens 1985-2, 47) and of course of the evil dwarf Quilp.

conception of the novel.[12] There is only one, very laudatory, specific mention of Dickens in Gogol's letters. Fedor Buslaev, a close friend of Gogol's, mentions that he had read Dickens in the winter of 1840-1 (Buslaev 1897, 258-9) while working on the revision of the first part of *Dead Souls*. Gogol probably discovered the increasingly popular author of *The Old Curiosity Shop* at a time when–it is important to note–he had already reached literary maturity. If the exact impact of Dickens's fiction on Gogol is hard to evaluate, it is very likely that it mainly served to reinforce Gogol's determination to explore grotesque expressivity.[13]

Dickens, for his part, had read (in French) at least one of Gogol's short stories, "Taras Bulba."[14] The question of their mutual influence is minor when compared to that of their concomitant tendency, in a prose generally considered as "realistic," to resort to particular devices opening up a dimension governed by fantastic uncertainty and grotesque distortion. For example, interstices in the excerpts quoted above lead to the superposition of several scenes. The vision of the greasy marks left by the backs of travellers conjures up merchants drinking tea on market-days and the background of one of Gogol's Ukrainian stories.[15] The unexpected simile which tends to turn the teacups on the waiter's tray into as many "birds on the seashore" fuses together the enclosed space and the outside one, with the sea-gulls' cries probably brought to mind by the "leap[ing] and jingl[ing]" of the glass pendants.

One cannot fail to think of Dickens when reading Gogol's similes, which Nabokov has described as characteristic of his extraordinary evocative

---

[12] We know that Gogol had subtitled his novel "a poem" and that in an earlier, discarded version of Chapter 2, the authorial voice dedicated the work to "Shakespeare, Ludovico Ariosto, Fielding, Cervantes, Pushkin, all authors who represented nature as it was and not as some would have preferred it to be" (Gogol 1952, 35, my translation).

[13] Cf. Donald Fanger: "Gogol did read Dickens, at least once, but that was already near the end of his urban period, when any Dickensian 'influence' must have been corroborative, rather than productive–the recognition of a kindred artistic soul, a congenial but distant cousin." (Fanger 1998, 103). Alekseev remarks: "It is possible that Gogol's fiction may have paved the way for Dickens's popularity in Russia and influence on Russian literature." (Alekseev 1989, 193, my translation).

[14] As is made clear in a letter addressed to Bulwer-Lytton, dated October 25th 1867.

[15] As the description of Jaggers's office in Chapter 20 of *Great Expectations* conjures up the vision of Jaggers's unclean and frightened clients: "The room was but small, and the clients seemed to have had a habit of backing up against the wall: for the wall, especially opposite to Mr Jaggers's chair, was greasy with shoulders." (Dickens 1999, 130).

power,[16] because comical elements are often unexpectedly worked into their subtle lyricism. The association of teacups with "birds on the seashore" irresistibly mirrors the simile between Samuel Pickwick and his research field:

> There sat the man who had traced to their source the mighty ponds of Hampstead, and agitated the scientific world with his Theory of Tittlebats, as calm and unmoved as the deep waters of the one on a frosty day, or as a solitary specimen of the other in the inmost recesses of an earthen jar. (Dickens 1985-1, 68)

As the reader knows that Pickwick has a "bald head, and circular spectacles" (68), the image of the improbable aquatic animal with the childish name imposes itself. The comic tone of the narrative and the disquieting final note create the grotesque vision of Pickwick as a small fish trapped in a jar. Gogol's description of the parlour ends on the same ironic note and grotesque exuberance with the mention of the "nymph with [...] an enormous bust," a "freak of nature" apparently appreciated by Russian "art-lovers" who had travelled through Italy.[17]

Therefore, as early as Chapter One of *Dead Souls*, before the famous portraits in which Gogol shows the full extent of his genius, the representation of Russian mediocrity (celebrated by contemporary liberal critics as a faithful rendering of reality and a social indictment) proves to be essentially informed by grotesque aesthetics.[18] Nabokov greatly admired Gogol's "faceted eye" (Nabokov 1981, 25) which could both see and show what no other Russian writer had seen before, and thought that Gogol's "peculiar genius" had excelled in building "a fundamentally unreal world" (20). In *Dead Souls*, objects become characters of fiction and are at least as important as human beings. Conversely, reification and animalization participate in creating a universe where human beings are always seen from the outside and devoid of psychological or moral depth, mere puppets operated by some mysterious, invisible force. This is true of all the characters, from the hero (or anti-hero) Chichikov to the series of colourful individuals he meets while looking for cheap souls. It is true also

---

[16] Nabokov's main argument is that Gogol is anything but a realist (see Nabokov 1981).
[17] An example of Gogol's self-derision: though not a "grandee" himself, he was interested in painting and had taken classes in Rome.
[18] As defined by the Russian critical tradition, i.e. based on contrast and on the fusion of opposites. See L.E. Pinsky's definition, quoted by Bakhtin (Bakhtin 1984, 32, note 12). The grotesque is not here opposed to the sublime, as in Hugo's conception, but includes it.

of secondary characters like Chichikov's valet and coachman, and even of the numerous people who appear only briefly in the course of the story and yet remain vividly in the reader's mind.[19] An example of this is found at the end of Gogol's depiction of the little shops below the inn:

> In the corner-shop [...] or rather in its window, sat a *sbiten*-seller,[20] with a samovar of red copper, and a face as red as his samovar, so that at a distance it might have been supposed that two samovars were standing in the window, had not one of the samovars had a beard as black as pitch. (Gogol 2010, 4-5)

The grotesque arises here from the unexpected identification of the man with the object next to him, the colour red serving as ground of the metaphor. The narrative quickly moves away from the fleeting vision which, with many other such images, contributes to building the deeply corporeal and material world of Bakhtin's "grotesque realism."

When the narrator describes the land-owners approached by Chichikov as freaks of nature, the grotesque participates in the persistence of the fantastic atmosphere of Gogol's urban stories in the tale of rural life. In "The Nose" or "The Overcoat" the fantastic originates in an inexplicable incident in the ordinary hero's daily life. The dizzy heterogeneity produced by the grotesque in *Petersburg Tales* also creates such a moment of hesitation between reality and the unreal, which shows that it is impossible to dissociate the fantastic and the grotesque in the short stories. In *Dead Souls*, such closely-knit association persists, but it is the grotesque lack of substance of the characters which borders on the fantastic.

The grotesque unreality of such characters must be considered within the context of Chichikov's fraudulent venture. A would-be landowner buys "non-existent" goods (103-4; an adjective Chichikov uses twice to haggle the price) from serf-owners as dishonest as him who agree to sell such goods. Chichikov is a master of pretence and a shrewd dissembler like the anti-heroes in the Spanish picaresque tradition,[21] like Gil Blas or Tom Jones, with whom Russian readers were quite familiar. But in *Dead Souls* the hero's "qualities" serve his morbid trafficking; and Gogol displays his genius by constantly playing with the macabre situation and the porosity of the separation between life and death. The dead serfs have

---

[19] Nabokov calls them "Gogol's homunculi [who] seem intent on [staying in the book]–and do not" (Nabokov 1981, 21).

[20] *Sbiten* is a beverage made of water, honey, and spices. A samovar is a large tea-urn.

[21] On the diffusion of the Picaresque tradition in Russian literature, see Clerc 2012.

become mere goods, but their living "owners" are hardly more alive. The structure of the novel, which follows Chichikov's journey and introduces characters who quickly disappear (as though grounded on stretches of land rendered inaccessible by the vastness of Russian plains) contributes to turning them into mere illusions.

The reader thus meets Madame Korobochka in Chapter 3, "one of those women who own a small landed property, and cry over bad crops and losses, and hold their heads on one side, and meanwhile accumulate a little money in motley little bags, stowed away in the drawers of their commodes" (44). This obsessively meticulous woman, whose name means "little box," seems–like her house–made of carefully locked drawers. Gogol has here recourse to semantic and phonic associations in his characters' names, also one of Dickens's favourite modes of characterization.[22] In *Dead Souls*, such names point to animalization or reification, a significant component of Gogolian grotesque. One of Gogol's most famous characters is Sobakevich, whose name comes from "dog" but who is in fact both a hound and a gigantic, clumsy bear[23] as well as a formidable predator and a tough businessman. Everything about him is disproportionate, from his feet crushing his visitors' to his pantagruelic appetite. He and his room's heavy furniture are one and alike:

> Everything was durable, and clumsy in the highest degree, and had a certain strange likeness to the master of the house: in one corner of the room stood a walnut-wood desk with a swell front, mounted on four extremely awkward legs–a regular bear; the table, the armchairs, the common chairs–all were of the heaviest and most uncomfortable description; in a word, every object, every chair, seemed to say, "And I also am Sobakevich!" or, "And I also am very much like Sobakevich!" (98)

The character's physical features seem to have oozed disturbingly into his environment, thus erasing the frontier between the human and the non-human. The narrator observes:

> It seemed as though there were no soul at all in his body, or that there was one belonging to it, but not in the place where it should have been; […] it was […] enveloped in a thick shell–[so] that all which was rumbling about in its depths, produced absolutely no ripple on the surface. (103)

---

[22] Krook's name in *Bleak House* speaks for itself, Bella Wilfer in *Our Mutual Friend* is both a charming and strong-willed young person. Dickens uses onomastics even more extensively than Gogol.

[23] His first name, Mikhail, is also the Russian name for all bears.

What brings Sobakevich to life if his soul is not where it should be? Such unsettling merging of the inert with the living is achieved in *Dead Souls* through different means. Chichikov, for example, carries around a replica of himself: the travelling-chest where he keeps his money and property deeds, which has numerous compartments and a secret drawer which closes so fast one can't see what it contains. When Chichikov thinks it has been stolen from him, he becomes as mad as Molière's Harpagon shouting "ma cassette!"[24] as if he had lost his soul. The travelling-chest is therefore a portative soul, which like Sobakevich's is not found where the reader expects it to be. Underneath Chichikov's "peudo-Pickwickian rotundity of flesh" (Nabokov 1981, 26) there swarms something particularly disquieting. Humanity, for Gogol, remains alien and enigmatic, and to depict it he often combines fantastic effects with grotesque comedy. Chichikov's bouts of despair and rage are as excessive as his transports of delight. He keeps them to the privacy of his room and is depicted several times busy at his toilette, a rather plump grotesque hero putting on his suspenders or wearing nothing but boots, but always extremely satisfied with himself, and dancing the jig with very little lightness or grace (Gogol 2010, 140; 170).

There is something devilish[25] in this visitor nobody has met before, this ordinary, indefinitely adaptable, man (like his cousin the *picaro*). Chichikov is a rather amiable deceiver who is also a womanizer since once his schemes are discovered in N., rumor has it that he has eloped with the governor's daughter and is the devil himself, like Khlestakov, the hero of *The Revisor*. In *Dead Souls* as in his play, Gogol never brings in the supernatural directly, but it is secretly and powerfully present through the "estrangement" of many aspects of Gogol's grotesque narrative. The suggestion of the devil's presence, which constantly pervades Gogol's fiction from the Ukrainian stories (some of which are truly scaring) to *Petersburg Tales*, participates fully in such "estrangement." The world travelled by Chichikov, where appearances are deceitful and where incongruous hybridity appears in all shapes as in a painting by Bosch, is a hell where the visitor's schemes reveal that the living are more terrifying than the dead. The "dead souls" are those of fundamentally inhuman or sub-human characters only vaguely animated by greed. Comedy in *Dead Souls* is clearly sinister because, in the wake of the public's reactions to his great play *The Revisor*, Gogol perceived the sublime nature of a certain

---

[24] Molière, *L'Avare,* IV, vii.
[25] Nabokov calls him a "travelling salesman from Hades" (Nabokov 1981, 20).

type of ambivalent laughter.[26] Such ambivalent comedy is found when the miser Pliushkin, whose sex Chichikov at first cannot ascertain, is introduced. His description, which strongly focuses on one part of his face, creates an effect of grotesque obscenity:

> His face presented no special peculiarities; it was like that of many gaunt old men; only the chin projected very far in advance, so that he had to cover it with his handkerchief every time he wanted to spit, in order not to spit upon it; his small eyes had not grown dim, and they darted about from beneath his lofty, bushy brows like mice when they thrust their pointed noses out of their dark holes, prick up their ears, and blink, as it were, with their noses, as they peer about to see whether a cat, or some scamp of a small boy, be not hidden somewhere, and sniff the very air warily. (120)

It is impossible to determine what clothes he is wearing:

> By no possible means or effort could any decision be arrived at as to the material of which his dressing-gown had been concocted; the sleeves and the upper portions of the skirts were greased, and shining to such a degree that they resembled the Russia leather of which boots are made; behind moved four tails instead of two, from between which protruded bunches of checked cotton. Something, also impossible to distinguish, either a stocking, a bandage, or a belt, but certainly not a neckerchief, was knotted about his neck. (120)

Pliushkin brings to mind a character from Chapter 3 of *The Pickwick Papers*, Dismal Jemmy:

> It was a care-worn looking man, whose sallow face, and deeply sunken eyes, were rendered still more striking than nature had made them, by the straight black hair which hung in matted disorder half way down his face.

---

[26] At the beginning of Chapter 7, the authorial voice says: "Contemporary judgment does not recognize the fact, that elevated and enthusiastic laughter is worthy of standing on the same plane with elevated lyrical emotion, and that a whole abyss lies between them and the contortions of the buffoon of the booths! […] I have long been condemned by some wonderful power to go hand in hand with my strange heroes, to view all life as it passes pompously by, to view it through the apparent world of laughter and the tears which are invisible, unknown to it" (140). Bakhtin describes such laughter as "true ambivalent and universal laughter [which] does not deny seriousness but purifies and completes it, […] [which] purifies from dogmatism, from the intolerant and the petrified, […][which] liberates from fanaticism and pedantry [and] from fear and intimidation" (Bakhtin 1984, 122-3).

His eyes were almost unnaturally bright and piercing; his cheek-bones were high and prominent; and his jaws were so long and lank, that an observer would have supposed that he was drawing the flesh of his face in, for a moment, by some contraction of the muscles, if his half-opened mouth and immovable expression had not announced that it was his ordinary appearance. Round his neck he wore a green shawl, with the large ends straggling over his chest, and making their appearance occasionally beneath the worn button-holes of his old waistcoat. His upper garment was a long black surtout; and below it he wore wide drab trousers, and large boots, running rapidly to seed. (Dickens 1985-1, 103)

Similar modes of characterization are used by Dickens and Gogol: the emphasis placed on a physical incongruity which lengthens the character's face, the mention of remarkable details of his clothing–the tails of Pliushkin's dressing-gown, the ends of Jemmy's shawl–and the visual separation of head and body by odds and ends of material which turn the man into a scarecrow with a frightening head attached to a stick wrapped in rags. Jemmy and Pliushkin are spectral buffoons with fleshless faces which are little more than carnival masks. The ambivalence of the two characters (who provoke both terror and laughter) rises from their obvious proximity to death. Pliushkin is a rich landowner but also a hyperbolic miser and his serfs starve to death–hence Chichikov's interest in him. Jemmy, a strange character, plays bit parts in a theatre and appears in the story only to tell Pickwick and his friends about a pantomime actor's unhappy life and miserable death. Both the narrative of the clown's death and the analeptic one of Pliushkin's degeneration (Pliushkin became a miser after the death of a beloved wife) are quite touching. Gogol's narrator concludes that "inhuman old age" (Gogol 2010, 132) deprives man of the positive traits of human nature, which Gogol found so enigmatic. In both cases however, comedy soon takes over again when the narrator resumes the main story-line. During a classic scene, Pliushkin the offensive landowner suddenly understands that thanks to his visitor he won't have to pay taxes on his dead serfs and celebrates him as his benefactor before offering to sweeten his tea with old (and probably spoilt) sugar scraped off an Easter-cake (129). In the next chapter however, in a well-known digression, the narrator radically changes tones and again finds Hugolian accents to lament the writer's lot who–

[…] presumes to call forth into evidence […] all that terrible, agitating mire of petty details which enmesh our lives; all those depths of cold, disturbing, commonplace characters with which our earthly way […] is swarming. […] Contemporary judgment does not recognize the fact that

great depth of soul is required in order to light up the picture drawn from
the life of the lowly, and to convert it into a pearl of creative art.[27] (139-40)

Thus the grotesque aesthetics, of which Gogolian comic is an essential
aspect, concentrates on those interstices in realistic representation which
absorb common beliefs and values and from where emerge life so abject
and reality so monstrous (*poshlost* in Russian) that they verge on the
supernatural. In that sense, Gogol's "realism," tinged with Romanticism in
Petersburg Tales and with irrationality in *Dead Souls*, may appear as
fantastic. Russian playwrights and theorists of the 1920s labeled Gogol's
grotesque universe "fantastic realism."[28] His artistic description of reality,
unfettered by verisimilitude, influenced their avant-gardist conception of
staging.

Incessant energy runs through Gogol's infernal universe, leaving
nothing undisturbed, inverting top and bottom, good and evil, life and
death.[29] Thus the dead serfs are brought back to life (incongruous as it may
seem), first by Sobakevich when he tries to raise the stakes by mentioning
the dead men's expertise, then by Chichikov, rejoicing alone in his room
that business has been good, reading the list of dead serfs and marveling at
the unusual nicknames which point to their past idiosyncrasies: "Petro
Saveliev Despise-the-trough; Grigoriy Go-but-you-won't-get-there" (142-
3).

Gogol's imagination and verbal creativity operate this surprising
reversal of values which Bakhtin sees as corresponding to the carnivalesque
parody which "revives and renews at the same time" (Bakhtin 1984, 11).
The insistence on corporeal materiality and the fusion of opposite poles
are also found in Shakespeare and Cervantes and several writers of the
Spanish "Golden Age" ("*Siglo de Oro*") like Lope de Vega or Quevedo,[30]
as well as Sterne. These forms influenced in their turn the realistic
literature of the following centuries, which Bakhtin calls "realism of grand

---

[27] See previous footnote.
[28] On Gogol's "fantastic realism" and its links with the grotesque, again see Picon-
Vallin 1980.
[29] Bakhtin evokes the "merry plays of devils" found in Gogol's fiction, "which is
closely related in character, tone and function to carnivalesque visions of the
underworld and the demonic" (Bakhtin 1985, 30). About *Dead Souls,* he writes:
"A close analysis would reveal many traditional elements of the carnival
underworld, the nether regions of both the world and the human body" (32).
[30] Lope de Vega and Quevedo are listed in the French translation of Bakhtin's
introduction to his book, though they are not found in the English translation.

style" (52): Stendhal, Balzac, Hugo and Dickens, before "naturalist empiricism" (52) broke away from the tradition of the Renaissance.

Beyond their fantastic monstrosity, Gogol's characters in *Dead Souls*, like many of Dickens's, were born of "a special concept of the body as a whole and of the limits of this whole" (315), characteristic of the popular festive tradition: a body with no clear separation from other bodies or the cosmos, a body in a state of incompletion which is linked to the cosmos through its appendices and apertures (notably the nose, almost always of enormous size in Gogol's fiction, and the mouth). According to Bakhtin, the essence of laughter is found in the "bodily substance" lent to "nature and the cosmos" (336, note 9), and Gogol's grotesque laughter is a "zone of contact" (Bakhtin 1985, 36) between aspects of the cosmos which should not be separated, a "zone" open to interferences and cosmic circulation, dissolving norms (some of them literary) rather than questioning them. Looking at *Dead Souls* from the angle of the grotesque enables the reader to seize its kinship with Dickens's universe and gives the reader access to the spectacular hybridity of Gogol's fiction.

References

Alekseev, Mikhail. 1989. "Mirovoe značenie Gogolja" ("Gogol's Influence throughout the World"). *Russkaja literatura i ejo mirovoe značenie.* Leningrad: izd. Nauka.

Bakhtin, Mikhail. (1965) 1984. *Rabelais and His World.* Translated by Helene Iswolsky. Bloomington: Indiana University Press.

—. "Rabelais and Gogol: Verbal Art and Popular Humour." (1975) 1985. Translated by Peter O'Toole. *Australian Journal of Cultural Studies,* 3-1: 29-39.

Bryner, Cyril. 1963. "Gogol, Dickens and the Realistic Novel." *Slavic and East-European Studies,* Vol. 8, n° 1/2: 17-42.

Buslaev, Fedor. 1897. *Moi vospominanja (Memoirs).* Moskva: Lissaer i Gesel.

Clerc, Florence. 2012. "Le Rôle de la tradition picaresque dans la genèse du roman russe." In *Filiation, modèles et transmission dans les littératures européennes,* edited by Françoise Le Borgne, 285-96. Clermont-Ferrand: Presses Universitaires Blaise Pascal.

Dickens, Charles. (1837) 1985. *The Pickwick Papers.* Harmondsworth: The Penguin English Library. [1985-1]

—. (1841) 1985. *The Old Curiosity Shop.* Harmondsworth: The Penguin English Library. [1985-2]

—. (1861) 1999. *Great Expectations.* New-York: Norton.

Eichenbaum, Boris. 1963. "The Structure of Gogol's 'The Overcoat.'" Translated by Beth Paul and Muriel Nesbitt. *Russian Review*, Vol. 22, N°4: 377-99.

Fanger, Donald. (1965) 1998. *Dostoevsky and Romantic Realism: A Study of Dostoevsky in Relation to Balzac, Dickens and Gogol.* Evanston: Northwestern University Press.

Futrell, Michael H. 1956. "Gogol and Dickens." *The Slavonic and East European Review,* Vol. 34, n°83: 443-59.

Gogol, Nikolai. (1842) 2010. *Dead Souls.* Translated by Isabel F. Hapgood. London: Wordsworth Editions.

—. 1952. *Polnoe sobranie socinenij (Complete Works).* Vol. XXIV. Moskva: izd. AN SSSR.

—. 1966. *Oeuvres complètes.* Coll. "La Pléiade." Paris: Gallimard.

Kayser, Wolfgang. (1957) 1981. *The Grotesque in Art and Literature.* Translated by Ulrich Weisstein. New York: Columbia University Press.

Nabokov, Vladimir. (1944) 1981. *Lectures on Russian Literature.* Edited by Frederic Bowers. New-York: Harcourt.

Nivat, Georges. 1982. *Vers la fin du mythe russe. Essais sur la culture russe de Gogol à nos jours.* Lausanne: L'Age d'Homme.

Picon-Vallin, Béatrice. 1980. "Gogol, point de départ des recherches sur le grotesque au théâtre et au cinéma après la révolution russe, 1917-1932," *Cahiers du monde russe et soviétique*, Vol. 21, n° 21: 333-59.

—. 2004. *Meyerhold.* Paris: CNRS.

Shklovsky, Viktor. (1917) 1998. "Art as Technique." In *Literary Theory: An Anthology*, edited by Julie Rivkin and Michael Ryan, 15-21. Malden: Blackwell.

Slipchenko, Walter. 1966. *Proper Names in the Literary Work of Nikolai Gogol.* PhD diss. University of Manitoba.

Voguë, Eugène-Melchior. (1886) 2010. *Le Roman russe.* Paris: Classiques Garnier.

CHAPTER SIX

FIGURES OF THE GROTESQUE IN *THE SNOBS OF ENGLAND* / *THE BOOK OF SNOBS* BY WILLIAM MAKEPEACE THACKERAY

JACQUELINE FROMONOT

William Makepeace Thackeray's weekly chronicle entitled *The Snobs of England* was serialized in the satirical magazine *Punch* from 1846 to 1847 and then published in the following year as *The Book of Snobs*, a volume which retained 45 of the 52 articles in the original version. In this seminal text, Thackeray defines the snob as a vulgar, selfish and inauthentic being who strives for gentility, imitates the upper classes and tries to be accepted among their ranks through the meanest ploys. Therefore, he adds a new layer of meaning to the term, whose first occurrences in the 18th century simply denoted a social status. It referred to the man who, like a humble shoemaker, did not belong to the nobility, in accordance with one of the supposed etymologies of snob, a contraction of the Latin *sine nobilitate*. It also designated the *townsman*, as opposed to the *gownsman* in the sociolect of Cambridge with which Thackeray became familiar as an undergraduate. Hence it started to be a term of abuse, meaning a cad or low fellow, and in the wake of this evolution, Thackeray's use of the word in *The Snobs of England* clearly becomes morally connoted. This is made obvious as from Chapter One, in which the snob is emphatically taxed with baseness: "*He who meanly admires mean things is a Snob*" (Thackeray 1945, 68-70). The solemnity of this italicized preliminary definition does not totally reflect however the tone of the semantic analysis, for it is to be set against the derisive lightness of metadiscursive commentaries bearing on the item *snob*. What is thus called an "expressive monosyllable" (54) is made to sound strange, ridiculous and somewhat paradoxical by its peculiar quality as "a pretty little round word, all composed of soft letters, with a hiss at the beginning just to make it piquant, as it were" (446). Throughout his taxonomic enterprise, the author whom some critics once called the "Victorian Horace" intends to satirize snobs and snobbery at large. To this end he focuses on their grotesque dimension, in such a consistent way throughout that he truly builds an aesthetics and a poetics of the grotesque. In order to study their textual inscription, and more particularly their relevant stylistic traits, the present analysis hinges on two movements inspired from the anecdote in which the term "grotesque" originates, back in 15th-century Italy. First, the grotesque and its capacity to unsettle the observer or reader result from the irruption of an intruding element into a familiar background, which is reminiscent of the inadvertent discovery of Nero's *Domus Aurea* by a young Roman. Second, the grotesque and its picturesque aspect are methodically described, explored and assessed, just as was at the time the buried palace that was thought to be a cave (or "*grotto*" in Italian), decorated with extravagant ornaments, which explains the etymology of the term "grotesque."

The Grotesque and the Aesthetics of Irruption

This first part is therefore devoted to the sudden intrusion of the bizarre in an ordinary or harmonious context, a recurring textual arrangement so installed by the satirist as to create maximum impact on the reader.

Irruption of unexpected and heterogeneous elements

A logic of unpredictability prevails as early as in the text's original title, *The Snobs of England*, which may sound at first neutrally programmatic, but on closer analysis happens to be facetiously second-degree. Indeed, it is so worded as to constitute an intertextual reference to the series Mrs. Ellis devoted to the instruction of women: *The Women of England*, *The Mothers of England* and *The Daughters of England*, published in the 1840s. This underlying reference to the works of such a respectable tutelary figure emerges and creates a parodic sub-text which questions the apparent seriousness of the undertaking from its very beginning. As to the second version's main title, *The Book of Snobs*, it soon appears purposefully undermined too, although by a mechanism of a different nature–for playful Thackeray is never at a loss for redirection of meaning. From a simple denotative viewpoint, it soberly announces a treaty on snobs, until the subtitle "*By One of Themselves*" re-orients its epistemological value. Admittedly, the additional phrase and its emphatic reflexive pronoun "themselves" may at first glance certify the reliability of the analysis by stressing the closeness between the writer and his object. Yet this soon proves dubious, since the author, self-defined as a snob, necessarily falls into the category of vain and ignorant creatures. Actually, the comma between the two semantic units creates a pause thanks to which the former appears autonomous for a moment, before the latter theatrically introduces self-derision.

On macro-textual level, certain formal properties of the text create disjunctions of probabilities whose unsettling potential is amply tapped on. In the "Prefatory Remarks," for instance, style and content announce the depth of the purpose, until the next page eventually reveals its futility. This carefully-wrought movement asks for closer textual analysis. At first, a purple patch of considerable length bears on the evocation of historic figures which proved providential in their time:

> We have all read a statement [...] that when the times and necessities of the world call for a Man, that individual is found. Thus at the French revolution [...], when it was requisite to administer a corrective dose to the nation, Robespierre was found a most foul and nauseous dose indeed, and swallowed eagerly by the patient, greatly to the latter's ultimate advantage: thus when it became necessary to kick John Bull out of America, Mr. Washington stepped forward, and performed that job to satisfaction [...]. (50)

At last the main information appears in a brief, matter-of-course way to reveal that for the study of snobs, the author is the man of the situation (54). The impact of the mock-heroic configuration and its satirical tone is based on several devices, all aiming at imbalance meant to provoke uncomfortable laughter. The sheer grammatical sprawl of the sentences and their accumulation make the beginning grandiloquent, an effect destroyed by the trivial final disclosure. Indeed, the piling up of components that reveal the thematic subject and give the sentence its ascending curve postpones the appearance of the predicate and its anticipated end-weight; it also grants prosodic prominence to the theme, thus creating a horizon of expectation that is soon to prove deceptive. Also remarkable in the introductory passage in question is the fact that similar deceptive devices appear on the small scale of the paragraph, in a process of complexifying and convoluted *mise en abyme*. Here again, a string of appositives, synonymous equivalents that designate the writer's task, is meant to delay the revelation as long as possible:

> [...] I have a work to do–a work, if you like, with a great W; a Purpose to
> fulfil; a chasm to leap into, like Curtius, horse and foot; a Great Social Evil
> to Discover and to Remedy. (52)

The use of capital letters contributes to the stilted emphasis that is in addition heavy-handedly overstated by the metatextual comment "with a great W." The typographical flagging promotes the author's mission and sets off by contrast the mediocrity of the ultimate announcement, thus producing a disconcerting semantic discontinuity that points up to the grotesque. Finally, the epic tone itself is undermined by casual remarks, when for instance the hero of the American Revolution is said to have "performed that job to satisfaction" (50). A prominent figure is derided, a fate to which the author is soon to submit a few awe-inspiring military figures, in the wake of his "without a hero" motif, for that matter. The illustration on a wrapper to one of *Vanity Fair*'s monthly numbers features the Duke of Wellington as a ridiculously tiny character riding a donkey, while at the top of his column Admiral Nelson fares no better, as he stands piteously on his head (Thackeray 1983, 10)–for surely there is something carnivalesque in the grotesque. In brief, the preamble of the *Book of Snobs* is saturated with information that makes it monstrously profuse. This is meant to destabilize the horizon of expectation and impose a reorientation of the interpretation on a reader who is overwhelmed by the grotesque of this baroque or even rococo universe.

The cumulative structure, a recurring trait of the text, is not only a rhetorical tool aiming to achieve such profusion and procrastination; it also adds up to the grotesque effect whenever the unity of an enumeration is sapped by the presence of heterogeneous elements which make it sound bizarrely medley. This happens for instance in the depiction of an unscrupulous snob's efforts to take advantage of a weak woman. The satirist provides the following list of everything the scoundrel has wormed out of her: "He procured from her dinner, money, wearing apparel, spoons, implicit credence, and an entire refit of linen" (Thackeray 1945, 330). Carried away by his obsession, the snob is shown as a predator who lacks judgment in his compulsive desire to accumulate wealth and status. The heteroclite catalogue mixes concrete and abstract, small-scale and large-scale elements, thus creating a disturbing impression of confusion, typical of the snob's grossly mistaken values.

One might therefore conclude on this point that there seldom seems to be any grotesque element *per se*, at least in the Thackerayan universe. In other words, the grotesque does not result from isolated items taken separately; it is rather their troubling association and the constant semantic and rhetorical ruptures that generate its presence.

Irruption of anticlimactic elements

Textual instability verges on incoherence and tends to produce spectacular lapses which reinforce the comical dimension of the satire with burlesque consequences. The rhetoric of anticlimax in particular is purposefully exploited in the succession of two statements in Mr. Snob's account of a dinner with the Pontos. These "Country Snobs" are intent on keeping up appearances in spite of their meager income–quite in vain, since their gorgeously-clad servant soon betrays his condition as a stable boy:

> Stripes was in the livery of the Ponto family–a thought shabby but gorgeous in the extreme–lots of magnificent worsted lace, and livery buttons of a very notable size. The honest fellow's hands, I remarked, were very large and black; and a fine odour of the stable was wafted about the room as he moved to and fro in his ministrations. (264)

As the narrative unfolds, an apparently neutral voice juxtaposes two incongruous details which call for the reader's reinterpretation of the scene as farcical pretence. To drive the point home, Thackeray repeats the comic effect at the end of the same chapter, although with a variation, for this time it is the homodiegetic narrator himself who is forced to reorient his perception. When everyone has gone to bed, the following dialogue starts from one room to the next between the host and his guest: "'And are there Snobs in this Elysium?' I exclaimed, jumping into the lavender-perfumed bed. Ponto's snoring boomed from the neighbouring bedroom in reply" (274). The lofty representation that the narrator is trying to fit in–the mythological allusion and the bucolic reference–is blocked by a coarse noise that makes the scene even grotesquely obscene, because the indecorous, which should stay concealed, comes to the fore. Such anticlimactic devices are made even more theatrical when they are concentrated inside a single statement. For example, an exclamation caused by the sight of a cameo loses any laudatory value when the jewel is likened to a muffin, hence a bathetic effect: "What a cameo, the size of a muffin!" (176). The monstrous aspect of the outsized ornament thus prevails, starting a retrospective reinterpretation of the previous "What a..." exclamatory form, whose ambiguous polysemy is no longer operative. Once the asyndeton has been clarified, it becomes obvious that far from expressing admiration, the sentence reveals the astonishment of the observer, or even his aversion for the snobs' aesthetic choices. Devoid of refinement, the snobs make such a display of their riches that a cameo, usually renowned for its daintiness, has in this case extraordinary proportions that exclude it from the abstract sphere of the beautiful and place it in the trivial category of basic food. This is reminiscent of a similar process in the well-known passage of Charles Dickens's *Our Mutual Friend*, a novel peopled with vulgar *nouveaux riches* whom the writer lampoons just as ferociously. The Podsnaps' solid-silver forks are so ostentatiously big that the guests are forced to open their mouths wide– and give up all table manners (Dickens 1964, 154). Thackeray's scathing satire particularly targets the inordinate pretension of the Pontos, who in truth live an obscure country life in which "boots" replace "books," as is evidenced by the following pun based on phonological closeness, "Ponto's library mostly consists of boots" (Thackeray 1945, 280) and "I found poor Pon. in a study among his boots" (306). The subject of each sentence, "library" in the first and "study" in the second, calls for the predicate "books," an expectation that is entertained until the last-but-one letter, thus reinforcing the bathetic effect. The reader, in disbelief, has to go through the statement again to make sure that he has understood it correctly. The reading process is therefore no longer channelled by a left-to-right axis, but moves back and forth; the quest for meaning develops in unpredictable movements.

Finally, the logic of the unexpected is at its highest when it applies to the morphological level, thus revealing even more clearly the creative genius of Thackeray, for whom the existing lexis is not rich enough and so is in need of personalized developments in an infinite, quasi autonomous way. From the lexicalized item "snob," the writer coins surprising and unheard-of derivations by adding appendages, so to speak, like suffixes or substantives, with seemingly limitless productivity. For example, the "Snobonomer" (246) designates a sort of philosopher striving to examine the snob with a telescope; he can become a "Snobographer" (342) who writes a "Snobography" (320) as he discovers snob territory, aptly called "Snobland" (328) and claimed to be rich in snob material or "snobore" (54). These excrescences stem from the root "snob" in a quasi teratological way, and the resulting hybrid creations recall the chimera, an animal composed of a lion's head, a goat's body ending up with a dragon's tail–a strange composite creature whose grotesque dimension grows as the eye moves forth from head to tail, just like the Thackerayan text, which beats all prognoses as it goes forward.

Not only does Thackeray deride the figure of the author by taking the posture of a snob in the subtitle, but he also mocks the book as an object of reverence. In a London club's library, a visitor's attention is caught by a peculiar volume grotesquely equipped with a handle that triggers the opening of a niche:

[H]e selected Volume VII, to which he was attracted by the singular fact, that a brass door handle grew out of the back. Instead of pulling out a book, however, he pulled open a cupboard, only inhabited by a lazy housemaid's broom and duster [...]. (430)

The lever of the book, incongruous enough as it is, also happens to give access to a dark recess with nothing glorious about it, a find that turns the visit of the club into a farcical ride. In this respect, the scene can also be considered a re-enactment of the discovery of Nero's so-called "grotesque" palace, back in 15th-century Rome. Furthermore, Thackeray's fictional anecdote stands out as a clue to the whole text, emerging as the means to reveal a usually concealed or repressed reality. As the "broom and duster" placed in the secret cupboard seem to imply, there is a duty to clean the place, and more relevantly to the matter at hand, to wash the snob's dirty linen in public, however grotesque the result may be.

Poetics of the Exploration of the Grotesque

To this end, the satirist complements the grotesque aesthetics of irruption with a poetics of its exploration. Indeed, he spots it everywhere around him in the snob-ridden British society–or maybe he creates it owing to his biased, highly selective viewpoint. Accordingly Thackeray writes this series of literary portraits, a format perfectly suited for the initial weekly publication of same-size articles with a repetitive pattern. Programmatic titles announce the handling of particular categories of snobs, from "Military Snobs" (Chapter 9) to "Club Snobs" (Chapters 37 to 44), not to mention "University Snobs" (Chapters 14 and 15). The depiction hinges on three main rhetorical strategies: excess, paradox and the transfiguration of reality.

The focus on excess

First and foremost, the caricatural dimension of Thackeray's work unsurprisingly lies in the presence of excess in several respects, for in accordance with the etymology of the word, *carigare*, or "load," caricature tends to over-emphasize one particular trait to the point of making it disproportionately and preposterously salient. The technique finds an expression through a number of linguistic devices which conjure up the pictures of ludicrous and monstrous creatures in the reader's mind. For instance the writer exploits the singularizing power of adjectives, simple or compound, to blow up one snob's specific feature, and to this end he taps on the Germanic syntax of the premodification of nouns. Necessarily heading a nominal structure, determiners accumulate in front of substantives and so appear independent, free-floating items thrown into relief in the apostrophe: "O you crawling, truckling, self-confessed lackeys and parasites!" (328). Compound adjectives, which are information-packed, also prove semantically productive and their cumulative structure mimes the inflated ego they designate. Wealthy Goldmore's coachman is to be distinguished by his extravagant wig in the metonymic expression "floss-wigged coachman" (356), thus betraying his effort to ignore his own menial status and also confirming Goldmore's will to turn him into a piece of ostentatious display that reflects favourably on the employer's social status. A colonel falling into the category of "Continental Snobs" is designated by the phrase "salmon-coloured blood-shot face" (242), with special emphasis on his pinkish complexion, ridiculously associated with fish flesh. The renowned elasticity of the English language in word formation lends itself particularly well to this stylistic exercise, and it becomes difficult to recognize the *Peerage* through the compound-laden metaphor "gold-laced and liveried lackey to History" (396), or the promising young heir and his ginger beard, referred to as the "carroty-tufted hope of the family" (230). The cumulative process underlines the teratological dimension of the snob, but also his favourite haunts, like the Sarcophagus club, whose loads of decoration appear grotesque:

> The Sarcophagus displays every known variety of architecture and decoration. The great library is Elizabethan; the small library is pointed Gothic; the dining-room is severe Doric; the strangers' room has an Egyptian look; the drawing-rooms are Louis Quatorze (so called because the hideous ornaments displayed were used in the time of Louis Quinze); the cortile, or hall, is Morisco-Italian. It is all over marble, Maplewood, looking-glasses, arabesques, ormolu, and scagliola. Scrolls, ciphers, dragons, Cupids, polyanthuses and other flowers writhe up the walls in every kind of cornucopiosity. (428)

The descriptive statements repetitively make use of the copula "be" and as a result give a static evocation of the setting. However, the final verb of the passage, "writhe up," a phrasal verb that combines movement and direction, gives the eerie impression that the profuse ornaments have finally come to life, now invading the scene and saturating the surrounding space with their masses of curving foliage and floral elements. The passage climaxes with the neologism "cornucopiosity," a concentrate of linguistic extravagance. The lexicalized term "cornucopia," already complex in itself as it is a loan word composed of two welded Latin substantives, is now burdened with suffixation that turns it into a nonce-word. What follows is an unheard-of hybrid polysyllabic of outsized proportions or in other words a signifier whose morphological properties mime the multifarious excesses of its own referent, the mythological goat's horn that is traditionally represented pouring out all kinds of flowers, fruits and cereals. Thackeray sculpts the linguistic material to offer in this case what could be called a verbal gargoyle, both monstrous and grotesque.

The rhetoric of paradox

The fixed *décor* of the Sarcophagus is made to seem animated, a clash of opposites which is echoed by the numerous paradoxes at various levels of the text. First of all, they characterize Thackeray's study of snobs at large, with its opposition between the rationality of the project and the irrationality of the result. On the one hand, scientific rigour is claimed to be used in order to analyze the "specimen" (136 and 396) of snobs, painstakingly labelled and categorized into "relative snobs" and "positive snobs" for instance (56). The empirical paradigm, based on the method of natural sciences, is supposed to induce the essence of snobbery. The serious register however coexists with the farcical, hence the impression of irreducible confusion that critics have not failed to pinpoint. In addition, the author confesses his incapacity to define a snob when he finally comes to the somewhat disappointing conclusion that the social phenomenon at hand resists verbalization: "We can't define it, perhaps [...] but we *know* what it is" (444). He explains that the problem lies not only in the sharpness of his intellect–or rather its blunted edge–but also in the bulk of the work at hand, by admitting to the partial failure of his anthropological enterprise: "The labour is endless. No single man could complete it" (442). This finally reveals the grotesque at the root of a project meant to circumscribe a reality which is so multi-faceted that it includes the whole Creation and cannot spare anyone, however contrasted all the examined cases may be. Finally, the diagnosis rendered by the moralist is made of extremes that prove hard to reconcile, since eating peas with a knife is snobbish, as much as starving oneself daily to afford a carriage and horses for show. Hence the unsatisfactory levelling of all human weaknesses and the unusual medley including components ranging from mere lack of manners to despicable conspicuous consumption. This contributes to the grim and distorted representation of the British society that may have stamped Thackeray as a cynic, but is in fact the expression of grotesque playfulness on the part of the narrator, Mr. Snob, behind whom the author is hiding.

The rhetoric of paradox is the basic principle of composition of wholly-contained scenes, in which episodes of social life are complemented by the depiction of what happens backstage so as to denounce the ridiculous pretension of the "dinner-giving snob" for instance. The contrapuntal configuration appears in the following passage, a *scène de genre* that might have found an equivalent in William Hogarth:

> The host is smiling and hob-nobbing, and talking up and down the table; but a prey to secret terrors and anxieties lest the wines he has brought up from the cellar should prove insufficient, lest a corked bottle should destroy his calculations; or our friend the carpet-beater, by making some *bévue*, should disclose his real quality of green-grocer, and show that he is not the family butler.
>
> The hostess is smiling resolutely through all the courses, smiling through her agony; though her heart is in the kitchen, and she is speculating with terror lest there be any disaster there. [...]
>
> The children upstairs are yelling [...].
>
> The servants are not servants, but the beforementioned retail tradesmen.
>
> The plate is not silver, but a mere shiny Birmingham lacquer; and so is the hospitality, and everything else. (224)

The conjunctions "but" and "though" link but above all disjoin the two planes of reality, set against each other by a narrator whose omniscience makes it possible to oppose the snobs' outward serenity and their real anguish, appearance and reality, order and disorder. The observer systematically details all the actors of this grotesque farce, the parents, their children, the servants and even the plate, before the sweeping generalization "and everything else," a closing of the list which opens up the perspective and recalls the rhetoric of excess studied earlier on. There might also be a note of pity, possibly verging on indulgence, in his evocation of these miseries, confirmed by the concluding remark "And to think that all these people might be so happy, and easy, and friendly, were they brought together in a natural unpretentious way [...]!" (226). Such individuals cannot however be "brought together," and the world made up of antitheses cannot achieve synthesis. The resulting incomplete dialectic movement confirms the presence of unresolved conflicts that are part and parcel of the text.

At the microtextual level of this hastily written production which nonetheless proves highly-wrought, the grotesquely troubling coexistence of contraries is translated stylistically by the tropes of zeugma and oxymoron. Two elements of a different nature are thus treated as if they were equivalents owing to a common verb and a coordination in "If perseverance and forty thousand pounds down could have tempted him, Miss Lydia Croesus would certainly have been Lady Buckram" (98). The ferociously ironical association of a moral virtue and solid cash is meant to denounce marriage of convenience and the false values of notorious fortune-hunters. In the snobs' unnatural world, happiness depends on financial resources, so domestic bliss seems odd and even shocking in a penniless couple, as suggested by the oxymoronic combination of adjectives in "Mr. and Mrs. Gray, meanwhile, live […] in a most provoking and unnatural state of happiness" (348). An equivalent uncanny effect is used to challenge the notion of respectability in the phrase "those vacuous and most respectable men" (384). Thackeray plays on the two possible meanings of "and," both cumulative and adversative, in order to take the dominant social stance of a society that preposterously respects base characters. Oxymora combine apparently contradictory words, thus giving a complex, fantastic picture of the snob's universe when a guest of high rank is ridiculed through the reference to his "noble jaws" (82). The grotesque linguistic alliance of the man's nobility and the vulgarity of chewing and feeding is a humbling reminder of the human condition after all. As for the Pontos, who make a point of serving game in spite of their modest means, they are punished by the narrator, who rips apart their efforts with an amazingly economical technique. By calling the fowl "a corpulent sparrow" (282), he derisively activates an antiphrastic figure, before he lambasts the snobs' preposterous pretension to "swell to ox size" (322), a reminder of the well-known fable. The image of the small bird oddly striving for corpulence also gives rise to an uncomfortable feeling of the uncanny which redirects the concept of the grotesque, if only subliminally.

The transfiguration of reality

The troubling image of a corpulent sparrow is part of a linguistic transfiguration of reality that has pride of place throughout. It generates surrealistic effects, as in the following grotesque evocation of a debutante's toilette:

Miss Snobky
Habit de Cour, composed of a yellow nankeen illusion dress over a slip of rich pea-green corduroy, trimmed *en tablier*, with bouquets of Brussels sprouts: the body and sleeves handsomely trimmed with calamanco, and festooned with a pink train and white radishes. Head-dress, carrots and lappets. (86)

The outlay and wording of the passage fill most requirements of a social column; in addition, the specialized lexis referring to sewing techniques and different kinds of materials attests to its didactic seriousness. However, some elements give the passage an unexpected twist, for there is something unreal, or even surreal about them. The "nankeen illusion dress" might rather come from a fairy-tale, while the vegetables of the outfit have more to do with the pictorial universe of Arcimboldo than with a women's evening dress. The figurative meaning of "pea" in "pea-green" seems to have somehow become literal and proves pivotal in this respect. As a matter of fact, it paves the way for the mention of other actual vegetables in the composition of the outfit, as if the chronicler was from then on working under the influence of the logic of dream, with its typical condensations and displacements. In other words, the compound adjective "pea-green" provides a clue to the construction of the grotesque, according to which the use of incongruous material for a dress becomes possible. Miss Snobky is thus attired with a real basket of vegetables, but there is nothing in the text to signify that the description is anomalous, risible or grotesque. It imposes itself as being matter-of-course and self-evident, as do the fantastic creations of a dream. The same applies to many situations whose purported authenticity is nonetheless destroyed by their lack of verisimilitude. People whom the narrator claims he sees everyday are built as comic, even farcical characters, thus straining credibility–were it only on account of their programmatic names. It is to be expected that Mr. Biggs is a fat man, Lady Famish saves on food to afford a sumptuous carriage, and Lady Macscrew is avaricious–and Scottish! These onomastic creations transfigure those who people the British society and turn them into grotesques, all part of an originally serialized satire that gained popularity in unmatched fashion as it came out for over a year. Indeed, with his *Snobs of England*, Thackeray the chronicler emerges as the successful novelist he is about to become with *Pen and Pencil Sketches of English Life*, the future *Vanity Fair*–a truly fictional production which is nonetheless rich in grotesque "snobore" as well.

References

Dickens, Charles. (1865) 1964. *Our Mutual Friend.* New York: New American Library.
Thackeray, William Makepeace. (1848) 1945. *The Book of Snobs/ Le Livre des snobs.* Paris: Aubier.

—. *Vanity Fair, A Novel without a Hero* (1848) 1983. Edited with an Introduction by John Sutherland, with 193 Illustrations by the Author. Oxford and New York: Oxford University Press.

CHAPTER SEVEN

FROM "ABSOLUTE REALISM" TO NOCTURNAL GROTESQUE IN GÉRARD DE NERVAL'S *OCTOBER NIGHTS*

BÉRANGÈRE CHAUMONT

October Nights is a series of chronicles published in five installments in the newspaper *L'Illustration* from October 9th to November 13th 1852, then posthumously in book form in *La Bohème Littéraire*. The purpose of this largely autobiographical[1] and humoristic narrative seems simple at first: with "*nighttide* upon [him]" (Nerval 1999, 208) since he has missed the last train for the small town of Meaux, Nerval narrates a night spent wandering through Paris, killing time; then a chaotic expedition towards Creil in the area of Valois, where he hopes to join a friend on an otter-hunt. It is a derisory aim for a journey that never reaches its end, the narrator being placed under arrest for failing to show his passport to a *gendarme*. Contrary to Nerval's spatial choices for "Sylvie," another text from the Valois cycle published in 1854 in *Daughters of Fire*, Paris is here given pride of place. Fifteen chapters out of twenty-six cover the first Parisian night, whereas the narrative of the next two nights (made mainly of dream sequences) occupies far less textual space: three chapters are devoted to the narrative of the first night's dream and only one (Chapter 25) to the second. The two-fold journey through Paris and to his childhood's place is the occasion for Nerval's existential and literary experience of "realism" as he defines the term in the first chapter. His aesthetic credo, the narrative's leitmotiv, is first expressed after the reading in a café of an article published in Amédée's Pichot's *La Revue*

---

[1] The narrative remains ambivalent as it is poised between autobiography and fiction.

britannique, entitled "The Key of the Street," mistakenly attributed to Charles Dickens.[2]

For Nerval, realistic exploration as Dickens conceives it is the key that unlocks the underworld of the Parisian night to the *flâneur*, but it is also the key to clear-headed description and observation that make short shrift of novelistic narration and fiction. The aim is to reach "absolute truth" (205) which guarantees an authentic, daguerreotype-like representation of life (the daguerreotype being the early photographic process invented by Louis Daguerre in 1835). In Nerval's narrative, however, the outlines of the realistic picture are rapidly blurred and the chronicle becomes ambiguous. The grotesque, which corresponds to a posture "at odds with normality or rationality" (Peyrache-Leborgne 2012, 10, my translation) thus emerges from Nerval's narrative. Nerval's discreet reliance on the grotesque accounts for the disturbing feeling of estrangement felt when reading a chronicle presented as realistic. Nerval's text, indeed, works at the "distortion of a norm, of a reality whose traditional points of reference are by-passed" (15, my translation). Reality is distorted not only because Nerval questions and undermines literary realism through parody, but also because he seems to lose control over the world he depicts. Such a deeply unsettling metamorphosis of reality is probably due in part to the fact that Nerval's exploration of the city takes place at night, on the fringe of daily life and normality.

From Absolute Realism to Grotesque Estrangement

The very beginning of the chronicle is filled with numerous signs of allegiance to "absolute" realism, a British characteristic according to Nerval.[3] These Parisian October nights are indeed explicitly modelled on London nights: Nerval's narrator sets off with a *flâneur*, "one of those die-hard *badauds* that Dickens would call *cockneys*" (Nerval 1999, 205), who

---

[2] As Catherine Waters reminds us, "… it was not Dickens, but [George Augustus] Sala, who wrote the article entitled 'The Key of the Street' that appeared in *Household Words* on 6 September 1851. It was this narrative of his 'enforced perambulations of the thoroughfares of the metropolis' that first brought Sala to Dickens's attention and led to his regular employment as a contributor." (Waters 2008, 65). The phrase "the key of the street" itself comes from Dickens, however. It is used in Chapter 47 of *Pickwick Papers*. Job Trotter, locked out of the prison, is said to have "the key of the street." See also Sheringham 2010, 37-44.
[3] Nerval writes: "How lucky the British are: they manage to write and read entire chapters of first-hand observation unencumbered by the slightest contrivance of fiction!" (205)

will be his *cicerone* and the English mentor's diegetic double. The two friends start out in search of a place to dine, and thus walk past several renowned places of Parisian nightlife entertainment. Their perambulation is brought to a close at the market of *Les Halles*, before the narrator is finally able to catch the seven o'clock train for Strasbourg. The scenario of their expedition is similar to that of "The Key of the Street," in which the night-time *flâneur* ends up in a pub inside Covent-Garden market. Like the original text, Nerval's account oscillates between diary-entry, travel-writing, journalistic chronicle, scenes from nightlife and physiology of the underworld. The exploration of urban nights is even presented as part of a writer's calling and mission. Besides the English article, Nerval was also undeniably inspired by French sources for his Parisian night-time realism. The main reference is without doubt to Nicolas Restif de la Bretonne, author of *Nuits de Paris, ou Le Spectateur nocturne* (*Parisian Nights, or the Night Spectator*, 1788-94), who will be one of the *Illuminés, ou Les Précurseurs du socialisme* (*The Illuminati, or The Precursors of Socialism*) portrayed by Nerval as early as 1850. The other key reference, when one thinks of the Parisian night-world of the 19th century, is to the socialist novelist Eugène Sue, whose *Mystères de Paris* (*The Mysteries of Paris*), published in the weekly magazine *Journal des Débats* (*Journal of Debates*) in 1842-3, is the paragon of French serial fiction. In his *Mystères*, Sue transposes the exoticism of his earlier sea narratives to the city of Paris, which he depicts as a place of uncanny violence. The first part of this very long serial takes place in a *tapis-franc*, a low haunt where the ruffians of the *Ile de la Cité* meet at night. This early scene probably inspired Nerval's visit to Paul Niquet's establishment, a popular café of *Les Halles* which he leaves as someone is arrested in Chapter 15 of *October Nights*. Among other contemporary writers who inspired Nerval, one finds his friend Alexandre Privat d'Anglemont, a figure of the Parisian *Bohème*, a bard of nightly pleasures and the author of *Voyage à travers Paris* (*A Journey Through Paris*), published in the daily *Corsaire-Satan* in 1846. Middle-class readers were partial to picturesque urban narratives and the first instalment of Nerval's chronicle was published in the issue of *L'Illustration* in which the first volume of Edmond Texier's *Tableau de Paris*, with text and engravings, was also advertised. Twenty vignettes of "Paris by Night" by Eustache Lorsay were published in the first September issue of the magazine in 1852, with *topoi* found in Nerval's narrative: the fear of waking up one's porter (mentioned in Chapter 2 of *October Nights*), the old-fashioned cabaret and the café in *Les Halles*. The first stage of Nerval's journey thus leads him to give reportage on city night-life, as did both English and French contemporary realists, all adepts of the type of descriptive literature that Walter Benjamin later called "panoramic literature" (in Ferris 2004, 213). One may therefore assume that at the beginning of 1852 Gérard de Nerval was sincerely trying to adhere to realistic, even journalistic, writing, for him a new mode of expression.

Nerval was however also a well-known opponent of 19th-century realism, which he notably attacked in *Les Confidences de Nicolas*, the study devoted to Restif de la Bretonne mentioned *supra*, published in *La Revue des Deux Mondes* in August and September 1850, then in *The Illuminati* in November 1852. The chronological concomitance of the publication of *The Illuminati* and *October Nights* raises the question of Nerval's position as regards Champfleury's battle to champion realism in France, started in 1845. A week after the end of the serialization of *October Nights*, did Nerval wish to go back on his vindication of realism? The answer to the question is easy, since Nerval's adoption of realism is in fact satirical. The realistic enterprise of the first chapter is rapidly undermined by constant irony and by a dose of parodic excess, the two leading to the final aporia and the discarding of realism in Chapter 21. Nerval feigns to consider realism as the exact copy of reality in order to show that realism can never work.[4] The reader ends up with a fanciful daguerreotype in which the fragments of reality inserted in the narrative appear as bizarre and even grotesque, endowed as they are with a degree of estrangement. There is first the ridicule attached to the faithful reproduction of the price-list of different sizes of glasses of brandy (Chapter 11), then the inclusion in the text of other posters just as the narrator read them. They are the only fragments of reality which can be verified, but the narrator himself calls them "odd" or "bizarre." This is true first in Paris:

> Our attention was attracted by an odd public notice posted on the wall, listing the rules and regulations of a singing society. (Nerval 1999, 215)

Then in Meaux, where a merino-woman is exhibited as a monster:

> I took refuge in a café, where my eye was struck by a huge red poster which was couched in the following terms:
>
> BY PERMISSION OF HIS HONOUR THE MAYOR (of Meaux)
> WONDER OF WONDERS
> One of the most bizarre occurrences in Nature:

---

[4] This aspect has often been dissected by critics (see for example Mizuno 2005 and Blackman 1982).

A WOMAN OF GREAT BEAUTY
With a head of chestnut hair
That is in fact
THE FLEECE OF A MERINO (228)

The typography and presentation faithfully duplicate those found on the poster. The narrator adds in an ironic footnote: "Everything in this narrative being true, the author has deposited this poster at the offices of *L'Illustration*, where it is on view" (229). Realism supposedly offers a more authentic vision of reality, yet nothing real is visible and verifiable but words proving nothing: the existence of the poster does not guarantee that of the merino-woman. To simply transpose elements pertaining to reality to a text betrays a ridiculously narrow conception of realism. This Nerval shows at the end of the chronicle through the metaphor of the stuffed otter. The stuffed animal is the frustrating substitute of the initial purpose of the trip (otter-hunting), as well as the rigid and ridiculous image of what "absolute realism" creates. Experimenting with realism leads to absence of life.

As early as Chapter One, Nerval's irony in *October Nights* brings to the fore the important idea that true life is more bizarre than fiction:

Our neighbours [the British] have a talent for realism that delights in absolute truth. Indeed, novels will never be able to render life in all its bizarre complexities. [...] What novels can vie with the comic–or tragic–stories contained in a police gazette? (205)

His intuition is verified during the nocturnal visit to Paul Niquet's establishment:

If all these details were not exact, if I were not trying to daguerreotype the truth here, how much material for a novel could I gather from the examples of this derelict woman and this stupefied philosopher! [...] [from] low dives like these–the antechambers of Purgatory, [...] this Hell. (227)

The realism of *October Nights* is therefore that which unveils the unexpected present in the familiar world, the measure of estrangement found at the heart of daily-life, a first characteristic of 19th-century European grotesque, one present in Dickens's fiction too.[5]

---

[5] Michael Hollington writes about "a very important intersection of Dickens's work, where the [...] fantastic or the gothic comes into collision with the 'real' world of the city to produce the [...] art of the grotesque" (Hollington 1984, 24). The same could be said of *October Nights*.

The adjective "bizarre," which keeps cropping up in Nerval's chronicle, is perhaps what best justifies a new reading of *October Nights*, this time as a grotesque production. If today's theorists such as Régine Borderie usually distinguish between the bizarre and the grotesque (see Borderie 2011), the latter–in its larger sense–was often considered as synonym of the former in Nerval's time, as evinced by the omnipresence of the adjective "bizarre" in entries for "grotesque" in French 19th-century dictionaries. The *Littré* defines "grotesque" as "ridiculous, bizarre, extravagant"[6] and the *Larousse* as "bizarre, extravagant."[7] In the 1835 *Dictionary of the French Academy*, the adjective "bizarre" is first defined as the synonym of "capricious, weird, extravagant,"[8] which corresponds to the main perception of the grotesque by 19th-century intellectuals. The second entry, in accordance with the 18th-century meaning of the word, defines "bizarre" as "extraordinary, which departs from common practice or custom, surprising, inexplicable."[9] This second meaning raises the question of the perception of what is real and what isn't, which is linked to the grotesque as distortion of reality. In the representation of reality, what can one accept as "real" or authentic? "[...] What is real may not be real ... and this is not a joke,"[10] as the tramp in Gavarni's illustration for the fourth instalment of Nerval's text reminds us. In *October Nights*, the "bizarre" or "odd" fragments of reality correspond to contemporary definitions of the grotesque as weird, extravagant or close to caricature. But Nerval's bizarre is also rooted in ancient, decorative *grottesche* and thus relates to a superior, essentially aesthetic, grotesque. The grotesque originally falls within the province of fine-arts and is used in a text to create visualization (see Peyrache-Leborgne 2012). Nerval's chronicle revives this visual dimension and relies on two distinctive aspects of ornamental *grottesche* which inform modern literary grotesque: the monstrous and the arabesque. Philippe Morel gives a detailed description of the monstrous hybrids found in the grotesque of Roman times and of the Renaissance (Morel 1997) and Dominique Iehl explains how monstrous hybridity came to characterize literary grotesque (Iehl 1997). Nerval's text is punctuated by many popular shows, one of them the display of the merino-woman, an "anthropomorphous" monster, as Philippe Morel would call her (Morel 1997, 24). The universe of fun fairs

---

[6] "ridicule, bizarre, extravagant."

[7] "bizarre, extravagant."

[8] "fantasque, capricieux, extravagant."

[9] "ce qui est extraordinaire, ce qui s'écarte de l'usage ou de l'ordre commun, étonnant, inexplicable."

[10] "Le vrai peut quelquefois n'être pas vrai ... sans blague" (my translation).

crops up again when the narrator meets a "Savage" playing the drumbeats and a ventriloquist (Nerval 1999, 212-3), and reveals that the friend he wants to meet in Meaux "had formerly worked as a *Hercules* at fairs" (237). The merino-woman is a freak of nature, twice described as bizarre: "one of the most bizarre occurrences in nature" (228), "never before had Nature produced a creature this bizarre" (229). "Bizarre" here means "extra-ordinary," of course, but also "grotesque," a human-sheep hybrid, a debased version of Horace's sea-mermaid, turning the famous *desinit in piscem* into a facetious *desinit in ovem*. The grotesque, man-mimicking monkeys of rococo French *singeries* are here replaced by sheep. The merino-woman offers a combination of graceful womanhood and coarse animality, all the more striking as it incorporates a touch of the vegetal and thus brings to mind Arcimboldo's creations:

> This phenomenon [...] is possessed of a magnificent fleece of Barbary merino wool, chestnut brown in colour, and nearly two feet in length. Her hair grows like a plant, and upon closer inspection, the stems that support fourteen or fifteen branches can be observed. (228)

At a literary level the feminine hybrid may be (as in Horace) the image of the chronicle as a whimsical and capricious work of art, formally deconstructed, non-linear and lacking unity. This metaphorical reading of the merino-woman is supported by Nerval's mentions of Diderot and Sterne, two major authors of eccentric novels.[11] The allusion to Diderot in Chapter 2 does not refer to his most eccentric narrative, *Jacques le fataliste*, but the reference to *Tristram Shandy* is given prominence. In Chapter 22, the route that takes the narrator to Creil "twists and turns in every direction before making the enormous loop that finally takes you into Creil" (237), so much so that "the celebrated spiral that Corporal Trim traced in the air with his baton is no more whimsical than the itinerary you have to follow to get to one place or the other" (237).

Bizarre reality and formal eccentricities pave the way for the emergence of textual grotesque. From the beginning of the chronicle, the thread of the narrative is broken by preposterous digressions, as for example in Chapter 6, where the narrative is abruptly interrupted by the

---

[11] Daniel Sangsue has defined the eccentric narrative as discontinuous narrative lacking an overall structure. Chapter 10 of his book is devoted to Nerval (see Sangsue 1987). Dominique Peyrache-Leborgne has recently described it as the narrative counterpart of the ornamental arabesque (see Peyrache-Leborgne 2012, 375 and foll.). See also Muzelle 2006.

anecdote of the two philosophers from Marseilles who communicate only through onomatopoeia and whose friendship parodies that of the two night-time *flâneurs*. The chronicle follows an unpredictable path, the narrator accumulating "pranks" and "eccentricities" (209) like Saint-Cricq, the hero of the first digression (Chapter 4). But too many oddities mean that the serial will never reach its initial goal: just as the narrator can never reach Creil, the narrative will never be realistic. From deformed reality to twisted narrative, an excess of strangeness at the heart of everyday-life leads to the grotesque and questions man's perception of reality.

Nocturnal Estrangement and the Grotesque

October Nights is informed by the gradual intrusion of an antagonistic pole, a feeling of estrangement which has to do with night-time Paris. The nocturnal report is immediately considered as a journey into a foreign world and may read as a travel guide, for example in Chapter 5 where Parisian nights are compared to London nights. The references to foreign places and ancient times enable the narrator to describe Paris. In his mind, the "Dance Hall of the Dogs" in Chapter 8 resembles "the gymnasia of antiquity," and the ball itself can be assimilated to a Viennese "casual ball" (214). Nerval constantly needs to refer to foreign images in order to describe an increasingly unfamiliar reality. The feeling of alienation translates itself into radical estrangement with the intrusion of the fantastic. The constant reference to Dante's *Inferno* soon leads Nerval to equate the night-time population with infernal spectres. Later, in an allusion to Goethe's *Faust* (which Nerval translated in 1828), a young market girl of *Les Halles* is compared to a witch from Mount Brocken in a chapter entitled "The Charnel Houses." The narrator remembers that the Market of the Innocents is situated where an old churchyard used to be. That churchyard was famous for its 14th-century charnel houses, one of them adorned with a "Dance of Death." The memory of the charnel houses probably accounts for the fantastic allusions or images. Carried to its extreme, the bizarre night-time experience verges on the fantastic when the night becomes spectral, a metaphor conveying the protagonist's sense of unreality:

> I think it's time for me to proceed to the train station, carrying *the hollow phantom of this night* along with me in my mind. (227, italics mine)

When boarding the train for Meaux, Nerval gradually takes his readers to a different world. The French word for "dream" (*rêver*) comes from the

Latin *reexvagare*, meaning "to roam." Nerval moves from reality to
dreams. His chronicle literally becomes nocturnal since the last two nights
are narratives of dreams. The first one takes place on the second night,
when he arrives in Meaux. It is filled with "strange" (229) sensations, in
which tiny gnomes open his skull to try to surgically remove the seat of
objectivity (Chapter 18). The second one takes place on the third night,
when the narrator has just been arrested in Crespy-en-Valois for failing to
show his passport. In his dream, he appears before a classical tribunal and
is charged with being a "Fantaisiste! [a] Réaliste! [an] Essayiste!"[12] (241).
Both dreams are explicitly linked to the poetic reflection at the core of
Nerval's text since they are inserted in a journalistic essay and are
described as part and parcel of reality. Paradoxically enough, it is the first
dream which convinces the narrator that he should forsake his realistic
endeavour, the description of his vagaries being deemed too much of a
threat to his sanity: "Clearly this dream is too *outlandish*[13]... even for
me!" (232, italics mine). More than a clear rejection of realist aesthetics, it
is a disconcerting shift towards radical subjectivity, which makes Nerval a
unique case in the context of French Romanticism, as Claude Millet
explains:

> Realism for Nerval is less a matter of the vivid tension between reality and
> ideality which obsessed the other Romantics, as we have seen, but of the
> experience, no less traumatic, of chaos and of the confusing proximity of
> reality and fantasy, of objectivity and subjectivity. (Millet 2007, 191, my
> translation)

The question of the place of subjectivity in realism, asked *in fine* by the
critic-*cum*-dreamer, brings him closer to Dickens who, in virtually the
same year, raised that of "the Romantic side of familiar things" in his
preface to *Bleak House*.[14] But the originality of Nerval's conception of
reality appears at the end of the serial, where reality and dream cannot be
told apart. The end is endowed with such a strong dream-like quality that
it paves the way for *Aurélia*, whose subtitle is "Dream and Life." After the
first dream, the narrator of *October Nights* exclaims: "Let's stick around
then and try to extricate ourselves from this awful hotchpotch of comedy,
dream and reality" (Nerval 1999, 232). The disjointed and whimsical

---

[12] The French words are kept in Richard Sieburth's translation. "Fantaisiste," a
note indicates, "is roughly equivalent to 'humorist.'"
[13] The adjective used here reminds us of the definitions of "grotesque" found in
19th-century French dictionaries. Cf. *supra*.
[14] On Dickens and mid-Victorian realism, see for example Vanfasse 2004.

poetics of dreams then pervades the narrative of the following days, which switches abruptly from impressions to confessions, from memories to literary criticism, from the narrator's day-dreaming to his conversation with the *gendarmes*. Journalistic observation is contaminated by dreams, unpredictability becomes the rule and inconsistency makes the mundane uncanny. Is the realistic endeavour doomed to fail because it takes place at night? Nerval's choice of the daguerreotype as his reference inscribes failure from the start, since the daguerreotype cannot photograph reality in the dark.

October Nights chronicles a journey into estrangement and the narrator, who wished to explore nightlife reality, loses his bearings and sense of direction. Night-time conjures up the grotesque because it distorts perceptions and awakens fantasies. Pitch darkness is a *camera obscura* which favours the most fantastical phantasmagoria. The excursion to Meaux thus becomes a journey into an uncanny, dream-like world where the strangest people inhabit the most singular places, where extreme estrangement contaminates the narrator. The process starts in Paris where the narrator discovers an alien space with its specific language. Nightlife speaks *argot* (French slang):

> Pantin is the dark side of Paris–some would say the raffish side of Paris; but the slang term for it is Pantruche. (213)

During his exploration of Parisian nightlife, the narrator's de-familiarization leads him to unlearn his own mother tongue: "I'm afraid I'm no longer speaking French" (214). To roam through Paris at night means to be caught in a web of alienation, both from one's city and one's own self. In that sense, to be drunk ("être gris," literally "to be grey" in French) means to take on the colour of the night and to be dispossessed of one's individuality. The narrator experiences the fever of intoxication, the breakdown of reality and its adulteration by fantasy in Paul Niquet's establishment: "Finding myself among this strange *clientèle*, my head was beginning to swim" (237). His alienation reaches a climax in Meaux, as shown above, and he feels it an absolute necessity to come to his senses:

> … I'll stop here–It's far too difficult to go on playing the part of a realist. And yet it was the chance reading of a piece of Dickens that set me off on these divagations! ... A solemn voice is calling me back to my senses. (234)

Embarked on a realistic expedition, the narrator faces nocturnal estrangement which gradually reveals itself as Freudian uncanny and opens onto madness. Next to the humoristic tone of the text, night-time paves the way to the second pole necessary to the romantic grotesque described by Wolfgang Kayser, i.e. the feeling of alienation (Kayser 1966, 185). For today's reader who knows about Nerval's life and tragic end, the text's aberrations are the death knell for Nerval's failing reason. These *October Nights* of 1852 are "wasted nights," to use Nerval's title for the first part of *Sylvie*. The narrator does not only visit "Hell" (Nerval 1999, 227), he loses his mind in the labyrinth of his own inner night. More than a journey into Dantean infernal circles, the structure of this miniature night-time epic is indeed labyrinthine, a final image of the grotesque arabesque. Through the description of Piranesi's *Carceri* stairs, the first nightmare suggests a *mise-en-abyme* of both the narrator's erratic and aimless wandering through Paris and his disorganized narrative:

> Corridors–corridors without end! Stairways–stairways one ascends and descends and then reascends, stairways whose lowest steps are lapped by the black waves churned up by the waterwheels beneath the immense arches of a bridge … amid a maze of scaffolding! To ascend, to descend, to wander through corridors–and all this for eternities on end … (229-30)

This section of the dream conveys the narrator's distress at being trapped in the darkness of madness, alienated from reason and a stranger to himself. His anguish is literally illustrated at the end of the chronicle, when the narrator is unable to prove his identity. According to Claude Pichois, Nerval's realistic endeavour was both a therapeutic and literary attempt at ridding himself of the chimera haunting his mind (see Pichois 1993). But for want of stable objectivity and realism, the night-time dream pervades daytime reality and becomes insanity, a dark disease Nerval later tried to cure in the sanatorium of the aptly named Dr. Blanche ("White" in French).

Nerval both literally and metaphorically travelled to the end of the night. His literature chronicles his journeys both abroad and at home, notably his various forays into the Parisian night where he surveyed darkness and its mysteries until his death, one night, in a street of Paris. Etymological symbolism, which Nerval was partial to, would seem to show that the man was predestined to experience night life. From his patronymic, Gérard Labrunie ("brun" is French for "brown" or "dark"), to his pseudonym after 1836, Nerval, meaning "le Noir-Val" or "Black Vale" (the name of some land he inherited from his mother), he bore names which designate night as his domain.[15] From 1836 onwards, Nerval was by essence and by name a *noctambule*, a discreet and whimsical figure walking through the night who never hesitated to take part in the *Bohème* of the impasse du Doyenné, where he resided. One also has in mind the narratives of his journeys abroad and his numerous night-time expeditions through Vienna or Cairo and Stambul, published in his 1851 *Journey to the Orient*, of Baden and Brussels in *Lorely* (1852). He is also the author of a serial on London nightlife published in *La Presse* and *L'Artiste* in 1845-6, which includes elements later used again in Chapter 5 of *October Nights*. Nerval truly made night his province, to the point of being unable to forsake it during the last few years of his life. "The Universe lies in the night" as Nerval writes in Part One of *Aurélia* (Nerval 1999-2, 279). "Here I am, embarked on a venture where I lose myself and spend endless hours trying to find myself again. Would you believe that I can barely compose two lines a day, so overcome am I by darkness?"[16] he is said to have written in a letter to Louis Legrand in January 1855, the month of his death.

In order to find his way through such unyielding night, Nerval invented a new way of life and a new vision, that of "the eternal eyes which the Night hath opened within us," as Novalis would have phrased it in *Hymns to the Night*. The starting point of the eccentric wanderings, "The Café of the Blind," heralds a new vision and the exploration of a deeper and truer facet of reality. The end of *October Nights* announces *Aurélia*, a text Nerval called "supernaturalist" in his preface. Nerval is undoubtedly one of the precursors of French surrealism, and André Breton mentions him at great length in his *Manifeste du surréalisme*. *October Nights* participates in the elaboration of a new type of realism, based on the observation of what lies beyond exteriority and beyond the surface of consciousness. To a lesser degree, it is the nocturnal distortion of reality which turns this eccentric text into a grotesque narrative. When opting for mimetic realism the narrator paradoxically understands the paramount importance of daydreaming in literary creation. A nocturnal demiurge, Nerval lights up the night with cultural reveries and intertextual or imaginary literary chimera to turn it into a space of artistic invention. The result is a hybrid, grotesque text which goes beyond the simple chronicle to humorously look towards *ars poetica* and the short story, one of which "I," turned other in the night, would be the hero.

---

[15] And that before Aloysius Bertrand's *Gaspard de la Nuit*, which certainly owes a great deal to Nerval.
[16] Quoted in Barine 1897, 158, my translation.

A few years before Baudelaire, with *October Nights* Gérard de Nerval enriched the grotesque with night-time shadows, which–considering the initial, realistic, project–led him to probe mimetic representation, rendered impossible and yet advocated. In that sense Nerval is a perfect representative of European Romanticism. He uses grotesque aesthetics to depict reality as deformed and question conventional perceptions of reality. Night-time intoxication seems here to open onto the supernatural later found in the visions of *Aurélia*. This short serial sheds light on the link between realism, the grotesque and the nocturnal, but also between the grotesque and the bizarre, the fantastic and the oneiric, the latter closely linked to the radical otherness of night life. The bizarre, in Nerval's writing, is deeply original. It has nothing to do with opium- or alcohol-induced dreams or trances, as is the case with Théophile Gautier and the lesser French Romantic writers. It is not "artificial" distortion of reality. Grotesque distortion, in *October Nights*, is caused by reality itself. Nerval is thus implicitly closer to Victor Hugo, who in the preface to *Les Orientales* claims that the bizarre (which Edgar Allan Poe and Baudelaire see as the hallmark of genius) is an integral part of literature.

References

Barine, Arvède. 1897. "Essai de littérature pathologique." *Revue des Deux Mondes*, Vol. 144: 124-60.

Blackman, Maurice. 1982. "Charles Dickens et *Les Nuits d'octobre* : clés pour le réalisme nervalien." *Australian Journal of French Studies*, 29: 32-40.

Borderie, Régine. 2011. *"Bizarre, Bizarrerie." De Constant à Proust.* Grenoble: Ellug.

Ferris, David S. 2004. *The Cambridge Companion to Walter Benjamin.* Cambridge: Cambridge University Press.

Hollington, Michael. 1984. *Dickens and the Grotesque.* Beckenham (Kent): Croom Helm.

Iehl, Dominique. 1997. *Le Grotesque.* Paris: Presses Universitaires de France.

Kayser, Wolfgang. [1957] 1966. *The Grotesque in Art and Literature.* New-York: McGraw-Hill.

Millet, Claude. 2007. *Le Romantisme.* Paris: Le Livre de Poche.

Mizuno, Hisashi. 2005. "Nerval face au réalisme. *Les Nuits d'octobre* et l'esthétique nervalienne." *Revue d'Histoire Littéraire de la France*, 105, n°4: 817-41.

Morel, Philippe. 1997. *Les Grotesques. Les Figures de l'imaginaire dans la peinture italienne de la fin de la Renaissance.* Paris: Flammarion.

Muzelle, Alain. 2006. *L'Arabesque. La Théorie romantique de Friedrich Schlegel à l'époque de l'Athenaum.* Paris: Presses Universitaires de Paris-Sorbonne.

Nerval, Gérard de. (1852) 1999. *October Nights.* In *Selected Writings.* Translated by Richard Sieburth, 204-44. London: Penguin Books.

—. (1855) 1999. *Aurélia.* In *Selected Writings.* Translated by Richard Sieburth, 265-316. London: Penguin Books. [1999-2]

Peyrache-Leborgne, Dominique. 2012. *Grotesques et arabesques dans le récit romantique. De Jean-Paul à Victor Hugo.* Paris: Champion.

Pichois, Claude. 1993. "Notice pour *Les Nuits d'octobre.*" In *Œuvres complètes III* by Gérard de Nerval, 1092-6. "La Pléiade." Paris: Gallimard.

Sangsue, Daniel. 1987. *Le Récit excentrique: Gautier, De Maistre, Nerval, Nodier.* Paris: José Corti.

Sheringham, Michael. 2010. "'The Key of the Street': 'London' in the Construction of 'Paris.'" *Synergies Royaume-Uni et Irlande*, n°3: 37-44.

Vanfasse, Nathalie. 2004. "'Grotesque but not impossible:' Dickens's Novels and mid-Victorian Realism." *E-rea*, 2.1. http://erea.revues.org/500; DOI: 10.4000/erea.500

Waters, Catherine. 2008. *Commodity Culture in Dickens's Household Words: The Social Life of Goods.* Aldershot: Ashgate Publishing Limited.

CHAPTER EIGHT

THE *FLÂNEUR* AND THE GROTESQUE FIGURES OF THE METROPOLIS IN THE WORKS OF CHARLES DICKENS AND CHARLES BAUDELAIRE

ISABEL VILA CABANES

Both Dickens and Baudelaire are well-known for their penchant for the grotesque as well as for their fascination with the nineteenth-century city. The main object of this chapter is to analyse the many descriptions of grotesque inhabitants of the metropolis from the perspective of *flânerie* in Dickens's *Sketches by Boz* (1836) and *The Uncommercial Traveller* (1860-75), which provide examples of London *flâneurs*–namely, observing and meditating urban strollers–and compare them with the grotesque figures that the Parisian *flâneur* in Baudelaire's "Tableaux parisiens" (1861) and *Le Spleen de Paris* (1869) encounters in the streets. I will start by briefly contextualizing the grotesque in the modern epoch, focusing on particular aspects which I consider relevant for the understanding of grotesque art in modernity, and, specifically, in the *flâneur* works of Dickens and Baudelaire. Then, I will deal with the attraction of the London and Parisian *flâneurs* towards the freaks of the city and analyse the role these grotesque passages have in the *flâneur*'s vision of the world, examining, at a textual level, the different aesthetic devices which convey or emphasize the grotesque in selected passages of Dickens and Baudelaire. I will finally analyse how the grotesque images that these *flâneurs* describe in their sojourning through the streets influence the overall perception of London and Paris.

The Grotesque and the Modern Epoch

Already in the Romantic period there is a transformation of the way in which ugliness is perceived and a new sensibility for the supernatural and terrible is born. The Romantic aesthetics of the ugly challenges the classical canons of beauty and champions the idea that the beautiful can also emerge from repellent, sinister objects which become irresistibly attractive. Numerous aesthetic treatises such as Burke's *A Philosophical Enquiry into the Origin of Our Ideas of the Sublime and Beautiful* (1756-9), Schiller's *On the Sublime* (1800), or Scott's "On the Supernatural in Fictitious Composition" (1827) elaborate on the notions of beauty, the sublime and the grotesque. However, it is Victor Hugo who takes the grotesque to the foreground of modern aesthetics. In his much quoted "Preface to *Cromwell*" (1827) Hugo argues that, for art to be complete, both the grotesque and the sublime must coexist as they appear in nature: as a "harmony of contraries" in which the beautiful seems to blend with the ugly.[1] But most importantly, he claims that, even though the grotesque is already present in ancient art, "in the idea of men of modern times, however, the grotesque plays an enormous part. It is found everywhere; on the one hand, it creates the abnormal and the horrible, on the other the comic and the burlesque" (Hugo 2010, 365). Hugo understands the grotesque as an essential aspect of the modern genius and as a category by itself. He also observes that in modern art the grotesque is the source of both the terrible as well as the humorous. Indeed, many studies of the grotesque agree that, in terms of the reader's response, the experience of the grotesque is paradoxical. It relies on an "unresolved conflict" between its comic and repulsive elements, and, consequently, the reaction to the grotesque image is simultaneously one of laughter and one of disgust.[2] Traditional criticism has examined the grotesque focusing on either its repulsive or its ludicrous aspects depending on which appears more prominently. For instance, Kayser concentrates on the "horrific" character of the grotesque, while Thomas Wright emphasizes the burlesque side of it. However, I would argue, in line with recent theorists, that the key to the grotesque is the very "unresolved tension," since distinguishing between the comic or horrific in it neglects a quality that is fundamental to

---

[1] Note that the notions of sublime and grotesque are not always clearly distinguished in Hugo's "Preface," being at times opposite and at other times equivalent terms.
[2] See Thomson 1979, 20; Steig 1970, 260; Jennings 1963, 10; Harpham 1976, 464-5.

grotesque art.[3] The complex nature of the grotesque is finely realized in Dickens's characters. Even though they have often been classified as either comic or fearsome,[4] it is the tension between comicality and repulsion that makes grotesque characters such as Mr. Pecksniff or Mrs. Gamp successful.

Hugo also points out that, since the grotesque is "free and open" (Hugo 2010, 365),[5] it offers a wider range of representations of modern existence than traditional beauty. Certainly, the aesthetic panorama of the nineteenth century bears witness to a renewed interest in the grotesque as a component of fine arts, for such an imagery that can transgress established aesthetic boundaries proves to be the ideal means to portray an era marked by contradictions and conflict.[6] The triumph of the ugly and terrifying in the modern epoch has special significance in Baudelaire's œuvre. The grotesque is not just a prominent element of his poetry but also a central concern in his art criticism, for he devises a theory of the grotesque which is scattered throughout his writings. In the essays "On the Essence of Laughter" (1855), "Some Foreign Caricaturists" (1857) and "Some French Caricaturists" (1857) Baudelaire explores the dual and contradictory nature of grotesque imagery in the plastic arts. He refers to the grotesque as the "absolute comic," distinguishing it from the ordinary or "significative comic." The dualism of the "significative comic" is easily recognized: it is satirical and consists of "art and the moral idea." On the contrary, the dualism of the "absolute comic" is presented as a unity and "calls for the intuition to grasp it" (Baudelaire 2010, 157). According to Michele Hannoosh, the paradoxical appearance of unity of Baudelaire's conception of the grotesque results in an increase of the possibilities of interpretation.[7] This openness of meaning makes grotesque images suitable for depicting the paradoxes of modern experience.

---

[3] For instance Rocadio explains that the grotesque object is effective when the audience experiences a feeling of ambivalence caused by the continuous interplay between horror and humour (Rocadio 1990, 32-3).
[4] See Clayborough 1965, 201-22. He categorizes Dickens's grotesque characters into "celestial creatures" and evil villains.
[5] This recalls Bakhtin's notion of the "grotesque body" as unfinished and representative of the external world (Bakhtin 1984, 317).
[6] See Connelly 2009, 2-4 and Hannoosh 1992, 11.
[7] See Hannoosh 1992, 43-4. Although there is a similarity between Baudelaire's and Hugo's conceptualization of the grotesque, there are also important differences between them. For instance, while the grotesque and the sublime are separate, opposed terms for Hugo, the boundary between them in Baudelaire's work blurs. See Rollins 1976, 271 and Hannoosh 1992, 37-8.

The laughter at the grotesque object, Baudelaire says, stems from a simultaneous feeling of superiority with respect to that object and of inferiority with respect to the divine. Hannoosh maintains that Baudelaire's theory of the dualism of the comic is closely connected with his theory of modernity and the *flâneur*, since these concepts can only be fully understood in terms of dualisms (Hannoosh 1992, 4). For instance, modernity is defined by the fleeting and transitory as well as by the eternal and immutable. The *flâneur* is a central figure in this context. He is both subject and object, the self and the other. Accordingly, the artist-*flâneur* epitomizes the permanent condition of dualism of human beings: "the power of being oneself and someone else at one and the same time" (Baudelaire 2010, 165). In his rambles around the crowded metropolis, the *flâneur* has the ability to double himself and become the object he observes. As I will show in this paper, both Dickens's and Baudelaire's peripatetic narrators experience a *dédoublement* in their encounters with marginal, eccentric pedestrians.

Baudelaire often pairs the fantastic and surreal with the grotesque, but he also notes that for it to be successful the spectator/reader must still find a connection with reality: "This is a creation mixed with a certain imitative faculty–imitative that is, of elements pre-existing in nature" (157). Indeed, scholars such as Harpham insist that an object can be considered grotesque when it simultaneously causes not only laughter and revulsion, but also astonishment, creating a feeling of alienation from ordinary life.[8] The grotesque image produces instant estrangement from the familiar and breaks with the reader's expectations. However, a connection with reality must remain so that the reader is not left with a feeling of total absurdity (Harpham 1976, 462).[9] Harpham refers to this response of alienation as an "interval," a moment or pause which occurs when, despite having noticed the different elements which constitute the grotesque object, the reader

---

[8] See Harpham 1976, 463 and Steig 1970, 254.

[9] According to Harpham, if the bond with the familiar world is lost, the image is not grotesque anymore but absurd. It should also be noted at this point that the grotesque is a diachronic concept and the response of the reader depends on the historical and cultural background, and, therefore, the definition of what constitutes a grotesque representation lies in our "context of expectations" which changes through time. The present discussion about the grotesque and estrangement as well as the lines concerning its paradoxical nature are a revised version of the definition I give of the grotesque in a paper entitled "Reading the Grotesque in the Works of Charles Dickens and Jonathan Swift" due to be published in the proceedings of the conference *Texts, Contexts and Intertextuality: Charles Dickens as a Reader*, University of Vechta, Germany, 7-9 June 2012.

cannot yet reconcile them and fully comprehend them (Harpham 2006, 19). Defamiliarization from everyday existence is a recurrent device in Dickens[10] and Baudelaire, who can find a balance between the fantastic and the mundane in their grotesque representations. As I will show, alienation and a distanced standpoint towards the urban spectacle are also crucial strategies in the practice of *flânerie*. Detachment from the urban surroundings helps the *flâneur* to achieve a certain extent of objectivity towards the subject of his observation.

Dickens, Baudelaire and the Uncanny Metropolis

Since, in Baudelaire's words, it is "the ephemeral, the fugitive, the contingent" (Baudelaire 2010, 12) that define modern experience, the ever-changing metropolis becomes the optimal site for the development and observation of the modern era. His portrayals of urban landscapes and casual encounters in *Les Fleurs du Mal* elevate the genre of the *Tableaux de Paris* from the feuilleton to lyrical poetry. Later, Baudelaire pushes the topic of the city further with his prose poems, which represent his efforts to adapt language to the rhythm of urban life: "It was, above all, out of my exploration of huge cities, out of the medley of their innumerable interrelations, that this haunting ideal was born" (Baudelaire 1970, x). Language becomes a tool in the hands of the poet in the representation of the ever-changing and transitory character of city life.

Baudelaire also establishes an explicit connection between the grotesque and the modern metropolis in his discussion of Daumier's works: "Look through his works, and you will see parading before your eyes all that a great city contains of living monstrosities, in all their fantastic and thrilling reality" (Baudelaire 2010, 177). For Baudelaire, the modern city is an endless source of exotic and grotesque "living monstrosities," turning both into the subject and the object of art. The extreme conditions of nineteenth-century capitals create an environment which stimulates creativity. Dickens, in consonance with Baudelaire, notices in *Sketches by Boz* that the growing metropolis accommodates the most inspiring and fascinating people:

> There are certain descriptions of people who, oddly enough, appear to appertain exclusively to the metropolis. You meet them, every day, in the streets of London, but no one ever encounters them elsewhere; they seem indigenous to the soil, and to belong as exclusively to London as its own smoke, or the dingy bricks and mortar. (Dickens 1995, 303-4)

---

[10] See Clayborough 1965, 250-1 and Rocadio 1990, 49-53.

    The London of Dickens's urban sketches, like the Paris of Baudelaire's poems, is full of liminal figures that lurk around the streets, a space where horror and beauty coexist. As a matter of fact, the grotesque permeates almost every aspect of the world depicted in his sketches. In the papers of *The Uncommercial Traveller* the narrator portrays a city of mysteries and secrets dominated by infamous people and "corpses" which the narrator tries to decipher in his meditative walks, blending the comic and the grotesque in his accurate portrait of modern London. Michael Hollington, who traces Dickens's use of the grotesque back to popular theatre and the *commedia dell'arte*, his relation to literary tradition, and visual satire, points out that the influence of the latter is evinced in Dickens's interest in human physiognomy as the means to determine personality (Hollington 1984, 8; 14). In *The Uncommercial Traveller*, the narrator-*flâneur* claims that he "hold[s] physiognomy to be infallible, though all these sciences demand rare qualities in the student" (Dickens 1991, 351). The physiologies of the *flâneur* remind us of Simmel's theory of visual interaction in the metropolis. Simmel argues that, in an urban environment, seeing becomes more important than hearing (Simmel 1972, 360). All the chaos, crowds and traffic which characterize life in a modern city make the sense of hearing less valuable. In fact, Louis Huart comments in his whimsical *Physiologie du Flâneur* (1841) that this urban type "needs above all good eyes to be aware of every pretty merchant, every *grotesque face*, every baroque poster, and every fine leg which he encounters in the course of his rambles" (Huart 1841, 54, my emphasis and translation). Benjamin also suggests that the visual conditions of the modern urban existence described by Simmel explain the success of physiologies of the nineteenth century, among which the *flâneur* was a popular character:

> Simmel's apt remark concerning the uneasiness aroused in the urbanite by other people, people whom, in the overwhelming majority of cases, he sees without hearing, would indicate that, at least in their beginnings, the physiognomies <correction: physiologies> were motivated by, among other things, the wish to dispel this uneasiness and render it harmless. (Benjamin 1999, 447 [M16a, 2], 433-4 [M8a, 1])

    In the big city, where the appropriate conditions for the use of the eye are combined, *flâneurs* such as Dickens's uncommercial traveller or Poe's narrator in "The Man of the Crowd" (1840) focus their attention on grotesque and odd urban dwellers in an attempt to grasp the riddles of modern London. The Paris of Baudelaire is also replete with phantasmagorical figures which arouse the curiosity of the stroller, turning the metropolis into an almost unreal space. For instance, the narrator in

"Les Sept Vieillards" claims that the city furnishes the observer with the most exciting scenes: "City of swarming, city full of dreams / Where ghosts in daylight tug the stroller's sleeve" (Baudelaire 2008, 177).

Hollington states that Dickens's perception of grotesque art is derived from German Romanticism. Also, the emphasis on the use of imagination against a more realistic vision of the world is distinctive not only of Dickens's (Hollington 1984, 18-9) but also of Baudelaire's approach to the grotesque. Dickens's descriptions of the city, Hollington asserts, are endowed with high symbolic meaning, distancing him from Victorian realism and bringing him closer to Baudelaire's allegorical representation of the city (Hollington 2010, 86).[11] Their urban grotesque reveals a world of wonder in which every element becomes symbolic of the paradoxes of modern culture. To give an example, Hollington points out that both Dickens and Baudelaire regard the mud of the city as representative of human corruption (91). In fact, oxymorons, juxtapositions, hyperboles, and the technique of humanizing objects and dehumanizing people are frequent aesthetic devices employed by Dickens and Baudelaire in order to create grotesque images in their *flâneur* writings.

The *Flâneur* and the Monstrous Bodies of the City

The figure of the *flâneur* has become in recent years the focus of attention of both literary and sociological theory. This type that comes with the rise of the metropolis in the nineteenth century is a solitary person, usually male,[12] who walks aimlessly around the streets observing and reflecting upon the urban environment. The *flâneur* stands in a paradoxical position with respect to the crowd, for even though he is immersed in the multitude, he is not really part of it. He maintains a certain degree of distance with the urban spectacle and turns into a detached observer who experiences society in his own way. The anonymous streets are the perfect environment to let imagination run free, for the *flâneur* is inspired by the endless stimuli of the metropolis (Müller and Vila-Cabanes 2012, 229). From this privileged standpoint, Dickens's and Baudelaire's narrators offer extensive descriptions of urban landscapes and dwellers at different times of the day.

---

[11] According to Hollington, Baudelaire comments in the essay "Puisque réalisme il y a" that Dickens's "mystic eye" sets him apart from traditional realism.
[12] Although most scholars agree that there are instances of female *flâneurs* in the twentieth-century metropolis, there is still an ongoing debate on the possibility of a nineteenth-century female *flâneur*. For further information on the topic see Nesci 2007, Wilson 2001, Parsons 2003 or Wolff 1985.

The *flâneurs* of Dickens's and Baudelaire's later works present the metropolis as a sinister and surreal space where the comic and the grotesque merge. The urban peripatetic is indeed particularly attracted to marginal, extravagant figures: "Gripped by my fatal humours, I observe / singular beings with appalling charms" (Baudelaire 2008, 181). For instance, in the paper "On an Amateur Beat" and the poem "Les Petites Vieilles" both narrators describe old, grotesque, misshapen women. Baudelaire's stroller comes across these "hunchbacked and dislocated wrecks" and realizes that, despite their pathetic, almost inhuman appearance, they "were women once" (181). The narrator wonders about the past of these decrepit hags who "trudge on, without complaint, / Through the chaotic city's teeming waste / Saints, courtesans, mothers of bleeding hearts, / Whose names, in the past, everyone had known" (185). They arouse a melancholy feeling in the poet and remind him of the mortal condition of man, since they do not just represent themselves but are also symbolic of humanity as a whole. These repellent but fascinating creatures turn in the eyes of the poet into the "ruins" of the metropolis and become an allegory for the fleeting nature of modern urban life. Similarly, Dickens's uncommercial traveller encounters in the London streets an analogous "hunchbacked monster," going from mere observation to a state of reverie:

> What London peripatetic of these times has not seen the woman who has fallen forward, double, through some affection of the spine, and whose head has of late taken a turn to one side, so that it now droops over the back of one of her arms at about the wrist? Who does not know her staff, and her shawl, and her basket, as she gropes her way along, capable of seeing nothing but the pavement, never begging, never stopping, for ever going somewhere on no business? How does she live, whence does she come, whither does she go, and why? I mind the time when her yellow arms were naught but bone and parchment. Slight changes steal over her; for there is a shadowy suggestion of human skin on them now. (Dickens 1991, 367)

Even though this grotesque, ridiculous woman is portrayed as a repulsive being, she still captivates Dickens's narrator, who feels compelled to answer all the questions she raises in his mind. In both texts, the old wretches become an abstraction and, at times, act as doubles of the *flâneur*.[13] The uncommercial, in a self-reflective moment, depicts her as if

---

[13] For doubling in Dickens's *The Uncomercial Traveller* see Müller and Vila 2012, 237-8. For doubling in Baudelaire's poems see Hannoosh 1992, 349 and Wing 1997, 24.

"for ever going somewhere on no business" in a way analogous to himself, their slow pace contrasting with the frenzy of the city. Likewise, towards the end of "Les Petites Vieilles" the poet claims that the old freaks are his "fellow-minds" (Baudelaire 2008, 187). Both *flâneurs* paradoxically become observers and the object they observe, illustrating, as Hannoosh says, Baudelaire's theory of the dualism of the comic and grotesque as well as the dualism of modern existence. These anonymous women who have become invisible for the citizens are only perceived by other marginal urban figures. In "On an Amateur Beat," the uncommercial traveller remarks that the old woman is followed by a "lop-sided mongrel" which, "jogging eastward like [him]self, with a benevolent countenance and a watery mouth, as though musing on the many excellences of pork," (Dickens 1991, 368) turns into another double of the *flâneur* and the woman (Müller and Vila 2012, 238).

Hollington identifies Dickens's grotesque images with Bakhtin's notion of "grotesque realism," characterized by degradation, hyperbolism, and emphasis on an unfinished body (Hollington 1984, 5-6). For Bakhtin, the "grotesque body" is not an individual entity but it is limitless and representative of the external world. Descriptions of bodily functions, birth or old age, which are typical images of grotesque realism, appear frequently in Dickens's grotesque moments. For instance, the caricatural depiction of an extravagant and repellent passer-by that the uncommercial traveller offers in "Wapping Workhouse" illustrates Dickens's taste for absolutes and hyperboles as the means to reinforce the distorted and comic qualities of the grotesque object:

> A creature remotely in the likeness of a young man, with a puffed sallow face, and a figure all dirty and shiny and slimy, who may have been the youngest son of his filthy old father, Thames, or the drowned man about whom there was a placard on the granite post like a large thimble, that stood between us. (Dickens 1991, 18)

The bystander portrayed in this passage seems in the eyes of the *flâneur* no longer human but a "creature" or "apparition" which has taken the same shabby and dirty appearance as the Thames, emphasizing the darkness and bleakness of his surroundings. But excessiveness is not exclusive to Dickens's writings. In "On the Essence of Laughter" Baudelaire, for whom the grotesque is best expressed in the English and German languages, concludes that exaggeration and hyperbole can transform the "significative comic" into the "absolute comic" or grotesque. (Baudelaire 2010, 158-9). Accordingly, the grotesque passages of his poetic work are imbued with intense images which play with the boundaries between the comic and horrific to an extreme. In "Les Sept Vieillards" Baudelaire's *flâneur* provides a macabre but humorous description of an old, grotesque man: "You would not call him bent, but cut in two - / His spine made a right angle with his legs / So neatly that his cane, the final touch / gave him the figure and clumsy step / Of some sick beast, or a three-legged Jew" (Baudelaire 2008, 179). In these lines, the old man's decrepit appearance is conveyed by irony and humorous exaggerations, for he is not just represented as being hunchbacked but also as broken, so disfigured that he resembles a limping quadruped. Two common rhetorical devices employed by Dickens and Baudelaire in order to stress the grotesque are, as the earlier examples show, anthropomorphization and dehumanization. According to Nathaniel Wing, the grotesque creatures of Baudelaire's poems "evoke that ambiguity between man and beast" (Wing 1997, 28). Thus, the little old women appear dehumanized: they are "shrunken shades" and "marionettes" who crawl "like wounded animals" (Baudelaire 2008, 183; 187). Dorothy Van Ghent aptly explains how humanizing objects and dehumanizing people is an essential strategy in Dickens's works (Van Ghent 1950, 419). Descriptions of animals wandering around the city as if they were real people or monstrous bodies almost devoid of humanity abound in the papers of *The Uncommercial Traveller*. To give an example, in "Night Walks" the protagonist is surprised by "a thing" that looked "like a beetle-browed hair-lipped youth of twenty" (Dickens 1991, 140). Despite their disturbing physical outlook, grotesque urban types seem to hold some irresistible power over the peripatetic observer.

The Grotesque in the *Flâneur*'s Overall Vision of Paris and London

The atmosphere portrayed by Baudelaire's and Dickens's *flâneurs* is determined by the ever-present grotesque imagery. Not only are the urban inhabitants grotesque, but everything else seems to be tinged with decadence. The *flâneur* has an eye for the sombre and inscrutable nooks of the metropolis, since, as Baudelaire writes in the prose poem "Les Veuves," it is especially "towards these places poets and philosophers love to direct their avid speculations" (Baudelaire 1970, 22). Dickens's rambling narrator is likewise intrigued by concealed spaces, of which he describes every gruesome detail. For instance, in "London Churches" the uncommercial traveller notes that "rot and mildew and dead citizens formed the uppermost scent," (Dickens 1991, 96) accentuating the general theme of death which dominates the essay. For Dickens's peripatetic the

English capital is above all shabby. In "The Boiled Beef of New England" he complains that:

> The meanness of Regent-street, set against the great line of Boulevards in Paris, is as striking as the abortive ugliness of Trafalgar-square, set against the gallant beauty of the Place de la Concorde. London is shabby by daylight, and shabbier by gaslight. (Dickens 1991, 264)

Dickens, who had often visited Paris, considers London, by way of contrast, as an all-consuming and decadent space which becomes almost threatening. A similar tone of pettiness and secrecy is conveyed by Poe's narrator in his walk around London in "The Man of the Crowd." Michael Sheringham argues that Baudelaire's perception of Paris is influenced by the accounts of London in Poe's story and De Quincey's *Confessions of an English Opium-Eater* (1821), with which he was very familiar (Sheringham 2010, 39-40). Although the grotesque is also present in other French *flâneur* works such as Fournel's *Ce qu'on voit dans les rues de Paris* (1858), the images that Baudelaire's *flâneur* produces are highly disconcerting and verge on the supernatural. The Paris of his poetry is indeed as claustrophobic and miserable as Dickens's or Poe's London, illustrating the paradoxes of the modern epoch. According to Hollington, the metropolis in Baudelaire's and Dickens's writings after the late 1850s has a higher symbolic meaning and gains a melancholic tone as a result of their growing dissatisfaction with contemporary politics and life (Hollington 2010, 91-2). It seems that, even though the numerous grotesque images on which their *flâneurs* muse emphasize that distinctive feeling of awe of the modern metropolis, Baudelaire's representation of Paris still has a more serious and nostalgic touch than Dickens's picture of London, where the humorous often emerges.

References

Bakhtin, Mikhail. (1965) 1984. *Rabelais and His World*. Translated by Helene Iswolsky. Bloomington: Indiana University Press.

Baudelaire, Charles. (1845-60) 2010. *The Painter of Modern Life and Other Essays*. Translated by Jonathan Mayne. London: Phaidon Press.

—. (1857) 2008. *The Flowers of Evil*. Translated by James McGowan. Oxford: Oxford University Press.

—. (1869) 1970. *Paris Spleen*. Translated by Louise Varèse. New York: New Directions.

Benjamin, Walter. (1982) 1999. *The Arcades Project.* Translated by Howard Eiland and Kevin McLaughlin. Cambridge, Mass.: The Belknap Press of Harvard University Press.

Clayborough, Arthur. 1965. *The Grotesque in English Literature.* Oxford: Clarendon Press.

Connelly, Frances S. 2009. *Modern Art and the Grotesque.* Cambridge: Cambridge University Press.

Dickens, Charles. (1836) 1995. *Sketches by Boz.* Edited by Dennis Walder. Harmondsworth: Penguin.

—. (1860) 1991. *The Uncommercial Traveller.* London: Mandarin Paperbacks.

Hannoosh, Michele. 1992. *Baudelaire and Caricature: From the Comic to an Art of Modernity.* University Park, Pa.: The Pennsylvania State University Press.

Harpham, Geoffrey Galt. 1976. "The Grotesque, First Principles." *The Journal of Aesthetics and Art Criticism*, Vol. 34, No. 4: 461-8.

—. (1982) 2006. *On the Grotesque: Strategies of Contradiction in Art and Literature.* Aurora: The Davies Group Publishers.

Hollington, Michael. 1984. *Dickens and the Grotesque.* Beckenham (Kent): Croom Helm.

—. 2010. "'Petrified Unrest': Dickens and Baudelaire on London and Paris 1855-56." In *Synergies Royaume-Uni et Irlande*, 3: 83-94.

Huart, Louis. 1841. *Physiologie du Flâneur.* Paris: Aubert.

Hugo, Victor. (1827) 2010. "Preface to *Cromwell.*" In *Prefaces and Prologues to Famous Books.* Edited by Charles W. Eliot, 354-408. New-York: Cosimo Classics.

Jennings, Lee Byron. 1963. *The Ludicrous Demon: Aspects of the Grotesque in German Post-Romantic prose.* Berkeley: University of California Press.

Müller, Wolfgang G. and Vila Cabanes, Isabel. 2012. "Dickens's Uncommercial Traveller as a *Flâneur.*" In *Dickens's Signs, Readers' Designs: New Bearings in Dickens Criticism*, edited by Francesca Ortesano and Norbert Lennartz, 227-52. Roma: Aracne.

Nesci, Catherine. 2007. *Le Flâneur et les flâneuses: Les Femmes et la ville à l'époque romantique.* Grenoble: Ellug.

Parsons, Deborah L. 2003. *Streetwalking the Metropolis: Women, the City, and Modernity.* Oxford: Oxford University Press.

Rocadio, D. S. 1990. "The Comic, the Grotesque, and the Uncanny in Charles Dickens." PhD diss. University of East Anglia.

Rollins, Yvonne B. 1976. "Baudelaire et le grotesque." *The French Review*, 50, 2: 270-7.

Sheringham, Michael. 2010. "'The Key to the Street': 'London' in the Construction of 'Paris'." In *Synergies Royaume-Uni et Irlande* 3: 37-44.

Simmel, Georg. 1972. "Sociology of the Senses: Visual Interaction." In *Introduction to the Science of Sociology: Including the Original Index to Basic Sociological Concepts,* edited by Robert E. Park and Ernest W. Burgess, 356-61. Chicago: University of Chicago Press.

Steig, Michael. 1970. "Defining the Grotesque: An Attempt at Synthesis." *The Journal of Aesthetics and Art Criticism* 29, 2: 253-60.

Thomson, Philip. 1979. *The Grotesque.* London: Methuen.

Van Ghent, Dorothy. 1950. "The Dickens World: A View from Todgers's." *The Sewanee Review* 58, 3: 419-38.

Wilson, Elizabeth. 2001. *The Contradictions of Culture: Cities, Culture and Modernity.* London: Sage.

Wing, Nathaniel. 1997. "Baudelaire's *Frisson Fraternel*: Horror and Enchantment in 'Les Tableaux Parisiens.'" *Neophilologus* 81: 21-33.

Wolff, Janet. 1985. "The Invisible *Flâneuse.* Women and the Literature of Modernity." *Theorie, Culture & Society,* 2: 37-46.

Wright, Thomas. 1875. *A History of Caricature and Grotesque in Literature and Art.* London: Chatto & Windus.

CHAPTER NINE

THE CONSTRUCTION OF THE MONSTROUS IN CHARLES DICKENS'S FICTION FROM *THE OLD CURIOSITY SHOP* TO *A TALE OF TWO CITIES*

MAX VÉGA-RITTER

The grotesque is often defined as the combination of exacerbated opposites, bringing together the real and the imaginary, the past and the present, life and death. Often, it simply erases the boundaries between them. In this sense the grotesque naturally engages with the monstrous and masquerade and exhibition become defining marks. The monstrous also interconnects the normal and its opposite, radical transgression. Grotesque transgression of the norm may then take the form of excess, of *hubris*, and may also instil sex or love with criminal compulsion. Excess may come into being as a result of a driving desire but other contradictory forces may act against excess and seek to restrain it in order to counter the death drive[1] that is silently at work in the wings. In the contest between life and the death drive, the latter may be understood as the force that disrupts, distorts and degrades the former, turning the monster into an embodiment of horror and destruction.

As Michel Foucault argues in his *Lectures* (Foucault 2003), during the nineteenth century in the aftermath of the French Revolution, and well before the industrial revolution, the grotesque monster became an emanation of societal forces rising up from below. The monstrous embodied a people freed from bonds beginning to labour under new constraints in factories. To what extent may these grotesque monsters be understood as incarnations of the various forces constituting society? Do they represent repressed energies distilled into criminal impulses or

---

[1] Or death instinct. See Rycroft 1995 or Laplanche and Pontalis 1967.

pathologies? Are they to be understood as forms of human life gone awry? Can they simultaneously be viewed as attempts at creating new, prophetic forms of gendered life, breaking down age-old barriers and taboos? Does the monstrous figure nascent influences, groping their way towards new forms of expression? Do Charles Dickens's grotesque monsters finally retreat to the abyss from which they seem to have originated, for want of a political response to their quest or do they continue their existence in less sombre regions?

An overabundance of energy seems to animate many of Charles Dickens's characters. Heep in *David Copperfield* may be considered simply as a horrible villain or, conversely, as invested with a semblance of comic weight. Daniel Quilp in *The Old Curiosity Shop* is an example of similar ambiguity. "The dwarf" (Dickens 1986-1, 73) is the name Dickens gives him. He is a dwarf physically speaking but his thirst for power is great. Because his social background prevents him from building up his own power base, he revels instead in the terror he inspires, for example when he spends a whole evening smoking cigars and drinking, his gaze pinning his wife down in submission (83). Cruelty consists here in enjoying the spectacle of suffering. Quilp thus feels delight in inflicting harm on women and little girls especially, highlighting an inexorable urge for defiling innocence. In contrast to the biblical Daniel who stands up to the lion, Daniel Quilp is a ridiculous, hateful male tyrant reigning over weak or disarmed women and an abandoned and terrified little girl.

A remarkable aspect of Dickens's genius is that the sadistic and impotent dwarf's hunting-down of the little girl could appear almost comical were it not for her ultimate death. Overwhelming emotion is thus coupled with grotesque effect. It is true that Nell's death is steeped in almost sublime pathos–long-separated brothers engaged in long-running feuds are finally reconciled and a schoolmaster takes lavish and tearful care of a dying boy.

In the small cemetery where little Nell's body has been buried, a drama of conflicting feminine and masculine self-identifications appears to have been played out. Kit seemingly lays aside his own problems in the graveyard. He takes to the road again in search of new horizons, inspired by a burgeoning love for the maid-servant Barbara. This route later leads David Copperfield to Emily whose death is one moment imagined or even wished-for by David in Yarmouth in Chapter 3, or by some strange cruel quirk on the narrator's part, in order to save her from becoming a fallen woman.

The sordid den which is the dwarf's abode reflects the ignominy of his pursuits and of his social background. He is a scrap-dealer whose yard is a cemetery for dirty junk the river seems about to swallow up again. The boy who works for him is himself a kind of "amphibious" creature (73). These are the margins or the lawless depths of society, where no rule applies; in this murky world of crime and dishonesty, of survival by all ways and means, despair prevails. The Quilps come into the world in utter destitution and grow up in despair. Finally, the reader must needs conclude that the monster, having emerged out of the mud of the marsh which begot him, returns to it when he dies. From this perspective, the innocent, pure and ethereal Little Nell personifies the dream of impossible purity and love which however arouses the lust of monsters born of a violent and diseased society.

Quilp is not the only monster from down below, from society's furthest reaches. Sim Tapertit, Hugh and Barnaby, in *Barnaby Rudge*, seem to constitute a three-headed mirror image of Quilp. Hugh is a contradictory combination of towering strength and grovelling fear of authority. Tappertit is surprisingly proud of his legs, which are "curiosities of littleness" (Dickens 1973, 79). Barnaby, the demented backward child, carries a great banner alongside the leader of the mob of insurrectionists, "proud, happy, elated past all telling" (450). The three characters are embodiments of the conflicting forces defeating the power of reason and common sense through the violent uprising of the Dickensian mob. Hugh, an aristocrat's bastard child and a foundling, is born of the vices of a class which look upon themselves as above the dictates of law and order. Tappertit claims to uphold the rights of craftsmen who are the new representatives of the Levellers of old and other Covenanters. Barnaby carries in his very flesh and mind the stigma of his father's murder of his own employer. The unleashing of these illicit animal instincts brings about the violent turmoil which threatens to tear down the very fabric of society.

Yet, very clearly, this turbulence arises from society's own ills and wrongs. It originates in the abuses of aristocracy or in the illusions–or rightful hopes for more equality–of craftsmen and Protestant fanatics, in the violent uprisings of the desperate and destitute rabble as well as in a legitimate hunger for love.

The violent abuse also springs from the unleashing of prodigious energies until then unharnessed and sterile, which, thanks to the combination of opposing forces, seem to surge towards unprecedented peaks of violence. During the storming of Bedlam and Newgate, murderers and lunatics alike are set free. Institutions which are supposed to uphold and enforce law and order in society are overthrown in chaos.

That Dickensian monsters are mainly constituted by antinomic forces necessarily signifies that they are heading towards self-destruction and the tearing down of the mainstays of social life and order. Yet the riots bring to light untapped or wasted human qualities which lie dormant and which are contemptuously ignored. No reader would have imagined Barnaby capable of being one day at the root of a popular uprising, nor Sim Tappertit of playing a leading role in the riot, nor Hugh, a cowardly brute, of fighting. The novel ends with a sense of tremendous waste. Had this energy been harnessed by society, Dickens seems to suggest, it might have been put to use for the good of humankind instead of leaping into flames fanned by anger, contempt and transgression. Very tellingly, Hugo in *Les Misérables* and Dickens seem to agree on this particular point. The *Barnaby Rudge* riots suddenly take on the appearance of a great Carnival which turns social order into chaos and overthrows hierarchies, but to no avowed purpose. The sole aim seems to be the avid quest for riches which inevitably is doomed to failure.

Nevertheless, the rioters appear too helpless to fundamentally threaten established order; they never really kill anyone though they do expose society's deep-seated weaknesses. The Carnival reveals glimpses of what lies behind the masks. The long-pent-up forces, thanks to the momentary lifting of repression, are unleashed; the bringing down of the Inn's May-Pole and symbolical breaking down of Willet's patriarchal rule allow a new generation to rise to power and take over from the fathers.

The Carnival masquerade though continues to haunt the Dickensian scenario. The alliance of hostile opposite forces from below operates time and again. Uriah Heep is a case in hand. The narrator yokes together contradictory images: grasping Uriah's hand feels like holding a fish, he is seen jerking or writhing like an eel, which suggests sharp pain or intense suffering, violent contortions akin to fits of epilepsy. Epilepsy has long been described as a "sacred disease" or "*Haut Mal*" (Clair 2012, 61) sent by the Gods or by the Devil himself, bringing to the surface forces or energies that lie buried deep within the cortex and which are demoniacal, if only because of the tremendous energy they liberate in the human body. Incoercible force, energy and ambition are thus infused into Heep's body and soul. They disrupt his gestures and turn him into a man-animal hybrid. He is driven by a craving for power and wealth–and desires to possess the woman who represents them all. This lust wells up from the depths of his body, almost dislocating his limbs.

Heep is a monster from below, born of the putative rabble, embodying its anger and lust. His fellow prisoners know that he is one of them and they admire and love him intensely. They look up to him in veneration and identify with him. The gaolers look on him as a model prisoner for his humble, repentant attitude whereas his companions admire him for his pride which raises him far above the common mortals. He is imbued with a passion to dominate even when he faces utter defeat. He does not recognise his failure but views the world with contempt and condescension from the very depths to which his downfall has reduced him. Creakle, too, the former sadistic headmaster now become a Middlesex magistrate, expresses his deep admiration for Heep. Heep cannot help drawing attention to himself for he is a born actor playing all the roles in a single pantomime. He is at once a model prisoner and a hardened criminal. However, the true confrontation between the people from below and those from the upper reaches of society is carefully elided or repressed, buried out of sight, never even mentioned as a possibility.

Before *David Copperfield*, the premises of the monster from above had been explored with depth and clarity in *Dombey and Son*. The head of the firm "Dombey and Son" has settled on his own son as the means of making his dream of power come true. Little Paul is destined to be the reflection-extension of his father's power and the instrument of his will. Dombey's craving for power, wealth and mastery are all worked into the same delusional monomania. Little Paul though will fail and in dying, he will tear his father's dream to shreds. For the child resists his father's annexing, appropriating and phallicising through dreaming, or by overtly expressing his need for tenderness and passivity which are symbolically evoked by his illness. Simultaneously the father ignores, despises and persecutes his daughter Florence, first because she is a woman, secondly because he is jealous of the affection that unites brother and sister and escapes his control. With his wife Edith, the conflict between desire for domination and power and the desire to love come to a climax. Edith refuses to be the symbol and the expression of Dombey's power. She wants to be respected and loved. Even before he is ruined she crosses swords with him and flees from home destroying his hopes and trampling on his pride. Dombey dies murmuring his daughter's name, as if she had been the truest and most enigmatic part of himself, the part he treasured but also hated the most.

Thus, Dombey oscillates from hyper-masculinity to the most feminine of attitudes out of a mad craving for domination and possession that is defeated by a silent passion for its opposite–femininity and tender love (see Véga-Ritter 1985). Though no longer obscene, femaleness remains for Dombey an object of irrepressible repulsion and obsessive attraction. Repressed and detested femininity constitute the most deeply buried and most violently active aspect of Charles Dickens's grotesque monsters.

Indeed, the great Dombey not only collapses under the weight of *hubris* and self-contradictions, but he also submits to other characters. The world of *Dombey and Son* is not reduced to a circle of friends. It is also open to public spaces. It is populated by numerous men and women, young and old, whose crowd–or their mob–enter the novelistic scene as they do in Balzac's *La Comédie humaine*. Thus, former lovers, friends or relatives of the main characters, malicious, infirm, simple-minded or damaged people, shady schemers who live by their wits, street-urchins–in short, modern democratic urban reality, the *demos*, makes its appearance in the novel. Dombey the monster from above is bound, like Gulliver among Lilliputians, to many beings who all contribute to his ultimate paralysis and downfall, like horrible Mrs Brown, Rob the grinder, gentle, half-witted Toots, and a host of others.

In *Bleak House* the monster becomes rather more institutional. Not only does the Court of Chancery refuse to examine the cases that come before it, but it exacerbates them and leads to ruin those who rely on the judiciary. Suicide, madness (Miss Flite), despair, moral degradation and death (Richard Carstone) remain the only alternatives. There is at the very heart of this particular pillar of society, an inability to decide:

> Equity sends questions to Law, Law sends questions back to Equity; Law finds it can't do this, Equity finds it can't do that; neither can so much as say it can't do anything, without this solicitor instructing and this counsel appearing for A, and that solicitor instructing and that counsel appearing for B; and so on through the whole alphabet, like the history of the Apple Pie. (Dickens 1983, 146)

Perpetual oscillation between equity and statutory law reflects a conflict between different courts, the rights of individual litigants and the Court as authority or, more broadly speaking, between individual and collective wills. This inability to settle matters is catching and communicates itself to litigants, destroying their ability to assert themselves, enslaving them further to the institution and to the illusion of justice. Richard Carstone becomes a "self-destructive obsessional neurotic" (Caudill 1997, 121) who is subject to chronic indecision. Such indecision nevertheless serves one great cause: "The one great principle of the English law is, to make business for itself" (Dickens 1983, 603). The law ensures its own financial interest and works towards exercising and consolidating control over society.

This monster from above, unlike the one from below, comes up against no material opposition. Its *hubris* originates in the deployment of its internal contradictions which knows no inner or outer boundary. If the mechanism of the monstrous from below leads to self-destruction, that of the mighty monstrous, while lurking under a vestment of ostentatious respectability, rewards its supporters handsomely from the energies of those who get caught up in its web of fascination.

That "monster," as Miss Flite calls it (557), develops its network of power throughout society by means of a variety of agents or servants, the "lawyers." The Court of Chancery is primarily a male institution, managed exclusively by men and headed by the mightiest of them all, the Lord Chancellor. There are those who, like Tulkinghorn, are outright misogynists who see women as "too many" and "at the bottom of all that goes wrong in [the world]" (276). These men feel called upon to track the shady sides of human life, those that "provide power," for their "calling is the acquisition of secrets and the holding possession of power such as they give [them], with no sharer or opponent in it" (567). Others are sadistic servants of established order, affecting airs of bland joviality like Inspector Bucket who causes the death of the unfortunate Gridley but wishes he could have him resurrected in order to continue persecuting him. He tracks down Lady Dedlock but he is accompanied by her daughter in order to disarm any potential hostility. He makes a show of hypocritical cordiality towards George the Trooper when arresting him. Others like Vholes affect to serve the interests of their clients when their main concern lies in the consolidation of their own social respectability. They are predators hypnotising their victims. Vholes has "a lifeless manner and a slow, fixed way [,..] of looking at Richard [...] as if he were looking at his prey and charming it" (591). There is also a host of paranoid ambitious subordinates who, like Guppy, think that plots are being hatched against them everywhere. With their parasites or satellites like Jobling and Smallweed, they are all cogs in the one and same judicial machine. Between them they have society in their grasp, pushing and pulling levers, turning wheels and precipitating their prey into abyssal ruin.

The law and its representatives are all stamped with greed for power and a penchant for cruelty, corruption and hypocrisy. The district of Tom-All-Alone's is an illustration of the effect of the destructive cynicism of those supposedly upholding the Rule of Law. The powerful monster from above has no acknowledged adversary. Its *hubris* comes partly from the fact that its internal contradictions know no outer or inner boundary.

It has been argued (Manheim 1955, 21-43) that Charles Dickens was particularly concerned with the Father as an authority figure due to his own childhood experience. As Pam Morris shows (Morris 1991),[2] beyond the biographical father depicted by Charles Dickens there lies the law as a source of legitimacy fundamental to property, power and human rights. What Dickens is sharply and obsessively critical of is the essential arbitrariness of Justice and Law as self-perpetuating institutions. Dickens uncovers the mechanisms by which people bow down to the machinery of Law, falling under its fascination and thus confirming its rational delirium. However, most of the lawyers and their victims, from Pickwick to Jasper in *Edwin Drood*, display a sense of sexual insecurity or even uncertainty which is not merely a mockery of patriarchal power and its propensity to tyranny. In *Bleak House*, Jarndyce, Esther's generous protector, eventually withdraws from competing with his younger–and lesser-known to the reader–rival, Allan Woodcourt, after proposing to Esther. He remains unmarried, like Pickwick and a host of other characters in Charles Dickens's fiction.

In *Hard Times*, Charles Dickens creates a social and cultural monster. The schoolmaster stands for fact-worship as the only rule by which men should live. Nevertheless, facts are implicitly shown to be constructed as the example of the definition of the horse in Chapter 2 makes amply clear, it is an abstract concept. Facts are rational constructs. In fact, they bear the mark of patriarchal, capitalist as well as industrial domination. In the name of this principle Louisa's father refuses to answer his daughter's question "do you ask me to love Mr Bounderby?" He responds with a factual "Does Mr Bounderby ask [you] to marry him? Yes he does" (Dickens 1986-2, 133-4). The prospective husband is a rich and influential mill-owner. The word "love" is non-factual and thus irrelevant to the reference system within which Gradgrind has brought up his daughter. Hard facts are to be substituted for emotions and feelings as the foundation of marriage. Louisa is asked to contract a loveless marriage and this fact goes unnoticed by her father. The father-*cum*-schoolmaster sells his daughter to a rich elderly man in exchange for influence. He turns out to be the very ogre the third chapter mentions (54). The technocratic-utilitarian logic of the schoolmaster in alliance with patriarchal capitalist entrepreneurship thus constitutes the backbone of the monster from above.

In *Great Expectations,* published two years after *A Tale of Two Cities,* Magwitch and Orlick, like Quilp and Uriah, belong with the monsters

---

[2] See also Hirsch 1975.

from below. In contrast, Miss Havisham is a female monster from a world of wealth and power that captures Pip's heart and kindles envy and desire. Her social position enables her to play with Pip's expectations. Still more significantly, her position and affluence allow her to indulge her darkest fantasies and to avenge a man's insult to her wounded pride, in defiance of all established conventions. At one of the many levels of a symbolically rich text, Miss Havisham's wedding cake which has been left to rot, can be viewed as a metaphor for her wedding-day, and–perhaps–her wedding night, too, showing her angry frustration at the aborted love-making. The crawling insects around the mouldy cake: spiders with blotchy bodies, black beetles and mice, may be understood as a grotesque representation of patriarchal sexual power.

In *A Tale of Two Cities* the monsters from above and from down below join together, ferociously grappling with one another. In England, the Court of Justice and the Old Bailey and Newgate, the mainstays of established order, send daily cartloads full of men and women to their deaths or to the pillory. Quartering is "barbarous!" but

> "It is the law," remarked the ancient clerk. […] "Speak well of the law […] and leave the law to take care of itself. I give you that advice." (Dickens 1995, 62)

The aristocracy displays outrageous arrogance, multiplying extortion, abuse, unlawful gratification of their lust, and other atrocities. The Marquis de St. Evrémonde and his brother rape and murder a woman and kill her husband and her brother. The carving of the Gorgon's head on the wall of the castle, along with other figures of lions' mouths or wild animals, are arrogantly defiant representations of the ruthless rule of the upper class, of its violence and brutality. In different but ultimately identical forms, Newgate and the Bastille are places of extreme sadistic impulses under the guise of Law.

Nevertheless, the Gorgon's face is also the image of the people's hunger for revenge. Outbursts of furious enjoyment and mad frenzy at the centre have their symmetrical counterparts on the fringes of society. A funeral in London is an occasion for a kind of bloodthirsty carnival, triggering off bursts of rage against a hidden enemy or an alleged traitor. The infuriated mob turn against innocent bystanders, accusing them of being spies, these are then captured and physically ill-treated, amidst raucous, drunken celebration and obscene singing and dancing. The people give themselves up to grotesque Bacchanalian orgies.

On the other side of the Channel, similar scenes occur a little later. Women and men indulge in mass drunkenness, collapsing in pools of wine in the name of the Revolution. The violent expression of rage takes on a festive appearance while the revolutionaries gleefully slaughter their victims. The monsters from down below have seized power and the upper classes have now fled. Monsters have become indistinguishable.

Wild celebrations then break loose as hundreds of men and women dance to frenzied rhythms, sometimes together, sometimes apart, as though demented, and collapsing from exhaustion. These frantic and almost demoniacal dances are more brawls than happy romps. Grace and beauty, "warped and perverted" (289) make these trances the most unique and extraordinary of festivities. The decapitated head of the monster *par excellence*, the King's, is held up in display to the monsters from below.

With these events Charles Dickens considers the "law of contradiction" (283) that then reigned supreme. In Paris the Revolutionary Tribunal has as its paradoxical principle to be a tribunal applying lawless law. Prison, once the reviled symbol of tyranny and oppression, has become the ultimate institution, overcrowded with innocent people who are delivered into the hands of real culprits. Arbitrariness and cruelty are the characteristics of the new, established order which claims to eradicate the bloody abuse and despotism of the *Ancien Régime*. The guillotine is now a substitute for the crucifix. It is worn around the neck, instead of the crucifix (284). People bow down before it in veneration. It has replaced the original object of worship in a sort of farcical travesty of the revolutionary ideal, as a reproduction or caricature of the old religious order reeking of the Inquisition. A kind of general confusion comes into being.

The new monstrous and baroque authorities are described as advocating a wild pursuit of excess in a large, absurd and grotesque public parade. In response, the figure of the monster which combines opposites in the same confusion, gives rise to collective psychosis. There has now appeared the dreaded figure of the enemy, the traitor, the spy. Barsad is even a double agent.

Amidst this general confusion, the distinction between friend and foe has taken on dramatic significance, since that notion–in proportion as its meaning has grown intrinsically ambivalent and elusive–is nevertheless widely felt to be essential to the dispelling of all delirious fears and to the rational structuring of the world. Characteristically, it falls to Darnay to be the embodiment of ambivalent identity. Though an aristocrat, he rejects his social roots. A proponent of revolutionary ideas, he disapproves of the rabble's conduct. Though not English he has become an English bourgeois. Yet Darnay narrowly escapes being sentenced to death by the Court. He is arrested a second time in France, again accused of being a traitor, a falsely renegade aristocrat and a spy. He is saved by the sacrifice of an Englishman. Carton is his alter ego, the defector from the English side who becomes an ally. The rival in love has turned into a friend and is transformed into a sacrificial figure. Ironically, the revolutionaries execute a true Englishman and enemy in place of a Frenchman.

In the later Dickensian grotesque, the figure of the defector who does not betray but saves is a leitmotif. He can take on the identity of a mediator, a go-between, an honest broker, like Dr Manette, Charles Darnay or Sydney Carton in *A Tale of Two Cities* and Stephen Blackpool in *Hard Times,* or of a man of shifting identities, like John Harmon or the "Golden Dustman" in *Our Mutual Friend.* These men shuttle back and forth from one side to the other in order to transcend oppositions; they disarm hostility and dissipate lies and deceptions, errors, confusions and misconceptions. This versatility is the hidden core of the combination of opposites in the Dickensian grotesque which can culminate in the sublime or in depths of horror. Sublimity is attained only if the political dimension of events is entirely elided, of which *A Tale of Two Cities* is amply illustrative. Sydney Carton the Jackal unswervingly serves Stryver the Lion, his master, to whom he is strongly attached. Carton leaves the world to muddle through its mire of dreadful human and social conflicts. There is no political hope in Carton's death, nor does it constitute a political statement as to how the Quilps, Dombeys, Tulkinghorns, Vholeses, Saint-Evrémondes and Defarges of this world are to be eliminated.

Dickens's grotesque is frequently ambiguous and ambivalent. It is characterised by contradictory traits. The monsters carried along by the dynamics of conflicting emotions would be running headlong into the abyss of despair, were it not for Charles Dickens's sense of humour, in other words for his love of life and his passion for mankind.

References

Clair, Jean. 2012. *Hubris. La Fabrique du monstre dans l'art moderne.* Paris: Gallimard.

Caudill, David S. 1997. *Lacan and the Subject of Law. Toward a Psychoanalytical Critical Legal Theory.* New-York: Humanity Press International Inc.

Dickens, Charles. (1841) 1986. *The Old Curiosity Shop.* Harmondsworth: Penguin. [1986-1].

—. (1847) 1973. *Barnaby Rudge*. Harmondsworth: Penguin.

—. (1848) 2002. *Dombey and Son*. Harmondsworth: Penguin.

—. (1853) 1983. *Bleak House*. Harmondsworth: Penguin.

—. (1854) 1986. *Hard Times*. Harmondsworth: Penguin. [1986-2].

—. (1859) 1995. *A Tale of Two Cities*. Harmondsworth: Penguin.

Foucault, Michel. 2003. *Abnormal. Lectures at the Collège de France*. Translated by Graham Burchell with an introduction by Arnold Davidson. London & NewYork: Verso.

Hirsch, Gordon. 1975. "The Mysteries of *Bleak House*. A Psychoanalytic Study." *Dickens Studies Annual* Vol. 4: 132-52. Edited by Robert Partlow. Carbondale & Edwardsville: Southern Illinois University Press.

Laplanche, J.L and Pontalis, J.B. 1967. *Vocabulaire de la psychanalyse*. Paris: Presses Universitaires de France.

Manheim, Leonard. 1955. "The Law as 'Father.' An Aspect of the Dickens Pattern." *American Imago* 12: 21-43.

Morris, Pam. 1991. *Dickens's Class Consciousness: A Marginal View*. London: Macmillan.

Rycroft, Charles. (1968) 1995. *A Critical Dictionary of Psychoanalysis*. London: Penguin Books.

Véga-Ritter, Max. 1985. *Dickens et Thackeray, essai d'analyse psychocritique : des* Pickwick Papers *à* David Copperfield *et de* Barry Lindon *à* Henry Esmond. PhD diss. Université de Montpellier III.

CHAPTER TEN

AN "UNCANNY REVEL":[1]
THE POETICS AND POLITICS
OF THE GROTESQUE IN THOMAS HARDY'S
THE MAYOR OF CASTERBRIDGE

THIERRY GOATER

In Great Britain towards the end of the 19th century there was a growing feeling of anxiety, a loss of faith in the capacities of a changing society to offer man opportunities for fulfilment. Simultaneously in the novel an old debate between realism and idealism was revived: on the one hand, romance was perceived by authors such as Stevenson as a way to escape from the prevailing pessimism; on the other, under the influence of Zola and naturalism, realism took on an aggressive dimension (see Gilmour 1986, 180). Thomas Hardy did not believe mimetic or "scientific" realism could propose satisfactory answers. "Nothing but the illusion of truth can permanently please," he writes in "The Science of Fiction," "and when the old illusions begin to be penetrated, a more natural magic has to be supplied" (in Orel 1990, 135). Hardy's fiction stands half-way between romance ("magic") and realism ("illusion of truth"), as it were. The grotesque belongs to that romantic or magic vein which Hardy, like Dickens, uses to depict or rather reveal a chaotic and dissonant world. The grotesque had been forgotten since the Renaissance and was again brought into fashion by the Romantics (Rosen 1991, 43-5) owing to economic, social and intellectual upheavals questioning man's place in society and in the universe. However, the common use of the word "grotesque" is so loose and inaccurate that it is extremely difficult to define it in a satisfying way (see Rosen 1991, 5). To make things even more complicated, two major theories compete concerning the grotesque,

---

[1] Hardy 1985-1, 353.

Mikhail Bakhtin's, based on the carnival and its festive, joyful laughter, and Wolfgang Kayser's, focusing on the fantastic and the absurd.[2] The two approaches seem to be opposed and even contradictory. But, by essence, the grotesque precisely resides in a discrepancy between its components, hence a form of elusiveness.[3] While *The Mayor of Casterbridge* (1886) is considered as the archetype of the tragic English novel–as Hardy's great tragic novel at least–quite a few critics have underlined its grotesque features. In 1898 the novelist himself wrote: "All tragedy is grotesque–if you allow yourself to see it as such" (Hardy 1994-2, 72). This paper aims to show the poetics and politics of the grotesque in *The Mayor of Casterbridge* through the social comedy it presents, its writing technique based on disproportion and heterogeneity, and the mode of reception of the text, which is a key issue for Hardy as well as for the grotesque in general.

From Vanity Fair to Ruthless Carnival

A sense of the grotesque seems to have permeated 19th-century society, which is marked by perpetual change, threatened by chaos, and in which the impossible can come true and logic has gone mad.[4] Indeed, individual aspirations can easily jeopardize the community and its rules. In *The Mayor of Casterbridge* Hardy stages a discordant world resulting from exacerbated narcissistic desires. The novel's opening is emblematic in this respect. Henchard expresses his immoderate ambition from the outset: "'I'd challenge England to beat me in the fodder business; and if I were a free man again I'd be worth a thousand pound before I'done o't'" (Hardy 1985-1, 74). Such *hubris*, added to inebriation, drives the hero to sell his wife Susan and his daughter Elizabeth Jane during an improvised auction, thereby breaking fundamental social rules. Hardy presents a world where temptations are not to be resisted, an alienated world where man's soul is worth little in comparison with his social success. The writer revisits at

---

[2] See Bakhtin 1984 and Kayser 1982.

[3] For Rémi Astruc, those features are essential in the grotesque (see Astruc 2010, 37). Astruc's work mainly deals with 20th-century grotesque literature. However, it makes a valuable reappraisal of the phenomenon and offers relevant analyses for 19th-century literature.

[4] Those features are important in the grotesque according to Astruc (Astruc 2010, 53). Even though his remarks on the 19th century are based on the fall of the *Ancien Régime* in France, they can apply to a large extent to the social upheavals taking place in Great Britain.

one and the same time Bunyan's Vanity Fair and Thackeray's *Vanity Fair* (see Moore 1990, 82).

Discordance also derives from social transformations deemed abrupt or supernatural by the observer of the time who was used to a stable world. Henchard, the poor hay-trusser, becomes a rich corn merchant and the Mayor of Casterbridge. His success may not be quick but it seems that way to Susan and Elizabeth Jane when they come back to Casterbridge. To the reader, it seems rapid too because the narrator adopts the two women's point of view and uses an ellipsis ("Time, the great magician, had wrought much here," Hardy 1985-1, 101). As for Lucetta's social transformation, it is truly fast: the poor woman from Jersey turns into a rich woman after inheriting from her aunt in Bath. Farfrae's success occurs quite rapidly as well: after working for Henchard, he takes over from him as firm-owner and mayor. Social success is often obtrusive and loud, as is evidenced by the garish colours of the young Scot's new sowing machine ("The machine was painted in bright hues of green yellow, and red" 238), by the gaudy colours of Lucetta's dresses or by Henchard's clothes when he is powerful. And Lucetta's and Henchard's fall is as brutal as their success. Even before the episode of the skimmity-ride, the hero has gone bankrupt due to bad weather conditions and his own errors. He is replaced by Farfrae, and his past is exposed by Mrs Goodenough, the very woman who sold him furmity and alcohol at the fair of Weydon-Priors. The novel's very title, which can apply to both Henchard and Farfrae, suggests the instability of social status.

One gets the impression that social positions are roles played by the characters. Penelope Vigar is one of the first critics who pointed out the importance of theatricality in *The Mayor of Casterbridge* while evoking its grotesque features (see Vigar 1974). The grotesque universe, which proves to be a world of masks and pretence, has much in common with the world of the theatre (see Rosen 1991, 116 and Astruc 2010, 129). Casterbridge resembles a theatre where the worthies put on performances. The marketplace is presented as "the regulation Open Place in spectacular dramas" (Hardy 1985-1, 237). There Farfrae displays his intelligence and modernity through his new agricultural machine: "it had been placed there for exhibition" (238). As for Henchard and Lucetta, they interpret roles corresponding to their positive self-images. The banquet at the King's Arms is like a show put on for the population, as is suggested by an old man outside the hotel: "As we plainer fellows bain't invited, they leave the winder-shutters open that we may get jist a sense o't out here" (99).

This episode, in which Henchard is taking part in a public dinner at the King's Arms eighteen years after the sale of his wife and daughter, shows the hero's spectacular existence:

> Facing the window, in the chair of dignity, sat a man about forty years of age; of heavy frame, large features, and commanding voice; his general build being rather coarse than compact. He had a rich complexion, which verged on swarthiness, a flashing black eye, and dark, bushy brows and hair. When he indulged in an occasional loud laugh at some remark among the guests, his large mouth parted so far back as to show to the rays of the chandelier a full score or more of the two-and-thirty sound teeth that he obviously still could boast of. [...]
>   [He] sat before them, matured in shape, stiffened in line, exaggerated in traits, disciplined, thought-marked–in a word, older. [...] He was dressed in an old-fashioned evening suit, an expanse of frilled shirt showing on his broad breast; jewelled studs, and a heavy gold chain. (100-1)

As Mayor of Casterbridge, Henchard presides over the dinner and attracts all gazes, those of the guests as well as those of the people outside. He represents his fellow-citizens who elected him and plays at being Mayor. He only exists in representation, as Sartre would say (see Sartre 1981, 96). He plays the part corresponding to the "chair of dignity" in which he is seated. His clothes and accessories are in keeping with his office and social position but jar with his rough personality and physical appearance ("coarse," "rich complexion," "swarthiness," "bushy," "loud laugh"). He wears a "costume" corresponding to the word "custom" (etymologically speaking) and thus to his social status, but his garment is also the actor's costume. The passive form "he was dressed" instead of "he wore" may suggest a form of reification, of imprisonment in his role, which is confirmed by his attitude: "stiffened in line, exaggerated in traits, disciplined, thought-marked." The past participles, their semantic value and their sounds underscore rigidity. The character looks corseted in his clothes. Such rigidity is similar to that of the café waiter in Sartre's famous analysis (Sartre 1981, 96). Henchard plays the Mayor's role and his performance forces him to excessively discipline his personality. He constantly has to keep a check on himself, as is conveyed by phrases like "thought-marked" or "when he indulged in an occasional loud laugh." Indeed for a brief moment he reveals a part of his intimate self, in spite of his wish to conceal his past and secret identity. The terms "exaggerated" and "stiffened" perfectly correspond to the situation: Henchard is not only older; he is the somewhat grotesque caricature of a mayor; he has almost turned into a stiff and hollow puppet.

The same facticity is to be found in Lucetta, his former mistress. She is a theatrical, "protean" (Hardy 1985-1, 246) character who takes poses, plays one role and then another. Lucetta–or rather Lucette–Le Sueur would have people forget her modest Jersey origins and her past relationship with Henchard. She wants to acquire a new social status when she becomes Mrs Templeman's heir. She decides to take her name "as a means of escape from [hers], and its wrongs" (220). Her house in Casterbridge constitutes another mask: "The house was entirely of stone, and formed an example of dignity without great size" (210). Like her past lover, she buys herself a new "dignity." Marrying Farfrae, a promising young man with a spotless reputation, serves the same purpose.

The Mayor of Casterbridge prefigures the end of ontology, which is characteristic of 20th-century grotesque. Society takes the form of a theatre, in which appearance prevails over essence.[5] This is emphasized by Henchard himself: "'But it is not by what is, in this life, but by what appears, that you are judged'" (248). The novel presents a universe of multiple and shifting identities. Despite his efforts, Henchard's more intimate character shows through his costume. The discrepancy between being and appearance verges on the grotesque. Lucetta herself senses the split of the subject in such a world: "'But settling upon new clothes is so trying,' said Lucetta. 'You are that person' (pointing to one of the arrangements) 'or you are that totally different person' (pointing to the other)" (238). Her double identity is metonymically represented by her house, with its front full of dignity and its back connected with "the mansion's past history–intrigue" (212).

Hardy offers a bitter vision of existence associated with a masquerade or a puppet show, as in Kayser's grotesque universe (see Kayser 1982, 186). It is Henchard and Lucetta's dissembling and make-belief that the population of Mixen-Lane, the deprived and disreputable neighbouring village of Casterbridge, aims to expose. So as to punish Henchard, who chose Farfrae over him for the position of manager, Jopp discloses the content of the letters Lucetta wrote to Henchard at Peter's Finger inn. Jopp also longs to humiliate Lucetta whom he calls "the proud piece of silk and wax-work" (332). Nance Mockridge suggests organizing a skimmity-ride. Her idea materializes during the festivities for the visit of the Royal Personage in Casterbridge, during which Lucetta struts about on Farfrae's arm. Like Jopp, she craves to denounce her pretence:

---

[5] "The grotesque destroys being as essence" (Astruc 2010, 261, my translation).

"I do like to see the trimming pulled off such Christmas candles. I am quite unequal to the part of villain myself, or I'd gi'e all my silver to see that lady toppered–And perhaps I shall soon," she added significantly. (341)

The people of Mixen-Lane are about to take malicious pleasure in toppling Lucetta and Henchard, in removing their masks of dignity. The customers of Peter's Finger organize in the streets of Casterbridge a kind of grotesque carnival representing the former lovers under the form of effigies sitting in an improper position on a donkey. The skimmity-ride does present some of the festive and subversive features of Bakhtin's carnival, but cruelty seems to outweigh good humour, especially in Jopp's intentions: "To him, at least, it was not a joke, but a retaliation" (342). The consequences are dramatic, especially for Lucetta who watches the scene through the window of her house: "''Tis me!' she said, with a face pale as death. 'A procession–a scandal–an effigy of me, and him!' [...] 'She's me–she's me–even to the parasol–my green parasol!' cried Lucetta with a wild laugh as she stepped in. She stood motionless for one second–then fell heavily on the floor" (352-3). Before long she dies, following this emotional shock that leads to her miscarriage. No matter what Elizabeth Jane says, Lucetta cannot take her eyes off the ruthless spectacle which is aimed at her and which exposes her hidden identity and her repressed past. The grotesque episode highlights the conflict between a present and public identity and a past and secret one represented by the effigy. The shift from the neutral pronoun ("''Tis me!'") to the feminine pronoun ("'She's me'") is essential: the puppet is personified while Lucetta is reified; they are one now.

In Bakhtin's carnival, symbolic death results in rebirth, and humiliation leads to regeneration. In Hardy's novel, however, this is only partly true. The outcome of the skimmity-ride is Lucetta's real death and Henchard's hurried downfall. The novel ends in some new order with the marriage of Farfrae and Elizabeth, the two most balanced characters, those who best master their emotions and desires. As for Henchard and Lucetta, they serve as scapegoats or *pharmakoi* whose elimination should purify society (see Girard 1990). But such purification is probably superficial or temporary. Indeed, the society of Casterbridge offers the image of ubiquitous cruelty. The ruthless carnival towards the end of the novel and Henchard's atrocious deed in the first chapter are but two examples of it in a long and troubled history. The description of the back of Lucetta's house, in which theatre and cruelty are associated, foreshadows the skimmity-ride, the "rough jest" (Hardy 1985-1, 354) which violently puts an end to the social comedy performed by Henchard and Lucetta: "By the alley it had been possible to come unseen from all sorts of quarters in the town–the old play-house, the old bull-stake, the old cock-pit, the pool wherein nameless infants had been used to disappear" (212). Other places are associated with cruel practices. One is called Bull Stake: "A stone post rose in the midst, to which the oxen had formerly been tied for baiting with dogs to make them tender before they were killed in the adjoining shambles" (264). The novel's very last words intimate such cruelty is not likely to end with Farfrae and Elizabeth Jane's union: "[H]appiness was but the occasional episode in a general drama of pain" (411).

The Art of Distortion and Incongruity

For Hardy, only a personal vision, which he calls "the artist's idiosyncratic mode of regard" (Hardy 1994-1, 241), can give an appropriate account of a disturbing reality akin to the grotesque. Hardy's art is very different from mimetic realism and in August 1890 he wrote:

Art is disproportioning–(i.e. distorting, throwing out of proportion)–of realities, to show more clearly the features that matter in those realities, which, if merely copied or reported inventorially, might possibly be observed, but would more probably be overlooked. Hence "realism" is not Art. (299)

In those words, Michael Wheeler rightly reads "a personal manifesto for the grotesque" (Wheeler 1989, 180). The novelist's writing is indeed based on distortion and unusual combinations, which are distinctive patterns of the grotesque. Hardy's text "carnivalizes" itself,[6] i.e. turns into grotesque carnival. In *The Mayor of Casterbridge* disproportion is first to be found in the handling of plot and time. There is something grotesquely exaggerated in the misfortunes endured by Henchard and in the repeated unhappy coincidences of the story (Susan's choosing the very tent which will result in her unhappiness at Weydon-Priors; the concomitant returns of Susan and Elizabeth Jane on the one hand and Lucetta on the other, etc.). Hardy must have borrowed this vein from the Gothic and sensational novel. Distortion also concerns settings, for instance the remains of the Roman Amphitheatre or the *Schwarzwasser* where the hero walks after reading Susan's letter informing him that Elizabeth Jane is not his daughter:

---

[6] See Bakhtin 1998, 180. Bakhtin uses the term "carnivalization" to evoke the transposition of carnival into literature through generic and modal heterogeneity, polyphony, dissonances, etc.

Here were ruins of a Franciscan priory, and a mill attached to the same, the water of which roared down a back-hatch like the voice of desolation. Above the cliff, and behind the river, rose a pile of buildings, and in the front of the pile a square mass cut into the sky. It was like a pedestal lacking its statue. This missing feature, without which the design remained incomplete, was, in truth, the corpse of a man; for the square mass formed the base of the gallows, the extensive buildings at the back being the county gaol. [...]
The *exaggeration* which darkness imparted to the glooms of this region impressed Henchard more than he had expected. (Hardy 1985-1, 197-8, my emphasis)

The ruins of the priory and the gaol, the allusion to the gallows and the hanged man, the sounds of the river and the pervasive darkness create a gloomy, gruesome atmosphere reflecting the character's despair but also his crime and, more generally speaking, the brutal violence of Casterbridge. Hardy resorts to vivid and hyperbolic imagery. Likewise, to express the vice prevailing in Mixen-Lane, the novelist makes use of "exaggeration," depicting the haunt of the destitute and of the rabble "like a spit into the moist and misty lowland" or transforming it into a "mildewed leaf in the sturdy and flourishing Casterbridge plant" (328). Simile and metaphor are privileged tools of grotesque distortion in Hardy's writing.

Character drawing is concerned by distortion too. Like Dickens, Hardy makes a striking use of characters' names, which become grotesque through their harsh irony (Mrs Goodenough) or their crude violence (Nance Mockeridge). Moreover, some characters are extremely disquieting creatures:

Men were putting their heads together in twos and threes, telling good stories, with pantomimic laughter which reached *convulsive grimace.* Some were beginning to look as if they did not know how they had come there, what they had come for, or how they were going to get home again; and provisionally sat on with a *dazed smile.* Square-built men showed *a tendency to become hunchbacks*; men with a dignified presence lost it in *a curious obliquity of figure*, in which *their features grew disarranged and one-sided*; whilst *the heads of a few* who had dined with extreme thoroughness *were somehow sinking into their shoulders, the corners of their mouth and eyes being bent upwards by the subsidence.* (107, my emphasis)

Through the consumption of alcohol and food the guests of the dinner at the King's Arms turn into grotesque, twisted figures. Their metamorphosis started earlier on: "The younger guests were talking and eating with animation; their elders were searching for titbits, and sniffing and grunting over their plates like sows nuzzling for acorns" (101-2). The latter men are depicted as disgusting animals. The world of objects is also affected by such transformations. Farfrae's sowing machine, which will revolutionize agriculture, is weird: "[I]t resembled as a whole a compound of hornet, grasshopper, and shrimp, magnified enormously. Or it might have been likened to an upright musical instrument with the front gone" (238).

To some extent, Hardy's descriptions are reminiscent of some paintings by Hieronymus Bosch (1450-1516) or Pieter Brueghel (1525-1569).[7] The writer represents a world which has become monstrous, in which humans can turn into misshapen creatures, animals or objects. He creates a grotesque universe characterized by unlikely, supernatural metamorphoses and combinations (see Astruc 2010, 39).

Incongruity, which has been one of the basic features of the grotesque since it emerged as a motif,[8] is fundamental to a proper understanding of carnivalesque writing and of Hardy's aesthetics.[9] It is to be found in the treatment of characters and objects but also at the level of modes and genres. Hardy swiftly moves from realism to Gothic melodrama, from realistic presentation to surreal vision, often intermingling them. In itself the distortion of bodies and objects is a source of strangeness. In certain scenes, such strangeness turns into hallucinatory or phantasmagorical vision. It is true of the sale of Susan and her daughter at the fair of Weydon-Priors, of the *Schwarzwasser* scene, or of the skimmity-ride: "Lucetta's eyes were straight upon the spectacle of the uncanny revel, now advancing rapidly. The numerous lights around the two effigies threw them up into lurid distinctness" (Hardy 1985-1, 353). The adjective "lurid"–also used in the Weydon-Priors episode (78)–and the adjective "uncanny" convey the strangeness pervading a scene reminiscent of the paintings by James Ensor (1860-1949) teeming with carnival figures and grotesque masks. The theme of the double is also favourable to effects of estrangement. A short while after Lucetta's schizoid experience during the skimmity-ride, Henchard thinks he can see his double in the whirl of Ten Hatches Hole where he intends to kill himself. In fact it is his effigy thrown away in the stream by the organizers of the cruel farce. In Hardy's writing, as in Dickens's, the grotesque is close to the dark fantasy evoked by Kayser.

---

[7] Bosch's *Garden of Earthly Delights* or *Temptation of St. Anthony* and Brueghel's *Peasant Wedding* or *Fight between Carnival and Lent*.

[8] See the introduction to the present volume.

[9] Morton Dauwen Zabel was the first to point out this central aspect in Hardy's writing. See Zabel 1986.

Moreover, in *The Mayor of Casterbridge*, there is a constant and typically grotesque combination of the high and the low, the beautiful and the ugly, the tragic and the comic. Hardy refuses artificial classifications or generic hierarchies. Thus he juxtaposes and intermingles tragedy and farce, because in his view they are inseparable: "If you look beneath the surface of any farce you see a tragedy; on the contrary, if you blind yourself to the deeper issues of a tragedy you see a farce" (Hardy 1994-1, 282). The sale of Susan and her daughter, Henchard's humiliation by Mrs Goodenough and then by Farfrae during the festivities for the visit of the Royal Personage and the skimmity-ride are treated as farcical tragedies. John Paterson has aptly analysed the novel as a tragedy, drawing interesting parallels with Sophocles or Shakespeare (see Paterson 1959), but he probably underestimates its grotesque dimension.

Like Dickens's, Hardy's grotesque owes much to the Elizabethan playwright.[10] In a passage from *Far from the Madding Crowd* describing a gargoyle spurting out water on Fanny's grave and mocking Troy's remorse, Hardy writes:

> It has been sometimes argued that there is no truer criterion of the vitality of any given art-period than the power of the master-spirits of that time in grotesque; and certainly in the instance of Gothic art there is no disputing the proposition. (Hardy 1986, 241)

The novelist claims to draw his inspiration from a grotesque tradition he associates with the natural, organic form of the Gothic as well as with the stylistic liberty of the Elizabethan and Jacobean periods. Like Shakespeare's, his art is "radically impure" (Holbrook 2011, 174). Even if Shakespeare provides a tremendous support to the grotesque aesthetics, this "antirealist" art (Rosen 1991, 58, my translation) violates decorum and has shocked many readers and critics.

Hardy's grotesque "antirealism" is not gratuitous. Not only does it correspond to the author's highly personal vision but it aims at revealing reality. In *The Mayor of Casterbridge*, incongruous combinations and hyperbolic, supernatural or monstrous distortions serve a form of realism, which Bakhtin calls "grotesque realism," an intensified representation of reality. Through the transfiguration of reality, which he calls "imaginative revelation,"[11] Hardy unveils the mysteries of the human psyche and truths

---

[10] "The 'grotesque' for which Dickens and Hardy in particular find powerful Shakespearean precedents" (Poole 2011, 8).
[11] Hardy uses this phrase in his 1908 preface to *Select Poems of William Barnes* (Jones 1975, 510-1).

which are before our eyes but which we cannot see. Like the French poet Baudelaire, who thought that the role of caricature and the grotesque is "to represent his proper ugliness—both moral and physical—to man" (Baudelaire 1956, 135), Hardy shapes the horror of man and of the world. The novelist wishes to produce an effect, to leave a mark in his reader's mind and sensitivity.

"A Bewildered Child at a Conjuring Show"

Hardy was particularly sensitive to the *praxis* of reading and fully aware of the relation established between text, narration and reader. When he was blamed for enslaving himself to editors and publishers' demands and for yielding to sensationalism, he often replied that he merely wished to be a good storyteller, one whose stories could arouse the reader's interest. In February 1893 he wrote:

> A story must be exceptional enough to justify its telling. We tale-tellers are all Ancient Mariners, and none of us is warranted in stopping Wedding Guests (in other words, the hurrying public) unless he has something more unusual to relate than the ordinary experience of every average man and woman. (Hardy 1994-2, 15-6)

The narrator must be like the Ancient Mariner in Coleridge's famous *Rime*, who fascinates the Wedding Guest with his tale. The effect of the text requires a story which must be "exceptional," "unusual," which goes beyond ordinary experience through aesthetics quite distinct from mimetic realism. The grotesque, the art of disproportion, favours *aisthesis*, an essential aspect of aesthetic experience. It allows the artist to renew a perception dulled by habit.[12] This is how the grotesque and often melodramatic sensationalism of many episodes of *The Mayor of Casterbridge*, like the sale at the fair of Weydon-Priors, the Skimmity-ride or the visual distortions in many descriptions, can be interpreted. The purpose is to create surprise, to affect the reader by striking his imagination and arousing intense emotions through a tale relying on vivid imagery.

Emotion is of paramount importance in the grotesque, which is identified as much by an effect as by facts,[13] hence the great difficulty to define and express the grotesque which is manifested by "figures of

---

[12] Jauss 1998, 144. Jauss reminds us that the three key concepts of the aesthetic tradition are *poiesis*, *aisthesis* and *catharsis*.

[13] Astruc takes up and develops Kayser's ideas (see Astruc 2010, 31).

emotions" as much as by figures of speech (see Astruc 2010, 33). Hardy's novel arouses a wide range of emotions, from laughter to pity, distress and horror. The reader often wavers between opposite reactions. It is also what makes *The Mayor of Casterbridge* specifically grotesque. In his rich and powerful man's clothes early in the story, Henchard looks a little ridiculous but his successive degradations turn him into a tragic buffoon: "Now he wore the remains of an old blue cloth suit of his gentlemanly times, a rusty silk hat, and a once black satin stock, soiled and shabby" (Hardy 1985-1, 302). When reading those lines, the reader hesitates between laughter and pity. In the episode concerning Henchard's sale of his wife and child, the reader goes through similar emotional indecision:

> Up to this moment it could not positively have been asserted that the man, in spite of his tantalizing declaration, was really in earnest. The spectators had indeed taken the proceedings throughout as a piece of mirthful irony *carried to extremes*; and had assumed that, being out of work, he was, as a consequence, out of temper with the world, and society, and his nearest kin. But with the demand and response of real cash the jovial frivolity of the scene departed. A lurid colour seemed to fill the tent, and change the aspect of all therein. The mirth-wrinkles left the listeners' faces, and they waited with parted lips. (78, my emphasis)

Like the "spectators," the reader hesitates between "mirthful irony," "jovial frivolity" to start with and then the bewilderment or dread suggested at the end of the extract ("the jovial frivolity of the scene departed;" "they waited with parted lips"). He may even experience disgust, faced as he is with a deed breaking the symbolic order, deeply questioning his humanity and defiling him like an abjection (see Kristeva 2007, 80). According to Astruc, the abject analysed by Kristeva is one of the aspects at stake in the grotesque, a phenomenon which breaks boundaries and through which humanity is "carried to extremes" (see Astruc 2010, 93-100). In this scene the grotesque is also close to what Freud calls *das Unheimliche*,[14] something at once familiar and unfamiliar: such a grotesque scene may remind the reader of the force of the Id, of his own impulses.

The description of the remains of the Roman amphitheatre gives rise to mixed feelings too:

---

[14] In English "the Uncanny" (see Freud 1985).

Apart from the sanguinary nature of the games originally played therein, such incidents attached to its past as these: that for scores of years the town-gallows had stood at one corner; that in 1705 a woman who had murdered her husband was half strangled and then burnt there in the presence of ten thousand spectators. Tradition reports that at a certain stage of the burning *her heart burst and leapt out of her body, to the terror of them all,* and that *not one of those ten thousand people ever cared for hot roast after that.* In addition to these old tragedies, pugilistic encounters almost to the death had come off down to recent dates in that secluded arena […]. (Hardy 1985-1, 141, my emphasis)

The sense of the grotesque in the extract results from a hesitation between the terror created by macabre factual details reinforced by an abject precision, and the ridicule deriving from the prosaic parallel between the woman's heart and a roast of meat. This scene, during which Henchard and Susan meet again in a setting reminiscent of the violence of the opening chapter, gives rise to a similar feeling of unease.

In these episodes the reader is at a loss to express what he feels, for the grotesque is a peculiar emotion, a "*je ne sais quoi,* a shiver, a feeling of dizziness which can evolve to nausea and which can possibly be accompanied by laughter" (Astruc 2010, 31-2, my translation). It is a specific type of laughter, which tends to freeze or which is sudden, a type of laughter provoked by the grotesque according to Baudelaire.[15] In an episode of grim humour the reader is not far from laughing that way when Henchard reads to Farfrae–without mentioning any names though–the letters written by Lucetta and kept in the safe of his house. Just before, when Lucetta asked him to return the letters, Henchard was flabbergasted by such cruel irony: "A grotesque grin shaped itself on Henchard's face. Had the safe been opened?" (317). Henchard's "grotesque grin" or Lucetta's "wild laugh" (353) when she sees her effigy are similar to the grin of the damned, the grin of Melmoth which freezes one with terror and convulses one.[16] Hardy gives a perfect image of that grotesque grimace, freezing it in the keystone of the back door of Lucetta's house:

Originally the mask had exhibited a comic leer, as could still be discerned; but generations of Casterbridge boys had thrown stones at the mask, aiming at its open mouth; and the blows thereon had chipped off the lips

---

[15] (Baudelaire 1956, 143-5) The French poet's phrase is "*rire subit*" ("sudden laughter").
[16] Like all the followers of the satanic movement of French Romanticism, Baudelaire was very much influenced by C.R. Maturin's *Melmoth the Wanderer,* published in 1820.

and jaws as if they had been eaten away by disease. The appearance was so
ghastly by the weakly lamp-glimmer that she could not bear to look at it.
(211-2)

Like Elizabeth Jane, the reader is horrified at this grimacing mask–the
equivalent of the grotesque figures in Gothic cathedrals–which foreshadows
dramatic and tragic developments.

The reader's emotions are made all the stronger through Hardy's
spectacular writing. In Hardy's fiction, and particularly in *The Mayor of
Casterbridge*, there is at the narrative level a form of theatricality, at least
a visual, spectacular dimension, which is typical of the grotesque (see
Astruc 2010, 208). The scene of the sale in the opening chapter is
memorable because it is isolated as a result of the ensuing ellipsis, but also
because of the spectacle it represents:

> The *sight* of real money in full amount, in answer to a challenge for the
> same till then deemed slightly hypothetical, had *a great effect* upon the
> *spectators*. Their *eyes became riveted* upon the faces of the chief actors,
> and then upon the notes as they lay, weighted by the shillings on the table.
> (78, my emphasis)

The protagonists become "actors" and the people watching the scene
turn into "spectators." The effect on the reader is close to the one produced
on the "spectators." It is a good instance of Hardy's writing, which relies
on visual effects typical of pictorial art but also of the cinema: a subjective
shot adopting the point of view of the spectators ("the sight," "their eyes
became riveted"), a series of close shots on the protagonists' faces and
then on the banknotes and coins, which thus become symbols of Susan and
her daughter's reification, of the alienation of the hero and of the world.
Another of the writer's favourite devices is the "framing of a scene" (Page
1980, 80) consisting in isolating an element and in showing it to a
character or the reader, often through a window or a door. This way, many
scenes or descriptive passages of the novel seem to become self-contained
tableaux or "verbal pictures" (75) that remain in the reader's memory.

Hardy answered that his so-called "philosophy," which many objected
to, was "only a confused heap of impressions, like those of a bewildered
child at a conjuring show" (Hardy 1994-2, 219). Like Dickens and his
narrator in *David Copperfield*, Hardy kept intact the child's "power of
observation" (Dickens 1996, 21), his ability to be "bewildered" at a
"conjuring show." His reader can thus be a child again and be invited to an
"uncanny revel," a show which is full of unusual or disturbing emotions
and which has cathartic but also political virtues. Hardy was fully aware of

the central role played by emotions. In the "Profitable Reading of Fiction" he writes: "It is the force of an appeal to the emotional reason rather than to the logical reason; for by their emotions men are acted upon and act upon others" (in Orel 1990, 115). Through the emotions that it arouses and plays upon, Hardy's grotesque favours a communication allowed by aesthetic experience, which can then result in symbolic action (see Jauss 1998, 164).

It is no wonder that Hardy's readers are sometimes baffled. His writing outrageously distorts reality and crudely combines genres and modes. The novelist resorts to the grotesque so as to reveal and give form to the ever-changing 19th-century world, a world threatened by meaninglessness. No doubt it is also for him a means to exorcise the "ache of modernism" evoked in *Tess* (Hardy 1985-2, 180) but above all to think the unthinkable, the fragmentation of the world and of the subject, the inhuman, the abject, madness and death (see Astruc 2010, 251-64). *The Mayor of Casterbridge* is a literary carnival, a textual ritual, which allows the reader to experience chaos from a distance while sensing the threat involved (Astruc 2010, 102-3). Indirectly Hardy's grotesque posits a different world, too. Whatever some critics may think of his writing, Hardy's grotesque aesthetics presents a heuristic but also ethical and political dimension.[17]

References

Astruc, Rémi. 2010. *Le Renouveau du grotesque dans le roman du XXᵉ siècle.* Paris: Classiques Garnier.

Bakhtin, Mikhail. (1965) 1984. *Rabelais and His World.* Translated by Helene Iswolsky. Bloomington: Indiana University Press.

—. (1929) 1998. *La Poétique de Dostoïevski.* Paris: Éditions du Seuil.

Baudelaire, Charles. (1857) 1956. "On the Essence of Laughter." Translated by Jonathan Mayne, 131-54. New-York: Doubleday Anchor Books.

---

[17] For example, about the passage in which Hardy presents Henchard's will in *The Mayor of Casterbridge*, Gilmour writes: "Hardy's hawk's vision is compassionate, but it is not morally engaged in the way previous novelists were." And then he quotes P. N. Furbank: "A spectacle engaging our deepest feelings and appealing to our imagination but not capable of providing lessons... It can only confuse us to think of him in the humanistic and moralistic tradition of George Eliot and Dickens" (Gilmour 1986, 188). Such attacks are typical of the "humanist and liberal" criticism which has done so much harm to the evaluation of Hardy's art.

Dickens, Charles. (1850) 1996. *David Copperfield.* Harmondsworth: Penguin Classics.

Freud, Sigmund. (1919) 1985. "The Uncanny." In *Art and Literature.* The Pelican Freud Library Vol.14, 335-76. Harmondsworth: Penguin.

Gilmour, Robin. 1986. *The Novel in the Victorian Age: A Modern Introduction.* London: Edward Arnold.

Girard, René. (1972) 1990. *La Violence et le sacré.* Paris: Hachette Littératures.

Hardy, Florence. (1930) 1994. "The Early Life of Thomas Hardy (1840-1891)." In *The Life of Thomas Hardy.* London: Studio Editions. [1994-1]

—. (1930) 1994. "The Later Years of Thomas Hardy (1892-1928)." In *The Life of Thomas Hardy.* London: Studio Editions. [1994-2]

Hardy, Thomas. (1874) 1986. *Far from the Madding Crowd.* London and New York: Norton Critical Edition.

—. (1886) 1985. *The Mayor of Casterbridge.* Edited with an introduction and notes by Martin Seymour-Smith. London: Penguin Classics. [1985-1]

—. (1891) 1985. *Tess of the d'Urbervilles.* Edited by David Skilton with an introduction by A. Alvarez. Harmondsworth: Penguin. [1985-2]

Holbrook, Peter. 2011. "Thomas Hardy." In *Great Shakespeareans: Scott–Dickens–Eliot–Hardy,* edited by Adrian Poole, 139-82. London and New York: Continuum International.

Jauss, H. R. (1972-1975) 1998. *Pour une esthétique de la réception.* Paris: Gallimard.

Jones, Lawrence O. 1975. "Imitation and Expression in Thomas Hardy's Theory of Fiction." *Studies in the Novel,* N°7: 507-25.

Kayser, Wolfgang. (1957) 1982. *The Grotesque in Art and Literature.* New York: Columbia University Press.

Kristeva, Julia. (1980) 2007. *Pouvoirs de l'horreur: Essai sur l'abjection.* Paris: Editions du Seuil.

Moore, Kevin Z. 1990. *The Descent of the Imagination: Postromantic Culture in the Later Novels of Thomas Hardy.* New York: New York University Press.

Orel, Harold, ed. (1966) 1990. *Thomas Hardy's Personal Writings.* London: Macmillan.

Page, Norman. (1977) 1980. *Thomas Hardy.* London: Routledge & Kegan Paul.

Paterson, John. 1959. "*The Mayor of Casterbridge* as Tragedy." *Victorian Studies,* Vol. 3, N° 2: 151-72.

Poole, Adrian. 2011. "Introduction." In *Great Shakespeareans–Scott-Dickens-Eliot-Hardy,* edited by Adrian Poole, 1-9. London and New York: Continuum International.

Rosen, Elisheva. 1991. *Sur le grotesque: L'Ancien et le nouveau dans la réflexion esthétique.* Saint-Denis: Presses Universitaires de Vincennes.

Sartre, Jean-Paul. (1943) 1981. *L'Être et le néant: Essai d'ontologie phénoménologique.* Paris: Gallimard.

Vigar, Penelope. 1974. *The Novels of Thomas Hardy: Illusion and Reality.* London: Athlone Press.

Wheeler, Michael. (1985) 1989. *English Fiction of the Victorian Period: 1830-1890.* London and New York: Longman.

Zabel, Morton Dauwen. (1940) 1986. "Hardy in Defence of his Art: The Aesthetic of Incongruity." In *Hardy: A Collection of Critical Essays,* edited by Albert J. Guerard, 24-45. London: Prentice-Hall International.

PART III

RESISTING AND NEGOTIATING CHANGE

CHAPTER ELEVEN

"PRIMITIVE ELEMENTS
IN A MODERN CONTEXT":
THE GROTESQUE IN *THE MYSTERY
OF EDWIN DROOD*

ISABELLE HERVOUET-FARRAR

The grotesque plays a major role in *The Mystery of Edwin Drood*, the novel that Dickens left unfinished when he died in 1870. The word itself does not appear, although Dickens often used it in other novels like *The Old Curiosity Shop*, to name but one. However, Chapter 20 contains the phrase "the fascination of repulsion" (Dickens 1985, 234), echoing "the attraction of repulsion," which in the Dickens canon renders the fundamental ambiguity of the reception of the grotesque.[1] Geoffrey Harpham describes our reception of the grotesque in terms which cannot fail to recall Dickens's oxymoron: "The grotesque is always a civil war of attraction/repulsion" (Harpham, 1982, 9). Harpham's definition of the grotesque corresponds to numerous aspects of *The Mystery of Edwin Drood*, as this chapter intends to show: "The hypothesis before us is simple," Harpham writes, "the grotesque consists of the manifest, visible, or unmediated presence of mythic or primitive elements in a nonmythic or modern context. It is a formula capable of nearly infinite variation, and one which, rightly understood, illuminates the entire vast field of grotesquerie" (51).[2]

---

[1] The phrase is found in Chapter 23 of *The Uncommercial Traveller*, in which Dickens mentions his morbid fascination for "the churchyard of Saint Ghastly Grim" (Dickens 2012, 220-1), and is used extensively by Michael Hollington in *Dickens and the Grotesque* (Hollington 1984).

[2] Geoffrey Harpham's 1982 study of the grotesque concerns itself both with the *grottesche* of the Renaissance and more archaic grotesque forms like the *grotto-esque* or cave art. It shows that the grotesque ignores time and creates "images of

The first "elements" considered here are not as mythic as Harpham suggests. In *The Mystery of Edwin Drood* they are the remains of a distant, mainly Catholic, past which weaves acts of torture inflicted to screaming nuns and the despair of bored gargoyle sculptors. These echoes are still heard in 19th-century Cloisterham because the contemporary world has proved unable to shed its archaic past.

Critics have often considered the descriptions of Cloisterham as metaphoric representations of John Jasper's deeply divided self.[3] It is true that one of the most fascinating aspects of the novel is the representation of Edwin's uncle and probable murderer's split character. I wish here to discuss however how a slightly different approach leads to consider John Jasper's body as the literalisation–or visual representation–of the grotesque that endures in Cloisterham, in a scene which is so uncanny that it cannot fail to arrest the reader's attention, viz. the scene in which Grewgious tells Jasper that Edwin and Rosa broke off their engagement before Edwin's disappearance. I aim to analyse this scene in order to fully understand the sense of anxiety it conveys so as to show that in more ways than one, the grotesque in *Edwin Drood* is the sign of the literal endurance of primitive, unmediated elements "in a nonmythic or modern context."

Cloisterham Past and Present

The description of Cloisterham at the beginning of Chapter 3 is quite striking:

> An ancient city, Cloisterham, and no meet dwelling-place for any one with hankerings after the noisy world. A monotonous, silent city, deriving an earthy flavour throughout from its Cathedral crypt, and [...] abounding in vestiges of monastic graves. [...]
>
> A drowsy city, Cloisterham, whose inhabitants seem to suppose, with an inconsistency more strange than rare, that all its changes lie behind it, and that there are no more to come. [...]
>
> In a word, a city of another and a bygone time is Cloisterham [...]. Fragments of old wall, saint's chapel, chapter-house, convent and monastery, have got incongruously or obstructively built into many of its houses and gardens, much as kindred jumbled notions have become incorporated into many of its citizens' minds. All things in it are of the past. [...]

---

instantaneous process," (Harpham 1982, 11) in which time is compressed into "a single, ambivalent form" (63). See also the introduction to the present volume.

[3] See for example Frank 1984, 201-37.

> In the midst of Cloisterham stands the Nuns' House: a venerable brick
> edifice, whose present appellation is doubtless derived from the legend of
> its conventual uses. [...] Whether the nuns of yore [...] were ever walled
> up alive in odd angles and jutting gables of the building for having some
> ineradicable leaven of busy mother Nature in them which has kept the
> fermenting world alive ever since; these may be matters of interest to its
> haunting ghosts (if any). (Dickens 1985, 51-2)

Cloisterham is a city arrested in stasis, "a city of another and bygone
time," where historical evolution is negated or at least contested, reduced
as it is to the visual metaphor of the fragments of the Cathedral city walls
built into modern structures. The city appears as "a kind of palimpsest of
architectural styles from various periods of history" (Hollington 1984,
240). The palimpsestic effect is reinforced when the novel puts to the fore
the "incongruous" permanence of the past, for example with the mention
of "monkish trees" in Minor Canon Corner (Dickens 1985, 79), i.e. fruit-
trees planted by the Catholic monks, which implausibly still feed the
inhabitants of the early 19th century.

A few old stones and ancient fruit-trees, to which could be added the
"jumbled notions [...] [in] its citizens' minds," would probably not suffice
to turn Cloisterham into a grotesque city. The Catholic past however still
leaves its mark on present times in another, more gruesome, way:

> The Cloisterham children grow small salad in the dust of abbots and
> abbesses, and make dirt-pies of nuns and friars; while every ploughman in
> its outlying fields renders to once puissant Lord Treasurers, Archbishops,
> Bishops, and such-like, the attention which the Ogre in the story-book
> desired to render to his unbidden visitor, and grinds their bones to make his
> bread. (51)

The text here suggests that, like the fragments of old walls, other
remains are incorporated within modern structures. This time however, the
"primitive elements" are human remains (human ashes) swallowed by the
inhabitants of the city. Not only is the image more disturbing, it is also
more suggestive of the grotesque than that of the fragments of Catholic
walls because it has to do with food, with eating, with absorption by the
human mouth, "this wide-open bodily abyss" described by Bakhtin
(Bakhtin 1984, 317). The grotesque is here linked to the prospect of
cannibalism and is reminiscent of Kristeva's concept of "abjection" since
cannibalism blurs the distinction between self and other, subject and
object.[4]

---

[4] See Kristeva 1982.

Abjection however is here consistently played down. The narrator toys with images which strongly evoke cannibalism but are never *quite* to be taken seriously: the pies made with human ashes are "mud-pies" and therefore not destined to be eaten; the remains of "Lord Treasurers, Archbishops, Bishops, and such-like" serve as soil or fertilizer, but the abject image is deflated when a phrase from a very famous fairy-tale is used to narrate the ploughman's action.[5] The narrative paradoxically manages to conjure up cannibalism in a series of images which fail to induce the horror of abjection because they are linked to childhood. If the grotesque must always provoke laughter of some sort,[6] then the reader's smile is here facilitated by the harmlessness of the scene and the mention of childhood fun.

The primitive quality of such cannibalism borders on the mythic, as Harpham suggests about cave-art:

> Many of the cave paintings are not only as magnificent as works of art, but just as alienated as *grottesche*. And like *grottesche*, the cave paintings invoke, and thereby make ambivalently present and distant, an ancient code: they signify and embody antiquity, the origin. Cave art [...] reflects theology, and the rituals performed in the caves included inter-species intercourse, cannibalism, necrophagy, and sacrifice–all of which were intended to emphasize affinities with the natural world, and none of which is found in nature. (Harpham 1982, 64)

In Chapter 3 of *Edwin Drood*, the grotesque originates in the mixture of "sacred and unclean" (56) elements, i.e. of the innocent and primitive– thus almost mythical–dimension conferred to cannibalism, and the abject, revolting nature of the food ingested. Beyond that, the images of the walls and of cannibalism lead to the literalisation of the notions of progress and evolution. Evolution (understood as the transmission of knowledge and culture from one generation to the next) has become the grotesque absorption of abject food, the ingestion of the mortal remains of forefathers. The literal absorption of human ashes corrupts the notion of progress since historical evolution has been dramatically reduced, or, as

---

[5] Dickens here borrows the line from "Jack and the Beanstalk," one of his favourite fairy-tales. "Fee-fi-fo-fum /I smell the blood of an Englishman /Be he alive, or be he dead / I'll grind his bones to make my bread." "Jack and the Beanstalk" is mentioned again in Chapter 20 of *The Mystery of Edwin Drood*.

[6] As Harpham puts it: "For an object to be grotesque, it must arouse three responses. Laughter and astonishment are two; either disgust or horror is the third" (Harpham 1976, 463).

Harpham writes, time has been "rendered into space, narrative compressed into image" (11).

Evolution and progress exist only as literalised imagery because Cloisterham is arrested in a state of inertia or stasis. The inhabitants of Cloisterham have evolved, of course, and more often than not behave as 19th-century people. What is remarkable however is that the absorption of human ashes has not led to the disappearance of the dead. Nothing ever quite disappears in the world of *Edwin Drood*. Though omnipresent in the novel, death is strangely powerless to rid the living of the presence of the dead. The fictional universe is shaped by the uneasy coexistence of what is and what should no longer be. The dead's prolonged life eats away at the living, so much so that there is virtually no difference between the living and the dead. They are all dust, either "dust with the breath of life in it," or "dust of which the breath of life had passed" (Dickens 1985, 153). The metaphorical association of human beings and dust may appear as rather trite, yet it is one which Dickens's novel revives because the narrative repeatedly resorts to mentions of dust, sand, grit and the idea of grinding people alive,[7] thus suggesting that the world of the novel is one in which the living are constantly threatened to be ground into dust.

The dead feed the living–this the reader finds out in Chapter 3–but they appear as simply incorporated and gradually destroying the living from within. Just as the fragments of ancient walls become parts of modern buildings, the dead seem to have left fragments of their identity and behaviour in the living. In other words the dead haunt the living and determine their actions: when Rosa exclaims "I am a young little thing [...] to have an old heartache" (60), the Catholic nuns seem to have left within her the "ineradicable leaven of busy mother Nature" (52); the wretchedly uneducated children (Deputy and his acolytes) trying to survive in Cloisterham stone Jasper and Durdles "as if," the narrator says, "the days of St Stephen were revived" (77); and, as the narrator suggests in Chapter 3, "[old] jumbled notions have become incorporated into many of [the] citizens' minds" (52).

---

[7] For example: "The cramped monotony of my existence grinds me away by the grain," Jasper exclaims (48); "[Grewgious] was an arid, sandy man, who, if he had been put into a grinding-mill, looked as if he would have ground immediately into high-dried snuff" (109); "Fancy might have ground [Grewgious's voice] straight, like himself, into high-dried snuff (111); "[Neville's] daily life worn out grain by grain" (251); Billickin says: "'It is not [...] that I possess the Mill I have heard of, in which old single ladies could be ground up young (what a gift it would be to some of us)'" (261).

Such impossible survival of the dead, which becomes grotesque when it is more literal than fantastic, seems in part to originate in a pivotal element of the plot. The origin of the story (and of Jasper's murderous impulses) is indeed found in Edwin's and Rosa's dead fathers' wish that their children should marry. The haunting of the present by the past[8] thus stems from this absurd injunction and creates a universe pregnant with grotesque metamorphoses in which the dead plan out the lives of the living, a world ruled by what the text calls "strict fidelity to […] the dead" (Dickens 1985, 145).

The grotesque is linked to phases of dramatic change, to periods in history when fundamental beliefs are challenged.[9] It comes as no surprise that in the 19th century it should be linked to a feeling of alienation when one is faced with a society whose traditional structures have collapsed. Yet contrary to what the grotesque expresses in some of Dickens's other novels[10] it is conditioned in *Edwin Drood* by Cloisterham's refusal to accept that the world is changing. The permanence of the past provokes grotesque transformations because the people of Cloisterham reject change and modernity and consider that history has led to a state of perfection. Sapsea, the auctioneer and new Mayor of Cloisterham, the "jackass" (62), embodies all the practices and beliefs of a city ossified by the past's continuing presence. To him, nothing has changed since his childhood (64) and he refuses to have the train, that symbol of progress *par excellence*, pass through Cloisterham (83).

"Of all forms of ornament," Geoffrey Harpham explains, "the grotesque most fully embodies this tension between the archaic and the advanced" (Harpham 1982, 49). Such tension is at the core of the grotesque in *Edwin Drood*. The Catholic past is archaic, and because it haunts Cloisterham, the city itself is archaic, as its name reveals. The reader may then expect modern London and the British Empire (the other two *loci* of the novel) to be simply "advanced," but the novel does not always permit such simple categorization. London and the Empire (Egypt and India are mentioned in the novel) are imagined as places where one can escape Cloisterham's stifling atmosphere, but the illusion is not sustained for very long. London

---

[8] In his reading of the text, Lawrence Frank points to an intertextual reference that a lover of Gothic fiction cannot miss: the plot of *Edwin Drood* seems to have been conceived as a palimpsest of Lewis's *The Monk* (Frank 1984, 208-11), which would mean that the novel is haunted by the memory of an older one and that haunting in Dickens's novel is intertextual too.
[9] See for example Harpham 1976, 466.
[10] See Hollington 1984, 98-9.

in *Edwin Drood* is a place whose characteristics evolve according to which of its inhabitants (Princess Puffer, Grewgious, Tartar) the text considers, as Philip Collins has noted (see Collins 1994). In other words the metropolis is grotesque whenever its inhabitants are. Princess Puffer is "as ugly and withered as one of the fantastic carvings on the under brackets of the stall seats" (Dickens 1985, 279), and human bodies, in the London opium den, refuse to remain "separate and completed phenomen[a]" (Bakhtin 1984, 318). They become weak and soft and strangely resemble one another, in an "unclean spirit of imitation" (Dickens 1985, 39) which again points to Kristevan "abjection" and to the grotesque. The Empire provides the drug at the origin of this grotesque metamorphosis ("the woman has opium-smoked herself into a strange likeness of the Chinaman," 38), thus suggesting that London and the Empire can be grotesque in their own rights, as well as Cloisterham.

The fact remains however that *Edwin Drood* pits Cloisterham against other places. The grotesque originates in Cloisterham's relationship with the past, as we know, but the text also offers some of its most memorable images when the city has to deal with more present considerations, i.e. the exotic, the alien and its plans for the future. Fossilized between an archaic past and an unknown future, Cloisterham swallows the past as its inhabitants feed on the dead, and in a very similar fashion–as though through the mouth–the city also absorbs London and the Empire. Each of its inhabitants' longing for change or travel is stifled because the centripetal force exerted by Cloisterham is prodigious: most of the characters who live in London or the Empire end up in Cloisterham (this is true of Grewgious, the Landlesses, even Princess Puffer). Edwin is not allowed to leave and is probably buried or hiding somewhere in the crypt of the cathedral. Sapsea, once again, embodies Cloisterham's appetite for foreign "food" when he puts a finger on a foreign object and thinks that by so doing he can absorb the culture of the foreign country ("If I have not gone to foreign countries, young man, foreign countries have come to me [...] I see a French clock [...] I instantly lay my finger on him and say 'Paris!'" 64).[11]

Because they are thus devoured by Cloisterham, London and the Empire are not places of progress and evolution: behaving uncannily like

---

[11] Just as he is capable–*literally* capable, the text suggests–of inflating his mind in order to absorb another's in it: "When I had enlarged my mind up to [...] the pitch of wanting another mind to be absorbed in it, I cast my eye about for a nuptial partner." Sapsea's absorption of his wife's mind is so literal, so grotesque, so funny that the poor woman is reduced to idiocy and to repeating "Oh thou" throughout her married life (65-6).

the Cloisterham children, Belzoni eats the dead in the Pyramids–and almost fatally chokes on their dust (59). In *The Mystery of Edwin Drood*, the distant foreign, like the distant past, is reduced to a few features caught in a grotesque tableau which mixes them with elements belonging to 19th-century Cloisterham: the Cloisterham omnibus becomes an elephant,[12] or, a better example still, the famous incipit combines the past, the contemporary and the exotic in Jasper's nightmarish vision:

> An ancient English Cathedral tower? How can the ancient English Cathedral tower be here? The well-known massive grey square tower of its old Cathedral? How can that be [in London]! There is no spike of rusty iron in the air, between the eye and it, from any point of the real prospect. What IS the spike that intervenes, and who has set it up? Maybe, it is set up by the Sultan's orders for the impaling of a horde of Turkish robbers, one by one. It is so, for cymbals clash, and the Sultan goes by to his palace in long procession. (37)

Jasper, the Cloisterham Gargoyle

This blend of past and present, local and exotic, is also found in the novel's most fascinating character, John Jasper. Comparing the Renaissance *grottesche* to "grotto-esque" cave art, Geoffrey Harpham explains:

> Together, grotto-esque and *grottesche* provide us with a binocular view of grotesque. In fact, if we wanted to construct a system of classification for all grotesqueries, we could do no better than to begin with an elementary distinction between those like cave art, in which forms are compressed into meaningful ambivalence; and those in which, as with *grottesche*, forms are proliferated into meaningless ambivalence (Harpham 1982, 65).

That Jasper belongs to the first, "meaningful," mode of the grotesque, the "Gothic" or sombre variety, and not to the second, which Harpham also describes as the "Baroque, the light and funny, or the margin" (65),[13] is quickly apparent. The character offers a synthesis of all the sources of the grotesque found in *Edwin Drood:* in him the monks' former violence is exacerbated by opium and becomes fantasies of oriental tortures. If Jasper is a Dickensian gargoyle, he is not a funny one. Because he has internalized the carving of stone that the monks resorted to in order to

---

[12] "a short squat omnibus, with a disproportionate heap of luggage on the roof like a little Elephant with infinitely too much Castle" (83).
[13] Like Honeythunder for example, a dispensable character, typical of Dickensian farcical excess.

alleviate their boredom, he has metaphorically turned himself into a stone demon. Very early in the novel he suggests using his body as building material:

> "No wretched monk who droned his life away in that gloomy place, before me, can have been more tired of it than I am. He could take for relief (and did take) to carving demons out of the stalls and seats and desks. What shall I do? Must I take to carving them out of my heart?" (Dickens 1985, 48)

At first his words simply lead the reader to grasp the extent of the boredom and despair that the metaphor conveys. A literal reading of the metaphor, however, unveils the grotesque and striking reification of his body. It is important to note that Dickens encourages a literal reading of the segment. To the question Jasper asks, Edwin answers "I thought you had so exactly found your niche in life, Jack" (48). Dickens plays with the word "niche," which Jasper repeats and emphasizes ironically ("'A poor monotonous chorister and grinder of music–in his niche–may be troubled...'" 49), and thus invites us to take it literally and to consider that Jasper is indeed the "defaced statue" in the "broken niche" (42) seen by the Dean and the Verger when they look at Jasper's house a few pages earlier.[14] Finally, before Jasper describes himself as a gargoyle, the reader already suspects that he is one: very early in the scene, "Jasper's face" becomes "the Jasper face" (44) and is reduced to a terrifying mask (we will return to this further down) from behind which only "hungry, exacting, watchful" (44) eyes appear.

Chapter Fifteen offers a remarkable tableau in which Jasper's body visually reveals the grotesque of Cloisterham. Because Cloisterham will not take part in historical evolution, its inhabitants are first distorted–either inflated like Sapsea or eaten away like Jasper–and then reified or annihilated, ground to grit or dust, as we have seen. Here is part of the narrative of the scene in which Grewgious has come to inform Jasper that Edwin and Rosa broke off their engagement shortly before Edwin's disappearance. The reader is supposed to understand that Jasper has killed his nephew and suddenly realizes that the murder was pointless.

---

[14] This scene irresistibly evokes a scene found in Chapter 27 of *The Old Curiosity Shop*: Nell imagines that Quilp, who suddenly appears near her, is a statue come down from its niche. If Quilp is the gargoyle suddenly come to life, Jasper is the man who has sculpted himself into a monstrous grotesque.

Mr. Grewgious, alternately opening and shutting the palms of his hands as he warmed them at the fire, and looking fixedly at [Jasper] sideways, and never changing either his action or his look in all that followed, went on to reply.

"This young couple, the lost youth and Miss Rosa, my ward... [...]."

Mr. Grewgious saw a staring white face, and two quivering white lips, in the easy-chair, and saw two muddy hands gripping its sides. But for the hands, he might have thought he had never seen the face.

"–This young couple... [...]"

Mr. Grewgious saw a lead-coloured face in the easy-chair, and on its surface dreadful starting drops or bubbles, as if of steel.

"This young couple... [...]."

Mr. Grewgious saw a ghastly figure rise, open-mouthed, from the easy-chair, and lift its outspread hands towards its head.

"One of this young couple... [...]."

Mr. Grewgious saw the ghastly figure throw back its head, clutch its hair with its hands, and turn with a writhing action from him.

"I have now said all I have to say: except ... [...]."

Mr. Grewgious heard a terrible shriek, and saw no ghastly figure, sitting or standing; saw nothing but a heap of torn and miry clothes upon the floor.

Not changing his action even then, he opened and shut the palms of his hands as he warmed them, and looked down at it. (191-2)

The genre of such a scene is very difficult to define: the excerpt cannot be fantastic because the reader finds it impossible to hesitate and simply *consider* the possibility of the supernatural. There can be no doubt that the scene is realistic, and yet the principles of mimetic representation are ignored since the final image of Jasper's body ("nothing but a heap of torn and miry clothes") cannot be read metaphorically. Jasper's body has disappeared, Grewgious is not horrified, but the reader is. Because of its generic instability, the excerpt remains poised between excess (Dickens goes too far if the scene is realistic, Jasper's body should not disappear) and absence (if the scene is fantastic, fantastic hesitation should be possible). Jasper's body is not prone to swelling like Honeythunder's. It is withered, petrified and gradually annihilated as the scene draws to its close. It may call to mind Mrs Skewton's body in *Dombey and Son*, or Lady Tippins's in *Our Mutual Friend*, those two corpses hidden behind clothes and make-up. But in *The Mystery of Edwin Drood*, Dickens goes further than in the two previous novels: the human body is first reified and then disappears, there is no corpse left. Jasper offers here a grotesque, strikingly visual representation of the fate incurred by humanity in Cloisterham. Total annihilation threatens when stasis replaces evolution, when time is compressed into insignificance.

Jasper's petrified, eroded, then absent body evokes one of Durdles's "strange sights," (68) thus confirming that in *The Mystery of Edwin Drood*, there is little difference between the living (Jasper) and the dead ("the old chap" of the quote below):

> [Durdles] often speaks of himself in the third person; perhaps, being a little misty as to his own identity, when he narrates; perhaps impartially adopting the Cloisterham nomenclature in reference to a character of acknowledged distinction. Thus he will say, touching his strange sights: "Durdles come upon the old chap," in reference to a buried magnate of ancient time and high degree, "by striking right into the coffin with his pick. The old chap gave Durdles a look with his open eyes, as much as to say, 'Is your name Durdles? Why, my man, I've been waiting for you a devil of a time!' And then he turned to powder." (68)

The confrontation between Grewgious and Jasper is even stranger than Durdles's vision, however, in that it does not offer the consoling mediation of being the very unreliable narrative of an old drunkard. The scene is grotesque in that it resists closure and defies interpretation.

Childhood Terror

The obliteration of Jasper's body is deeply disturbing. However, the grotesque of the scene also has a more private origin. The scene is grotesque but not funny, and the reader experiences only the type of laughter described by Baudelaire, i.e. satanic laughter based on man's feeling of superiority (Baudelaire 1956, 116), a type of hilarity due to the reader's superior position and his childish satisfaction at realizing that Grewgious knows of Jasper's guilt and will see him punished. However, it appears that in Durdles's embedded narrative, the corpse's flesh disappears because Durdles–the Devil, or Death, or both, as Nancy Hill suggests (Hill 1981, 142-5)–has opened the coffin and looked at the dead man. The scene between Grewgious and Jasper is very similar: it is Grewgious's fixed gaze, as much as the news he has to bring, that causes the annihilation of Jasper's body, as is confirmed by the anaphora "Mr. Grewgious saw." The reader is confronted with a radically different and troubling perspective when perceiving that Grewgious and Jasper belong to the same mode of the grotesque, the gothic, the primitive, *literally* the unfinished, as the famous description of Grewgious's face shows:

> The little play of feature that his face presented, was cut deep into it, in a few hard curves that made it more like work; and he had certain notches in

his forehead, which looked as though Nature had been about to touch them into sensibility or refinement, when she had impatiently thrown away the chisel, and said: "I really cannot be worried to finish off this man; let him go as he is." (Dickens 1985, 109-10)

For a few moments, Grewgious, the slightly ridiculous but debonair lawyer, becomes an object of horror, reminiscent of what Dickens elsewhere called "the Mask." The "dreadful Mask" corresponds to one of Dickens's childhood fears. What is striking is that Grewgious's face is like a mask staring at Jasper,[15] and that Dickens's horror of "the Mask," when he was a child, came from its staring at him:

When did that dreadful Mask first look at me? Who put it on, and why was I so frightened that the sight of it is an era of my life? It is not a hideous visage in itself; it is even meant to be droll; why then were its stolid features so intolerable? Surely not because it hid the wearer's face. [...] Was it the immovability of the Mask? ... Perhaps that fixed and set change coming over a real face, infused into my quickened heart some remote suggestion and dread of the universal change that is to come on every face, and make it still? Nothing reconciled me to it. [...] The mere recollection of that fixed face, the mere knowledge of its existence anywhere, was sufficient to awaken me in the night all perspiration and horror, with, "Oh! I know it's coming! Oh! The Mask !" (In Wilson 1983, 11-2)

In the bizarre scene of confrontation between Jasper and Grewgious, therefore, Dickens offers two versions of the mask, this grotesque motif mentioned by theorists.[16] Jasper shows that there is *literally* nothing behind the social mask worn to hide the annihilation of humanity by stasis and boredom. Grewgious too, surprisingly enough, is the reified grotesque, though he belongs to a slightly different but equally disturbing type, originating as he does in a more personal source of anguish. He is perhaps the last character to wear the Dickensian "Mask," bearing witness to the persistence of childhood terror within the ageing novelist and thus to the emergence of the grotesque in *The Mystery of Edwin Drood* as persistently linked to the "unmediated presence of [...] primitive elements in a modern context."

The grotesque is such an essential aspect of *The Mystery of Edwin Drood* perhaps because, as an uncompleted work, the novel remains "a

---

[15] Just as Jasper's face is a mask staring at and devouring Edwin in Chapter 2, with his "hungry, exacting, watchful" eyes (44). See *supra.*

[16] See for example Bakhtin 1984, 39-40 and Harpham 1976, 462; 466.

fragmented text in search of a master principle" (Harpham 1982, 43). Because we can never be sure of what Dickens intended to show had the novel been finished, the symbolic dimension of the elements that compose the remaining text is difficult to grasp with absolute certainty, even if critics have always hypothesized on the subject. The symbolic dimension being left unclear, the literal dimension is given pride of place and, with it, the indecision or ambivalence of the grotesque.

References

Bakhtin, Mikhail. (1965) 1984. *Rabelais and His World*. Translated by Hélène Iswolsky. Bloomington: Indiana University Press.

Baudelaire, Charles. (1857) 1956. "On the Essence of Laughter." In *The Mirror of Art, Critical Studies by Charles Baudelaire*. Translated by Jonathan Mayne, 131-54. New-York: Doubleday Anchor Books.

Collins, Philip. (1962) 1994. *Dickens and Crime*. London: Palgrave Macmillan.

Dickens, Charles. (1870) 1985. *The Mystery of Edwin Drood*. London: Penguin Classics.

—. (1860) 2012. *The Uncommercial Traveller*. Gloucester: Dodo Press.

Frank, Lawrence. 1984. *Charles Dickens and the Romantic Self*. Lincoln and London: University of Nebraska Press.

Harpham, Geoffrey Galt. 1976. "The Grotesque, First Principles." *The Journal of Aesthetics and Art Criticism*, Vol. 34, No. 4: 461-8. Stable URL: http://www.jstor.org/stable/430580. Accessed: 01/08/2012

—. 1982. *On the Grotesque: Strategies of Contradiction in Art and Literature*. Princeton: Princeton University Press.

Hill, Nancy K. 1981. *A Reformer's Art: Dickens' Picturesque and Grotesque Imagery*. Athens and London: Ohio University Press.

Hollington, Michael. 1984. *Dickens and the Grotesque*. Beckenham (Kent): Croom Helm.

Kristeva, Julia. 1982. *Powers of Horror. An Essay in Abjection*. Translated by Leon S. Roudiez. New-York: Columbia University Press.

Wilson, Angus. (1970) 1983. *The World of Charles Dickens*. London: Panther Books.

CHAPTER TWELVE

ARTS OF DISMEMBERMENT:
ANATOMY, ARTICULATION,
AND THE GROTESQUE BODY
IN *OUR MUTUAL FRIEND*

VICTOR SAGE

Synechdochic Dismemberment

Dickens's first recorded, fully-fledged letter, written in 1825 or 1826 at the age of 13 or 14, to one Owen Peregrine Thomas while they were at Wellington House Academy, features the appearance of an anatomical theme in a series of coded schoolboy jokes about books:

> Tom
> I am quite ashamed I have not returned you your Leg but you shall have it by Harry tomorrow. If you would like to purchase my Clavis you shall have it at a very *reduced price.* Cheaper in comparison than a Leg.
>> Yours &
>> C. Dickens
> PS. I suppose all this time you have had a *wooden* leg. I have weighed yours every Saturday night. (In Slater 2009, 2-3)

If these are grammar books–as Michael Slater suggests, after Forster[1]–then the heavy Leg is "the Law or Laws of" (i.e. Lex, Legis; or Leges), and the Clavis is the "Key to" the subject of Grammar. If so, the latter is lighter, not such a weighty tome, as the Leges. Whatever the case, there is

---

[1] Slater notes that Forster has spotted that there is "some underlying whim or fun in the "Leg" allusions" (Slater 2009, 3), but beyond decoding the grammar book allusion, he doesn't say what that "whim" is.

a figurative tendency for the Leg to escape the body, the part to be separated from the whole, and the prosthesis, the very symptom and confirmation of that separation, makes its dishevelled appearance in the letter's postscript. We might describe a borrowed leg, a wooden leg, and perhaps a small connecting bone (Lat. *Claviculus*: "little key"), as dispersed synechdoches, parts delegated to stand for an absent whole. But I note also the economic register: they are also items that acquire their value, either from weight, or scarcity, in a system of schoolboy exchange, between Tom, Dick, and Harry.

Anyone who enjoys reading Dickens will no doubt already have made their own anthology of characters and episodes which feature the sudden intrusion of the Leg, but let me venture on one or two early ones from the 1840s, to remind us of the strangely absurdist, and apparently inconsequential, use of this limb, which itself forms a legacy in English popular satirical comedy, if we think of Spike Milligan and *The Goon Show*, or the giant Foot and Leg which drops with an obscene squelching noise to terminate Terry Gilliam's opening montage in *Monty Python's Flying Circus*, or the recurrent "magazine feature" in that comic series of a collection of "Silly Walks."

First of all, Chapter 9 of *Martin Chuzzlewit*, published in 1844, contains a classic example in Mr Pecksniff's after-dinner speech over the bannisters at Todgers's Commercial Boarding House, Pecksniff who, after having been carried up to bed by the clerks Jinkins and Gander, much the worse for drink, was seen to "flutter on the top landing," making persistent attempts to engage the company below with a dissertation on the nature of the Leg:

> "This is very soothing," said Mr Pecksniff, after a pause. "Extremely so. Cool and refreshing, particularly to the legs! The legs of the human subject, my friends, are a beautiful production. Compare them with wooden legs, and observe the difference between the anatomy of nature and the anatomy of art. Do you know," said Mr Pecksniff, leaning over the bannisters, with an odd recollection of his familiar manner among new pupils at home, "that I should very much like to see Mrs Todgers's notion of a wooden leg, if perfectly agreeable to herself." (Dickens 1959, 152)

The leg here has suddenly made a festive escape from the less than rigorous control of Pecksniff's discourse, and the reader gains a fleeting glimpse of what might actually be on his mind through the sign system of his body. The narrator's delicate reference to "strangely attired" suggests the good man's trousers have been perhaps loosened by Jinkins and Gander–who "made him as comfortable as they could" (151)–and have become dislodged in his sudden resurrection. We have already earlier seen him slip an arm round the redoubtable widow, Mrs Todgers, which she has affected not to notice. These two facts help to explain the subtext of his sudden rhetorical lurch from nature into art, from the leg fleshly to the leg wooden: he seeks with all the cunning of the drunk to cover his own urge to violate propriety, which the mention of Mrs Todgers's idea of the fleshly item would certainly do, especially from one leering over the banisters in a state of gross sartorial disarray. But Pecksniff's lack of sobriety interferes with his grasp of linguistic register, and, doubled into two anatomies, the "leg" escapes all Pecksniff's attempts to confine it, and is flourished in a free space of absurdity. The "anatomy of art," I shall argue below, is thus an art of anatomy, of dismemberment, an art that simultaneously makes and breaks a synechdoche.

Another slightly earlier example of synechdochic dismemberment is that of Scrooge, who, when confronted by the ghost of Christmas Past, locates its strangeness, not in the fact that it has a great candle-snuffer for a cap, but in its lower anatomy:

> Even this, though, when Scrooge looked at it with increasing steadiness, was *not* its strangest quality. For as its belt sparkled and glittered now in one part and now in another, and what was light one instant, at another time was dark, so that the figure itself fluctuated in its distinctness: being now a thing with one arm, now with one leg, now with twenty legs, now a pair of legs without a head, now a head without a body: of which dissolving parts, no outline would be visible in the dense gloom wherein they melted away. And in the very wonder of this, it would be itself again, distinct and clear as ever. (Dickens 1960, 25)

The allegorical form here makes explicit an indeterminate relationship between part and whole–"dissolving parts" a simultaneous allusion to the magic lanthern's "dissolving views"[2]–and the legs of the figure are the chief agents in the constant metamorphosis of its form: "now with one leg, now with twenty legs, now a pair of legs without a head." It's almost as if Scrooge were looking for the first time at the form of a creature, unable to discern its species or features–and yet, the allegory insists, this is the image of his own past–so alienated is his vision of the world, it is as if his own memories no longer belong to him and have become bodiless and exotic. The leg threatens to rebel against the body, the parts against the whole. The Grotesque Body is present here, but the moral allegory of *A*

---

[2] See Dickens 1998, 14-5 for a discussion of this phrase, and Dickens's enthusiasm for the technique.

Christmas Carol makes sure it is not in a purely comic form. The comic counterpart to this bizarre and disturbing image in the text is segregated to the behaviour of Mr Fezziwig's leg at the Christmas dance of his employees, which is an example of the old, eighteenth-century grotesque of Dickens's earlier novels.

Finally, on the subject of the segregation of comic and satiric effects of corporeal dismemberment, one more famous example, from *Hard Times*: the "Hands" of Coketown. This synechdoche of an absent, and therefore sick, Body Politic is often related, quite rightly of course, to the idea of the alienation of the industrial process; and the grotesque aspect of dismemberment is minimised. But Goldberg notices that Dickens is also employing a grotesque image of body parts that are reanimated in another part of nature:

> The best large-scale illustration of the crazy upward and downward mobility which operates in Dickens's world occurs in his treatment of Coketown's "hands," who are reduced by the system of utility and the dehumanising linguistic shorthand which stems from it to simply "hands" and "stomachs" like the "lower creatures of the seashore." (Goldberg 1972, 216)[3]

There is just a glimpse here of Dickens's awareness of the context of Natural History.

The Grotesque Body and the Uses of Natural History

Bahktin's account of the Grotesque Body of the Medieval period in his book on Rabelais involves several repeated features: (1) "fanciful Anatomy" (Bakhtin 1984, 346) or "wild anatomical fantasy" (345); (2) "members, organs and parts of the body (especially dismembered parts)" (317-18), and (3) the movement downward into the "lower bodily stratum" (353).[4] To be clear, I want to add to his account of these characteristic movements of the Grotesque Body, a variation which I shall call the *disjecta membra* effect, the scattering or dissolving of Limbs, a comic version of the Orpheus myth, and its corresponding narrative counter-movement, the profane resurrection. The apotheosis of this process is in the novel *Our Mutual Friend,* an encyclopaedia of the Dickensian

---

[3] I am indebted to Chapter 10: "The Grotesque," from which this quotation comes.
[4] Bakhtin is discussing a variety of different forms here, including the so-called "Indian Wonders" and the Italian Comedy of the Middle-Ages. He picks out recurrent patterns across different eras, cultures, and genres.

grotesque, in the figure of Silas Wegg, whose wooden leg has mounted a coup against his organic body, and is "evolving," rather alarmingly:

> Sooth to say, he was so wooden a man that he seemed to have taken his wooden leg naturally, and rather suggested to the fanciful observer, that he might be expected–if his development received no untimely check–to be completely set up with a pair of wooden legs in about six months. (Dickens 1989, 46)

Our Mutual Friend employs what its narrator refers to as a "timber fiction" (303) in a variety of contexts as a parody of "growth." Wegg later "modestly remarks on the want of adaptation in a wooden leg to ladders and such-like airy perches..." (303). The use of the word "adaptation" pinpoints the natural history context, but it seems here to refer to the development of a limb, not an organism.

The context of a topical joke like this is a parody of the organic metaphors of growth and development left over from the optimistic rhetoric of mid-century Social Darwinism; and the Grotesque Body's dismembered and dispersed anatomy is used to puncture the neat elision of the natural and the cultural in writers like Herbert Spencer and George Henry Lewes. Lewes used that elision after Dickens's death, to cut him down to size; writing of him, for example, that he was unable to create true character-development:

> It is this complexity of the organism which Dickens wholly fails to conceive; his characters have nothing fluctuating and incalculable, even when they embody true observations; and very often they are creations so fantastic that one is at a loss to understand how he could, without hallucination, believe them to be like reality. (Lewes 1961, 65-6)

The answer to the question posed here is that Lewes, anxious to promote George Eliot, employing the premise of organic growth and development as the mimetic template for aesthetic realism, was (perhaps deliberately) looking in the wrong place. From the point of view of "development," it is not the organism that interested Dickens so much as the organ.[5] Lewes knew perfectly well that from July 1842 onwards, when

---

[5] Sally Ledger makes an interesting point about the meaning of "development" by the time Dickens comes to write *Our Mutual Friend* in the 1860s: she suggests that "his later invective, in 1864-5, needs to be understood as part of a wider Social-Darwinian account of the struggle for existence, and secondly in terms of the ontological shift effected by Darwin, which, in the end, removed the possibility of Providential design" (Ledger 2011, 367).

they met in the Green Room at Drury Lane, Dickens's allegiances in Natural History debates were to his friend and fan, the anatomist and palaeontologist, Sir Richard Owen, and for twenty years afterwards *Household Words* and *All The Year Round* employed a group of journalists, who could all write in the Dickens manner, to boil down Owen's scientific papers. Owen, who has been rehabilitated since the early 1990s, after a period of eclipse, was in his first phase a Cuverian functionalist, tracing the development, not of the organism, but the adaptation of the limbs and organs. Owen then emerges as a transcendental morphologist in the late 1840s, seeing the development of the human skeleton in relation to a coelocanth-like Archetype, after Goethe and his followers, and was discredited by Huxley in the Hippocampus Minor dispute at the Royal Society in 1859, an event which made not one jot of difference to Dickens's championing of him as a populariser of science (see Padian 1997). Owen was an anatomist, a bone-man, and a popular national figure, "Professor Owen," thanks in part to Dickens's loyal publicity for him. He was nicknamed "the British Cuvier" because, like the great Baron, he was an expert in articulation and the reconstruction of palaeontological specimens. Claudia Cohen sums up the prestige of this activity, in a fashion which suggests some interesting overlaps with Bakhtin's dynamic of the Grotesque Body:

> Using the device of the synechdoche, Cuvier presented with great confidence one of the most powerful and enduring images connected with the palaeontological profession: the spectacular process of reconstruction, which, starting from a small part, produces a giant creature. It is a prodigious alchemy, akin to the myth of the phoenix arising from its ashes, or the resurrection of the dead. (Cohen 1994, 116-7)[6]

When the narrator in Chapter 2 of *Our Mutual Friend* refers to the excessively tall and bony Mrs Podsnap as "a fine woman for Professor Owen," he is probably assimilating her to *Dinornis,* the eight-foot Giant Extinct bird, the Moa of New Zealand, which Owen reconstructed from a single bone sent to him by a missionary.[7] Such allusions are part of a complex series of designed overlaps in the rhetoric of *Our Mutual Friend* between Victorian society's proliferating division of labour, the notion of

---

[6] Quoted in Ulrich 2006, 40.
[7] There is a famous photograph of Owen standing next to his articulated reconstruction, his outstretched hand on its upper thigh, which appears virtually level with his shoulder. In the other hand, he holds the original fragment of a femur from which he deduced the rest of the body-form. See Rupke 1994, 126.

"Progress," and what those arch-consumers, the Veneerings, term the "bran-new." The movement revealed by the John Harmon case is backwards and downwards into the primeval slime of a society that sees itself as in the forefront of progress.[8]

Dickens, Owen and Carlyle were all in the Athenaeum, a set of metropolitan "radicals" in the Victorian sense; i.e. individualists, often "self-made," as Dickens and Owen were at least, who were not necessarily aligned with the Bishop of Oxford and the donnish anti-Darwinian Christian arguments from design, though Owen's drubbing at the hands of Huxley tended to tar him with that brush. Carlyle is often seen as the very embodiment of an independent metropolitan culture, the great mediator of German Romanticism to the Victorians, a proponent of a "metaphysical, yet secular intellectual culture" to use Ulrich's phrase, to which Owen also belonged.[9]

It is Carlyle who, through the writings of his German visionary Professor Teufelsdrockh, takes the neo-classical cliché "Expression is the dress of thought" from Hobbes and Locke, Dryden and Pope, and deconstructs it in *Sartor Resartus,* in such way that very little of this traditional badge of articulacy is left standing. In its place, there is an anatomical reconstruction of language:

> Language is called the Garment of Thought: however, it should rather be, Language is the Flesh-Garment, the Body, of Thought. I said that Imagination wove this Flesh-Garment; and does she not? Metaphors are her stuff: examine Language; what, if you except some few primitive elements (of natural sound), what is it all but Metaphors, recognised as such, or no longer recognised; still fluid and florid, or now solid-grown and colourless? If those same primitive elements are the osseous fixtures in the Flesh-garment, then are Metaphors its muscles and living integuments. An unmetaphorical style you shall in vain look for. is not your very *Attention* a *Stretching-to*? (Carlyle 1987, 57)

The metaphor of "Thought's-Body" is substituted at all levels for the stable, decent metaphor of "dress" and the Result is that "articulation" becomes a grotesque and unstable play on words, that irresistibly suggests the image of an anatomical representation of the Body.

---

[8] For further discussion of the increasingly social aspect of Dickens's grotesque as he absorbs the work of Carlyle, see Goldberg 1972, Chapters 2 ("Romantic Inheritance") and 10 ("the Grotesque"). See also Sage 1999.

[9] Owen had learnt German from his youth; and he had a first-hand knowledge of the German sources for his work. See Rupke 1994.

This question of "articulation"–i.e. the playful relation between discourse and anatomical reconstruction which has long been recognised as one of the main themes and sources of the humour of *Our Mutual Friend*–also enters the question of the parody of the Body Politic in that novel. Venus advertises himself as an "Articulator of Human Bones" and Wegg, trying to flatter him, at one point describes him as having "the patience to fit together on wires the whole framework of society–I allude to the human skellinton..." (Dickens 1989, 478), which hints at a political dimension of the term "articulation," as, in this case, the *danse macabre* of the Body Politic's bony frame.

Articulation

There is also a conjunction in other parts of Victorian culture between the anatomical theme of "articulation" and the discourse of history: articulation also means "historical reconstruction" on the model of the "prodigious alchemy" of palaeontological reconstruction. Carlyle also met Owen in 1842 in August and he visited him at the Hunterian Museum at the Royal College of Surgeons, where he was shown the collection. Carlyle was in the throes of a book about Cromwell and the Civil War at the time, oppressed and somewhat tormented by the historiographical problem of how to reconstruct the past, and yet leave it *as* the past; and, as he grew excited about Cuvier and Owen's work, the palaeontological tropes in his own writing increased. He imitated the anatomical reconstructions of Georges Cuvier and Richard Owen, while simultaneously refusing as a romantic fantasy the idea that such palaeontological reconstructions actually made the past come alive.[10]

They were just beginning to dig the battle site of Naseby at the time in the early 1840s and Carlyle, who had begged a tooth, which he kept in the drawer of his desk, wrote to Edward Fitzgerald on whose land the site of the battle lay: "To think that this grinder chewed its breakfast on 14 June

---

[10] "It is precisely Carlyle's self-consciously conflicted view of historiography that allows him to be represented in both of these ways, as an artist/scientist deploying the logic of synechdoche to generate miraculously the whole from the part, and as a writer/historiographer who self-consciously foregrounds the limitations of such synechdochic historical representations. Caught between the desire for a full, unmediated apprehension of the past and the self-conscious awareness that such an apprehension is utterly impossible, in the fall of 1842, Carlyle began to reconceive his approach to the past in paleontological terms, as he searches for a way to work through his conflicted desires and reach a solution to his Cromwell dilemma." (Ulrich 2006, 41)

1645, and had no more eating to do in the world, or service farther there, till now, to lie in my drawer and be a horror! For one thing, I wish you would not open any more mounds till I can be there too; it would have been worth a longer journey to see those poor packed skeletons ...!" Despite Carlyle's compassionate enthusiasm for articulation here, commentators tend to think that he recognises that the whole which is implied by the discovery of a "part" is not simple, but that a trope of synechdochic reconstruction dominates his writing up to the pamphlet, "Past and Present," written in 1842-3, a pamphlet whose critical force had a great deal of influence on the earlier Dickens.[11] Indeed, the latter told Carlyle that he knew some of his pamphlets off by heart.

Of course it is twenty years later when Dickens is writing *Our Mutual Friend.* But in the meantime his journalists have carried on faithfully reporting Owen's work as it came out, along with other works of natural history, which included Darwin's *Origin of Species* too in July of 1860. Suffice it to say that perhaps the most extended set of dispersed synechdoches in Dickens is the shop of the "anatomist," Mr Venus, a figure commentators have long identified as an affectionate parody of Owen. We know that there is a biographical origin for this shop, if not the character: Marcus Stone, his young illustrator, when Dickens was stuck for an incident for the underplot, took him to the shop of one Willis in Seven Dials. But one can see that there is a rich set of allusions to other contexts at work in his treatment of articulation. The shop is famously a panorama of spare-parts:

> "You're casting your eye round the shop Mr Wegg. Let me show you a light. My working bench. My young man's bench. A Wice. Tools. Bones, warious. Skulls, warious. Preserved Indian baby. African ditto. Bottled preparations, warious. Everything within reach of your hand, in good preservation. The mouldy ones a-top. What's in those hampers over them again, I don't quite remember. Say, human warious. Cats. Articulated English baby. Dogs. Ducks. Glass eyes, warious. Mummied bird. Dried cuticle, warious. Oh dear me! That's the general panoramic view." (81)

The list is a series of parts waiting for (w)holes in which to fit. This is a vision of pure contingency, of an inarticulate landscape of objects, whose only achievable linguistic form in this passage is the list. The counterpart to this post-imperial scattering of body-parts, the whole to which these anatomical items quietly yearn or point, is a form of resurrection. And the reader is given a glimpse of this at the end of this

---

[11] See Ulrich 2006 for these details about Carlyle.

chapter: as Wegg leaves the shop after his first visit, he feels a slight
unease about what he perceives as movement behind him:

> Mr Wegg, looking back over his shoulder as he pulls the door open by the
> strap, notices that the movement so shakes the crazy shop, and so shakes a
> momentary flare out of the candle, as that the babies–Hindoo, African and
> British–the "human warious," the French gentleman, the green-glass-eyed
> cats, the dogs, the ducks, and all the rest of the collection, show for an
> instant as if paralytically animated... (85)

The chapter is called "Mr Wegg looks after himself," a phrase which
refers, beyond his rampant egoism, to his Anatomy; to the fact that he is
visiting in order to buy back his leg which has been purchased by Mr
Venus as part of a "job-lot," an article to which he refers in such a
intimately synechdochic fashion that its identity is never in doubt, despite
its grammatical impossibility:

> "Where am I?"
> "You're somewhere in the back shop across the yard, sir; and, speaking
> quite candidly, I wish I'd never bought you of the Hospital Porter."
> "Now look here, what did you give for me?"
> "Well" replied Venus, blowing his tea, his head and face peering out of
> the darkness, as if he were modernising the old original rise in his family:
> "you were one of a warious lot, and I don't know."
> Silas puts his point in the improved form of "What will you take for
> me?"
> "Well," replies Venus, still blowing his tea, "I'm not prepared, at a
> moment's notice, to tell you, Mr Wegg."
> "Come! According to your own account, I'm not worth much," Wegg
> reasons persuasively.
> "Not for miscellaneous working in, I grant you, Mr Wegg; but you
> might turn out valuable yet as a"–here Mr Venus takes a gulp of tea, so hot
> it makes him choke, and sets his weak eyes watering: "as a Monstrosity, if
> you'll excuse me." (82)

The dispersal of the integral, organic Self, and the image of the Body
as its guarantee, threatens here to increase just at the point of containment,
with the mention of "Monstrosity," which is the explicit point of entry of
the Grotesque Body. Here, it implies the popular world of the circus. And
this movement accompanies, on the one side, the dynamic of commercial
haggling. The counterpoint being the brief parodic appearance of Venus
Anadyomene, or Venus Rising, in the steam of the tea, like the spray of
the Aegean, one of the points of maximum beauty in the Western

tradition's representation of the integrality of the human body and the human soul.

Not all severed limbs, of course, have the same effect on the viewer. Consider the shift of tone in the following brief moment, still in Venus's shop. Wegg encounters something at about knee-height in the half-dark: "On his taking the candle to assist his search, Mr Wegg observes that he has a convenient little shelf near his knees, exclusively appropriated to skeleton hands, which have very much the appearance of wanting to lay hold of him" (80-1). Here, in Dickens's humour, there is just a playful flicker of fear, of the uncanny; which gives us a different tradition of dispersed synechdoche, the Gothic. Severed legs are Grotesque; severed hands are Uncanny. I'm thinking here of the disturbing chapter in Sheridan Le Fanu's novel, *The House By The Churchyard* (1863), of a house haunted by a "Hand," of the adaptation of that motif into "The Beast With Five Fingers," by W.F. Magee, a famous horror story of the late Victorian anthologies; a motif which was eventually adapted into a late German expressionist movie, "The Hands of Orlac." The Victorians were peculiarly sensitive to hands as the vehicle of emotion and inner feelings of all kind–witness Tennyson's "In Memoriam," a poem which is an encyclopaedia of the power of that particular affective synechdoche. The "severed hand" is a sub-motif in the Gothic tradition, which implies a dispersal of the most emotionally intimate organ in human bodily self-image, beside perhaps the eyes, which figure in Hoffmann's famous story, "Der Sandmann," and in Freud's psychoanalytic reconstruction of the "case" of castration-fear, which he thinks it recounts. There are also earlier French examples of the "severed hand" motif as a frightening image, and this particular dispersal is connected with Guy de Maupassant too.[12]

Bakhtin's historical account of the fortunes of the Grotesque in the 19th century registers an overlap between what we would perhaps now call the Gothic or Fantastic and what he labels comprehensively as the Romantic Grotesque, that is, the "expression of [a] subjective, individualistic outlook

---

[12] See Milner 1971, Vol. 1, 483, for some instances of the motif in the French *Fantastique* of the 1830s; Milner suggests a relation between Nerval's *La Main de gloire* and the Satanic bargain of a hand in a gruesome tale called *Dieu et le Diable* by Alphonse Karr; also see 530-2 of that same volume on Gautier's obsession with hands (as "la griffe de Satan") in various of his tales. For Maupassant, see the introduction to Maupassant 1989, xv, where it is claimed that Maupassant's morbidity was encouraged by Swinburne, who presented him with the mummified hand of a parricide "as a reward for helping to rescue him from drowning near Etretat."

very different from the carnival folk concept of previous ages, although still containing some carnival elements" (Bakhtin 1984, 36), in which "laughter is conquered by fear." And he traces this new movement to Sterne's "peculiar transposition of Rabelais' and Cervantes' world concept into the subjective language of the new age" (36). The difference he maintains between "the black or Gothic Novel" and the New Grotesque is a relative one, between the predominant effects of Fear and the Uncanny in the case of the Gothic, and Laughter in the case of the Grotesque. The culmination of this overlap, after the *Sturm und Drang* dramatists (Lenz, Klinger, the young Tieck), is the work of Hippel, Jean Paul and Hoffmann "who strongly influenced the development of the new grotesque in the next period of world literature" (36). Both modes are thus for Bakhtin varieties of each other, which he calls the Romantic Grotesque; and both are rebellions against the classicism and cold rationalism of the eighteenth-century Enlightenment aesthetics. And both modes centre on the centrifugal *danse macabre* of synechdochic dis-articulation, and its concomitant resurrection.

"Paralytic Animacy" and Romantic Grotesque: The Case of Mr Dolls

Our Mutual Friend illustrates abundantly this overlap between the two modes of the Romantic Grotesque: the presence of the Grotesque Body in both the humorous grotesque and the gothic modes. I shall finish this discussion with the theme of "paralytic animacy" and the treatment of a minor character, called "Mr Dolls." Mr Dolls' real name is probably Mr Cleaver, but this is the name he is given by Eugene Wrayburn, because he recognises him as the father of Jenny Wren, otherwise known as Fanny Cleaver, the crippled dolls' dressmaker, in whose premises Lizzie Hexam, to whom Wrayburn is immensely attracted, at one time takes up residence. Mr Dolls is a dead-living man, one of the many walking corpses in this novel, an advanced alcoholic whose life has been preserved by his daughter, Jenny Wren, who rules him with a rod of iron. When Lizzie, in despair at the social gulf between them and terrified by the murderous attentions of Bradley Headstone, runs away from Eugene to a secret location on the river, her whereabouts are known only to Jenny, and the benevolent Jew, Riah. Letters, however, pass between Lizzie and Jenny. Mr Dolls, sensing a bargain, sells the information of Lizzie's whereabouts to Eugene for fifteen shillings' worth of rum, which will result in his long overdue death. Mr Dolls staggers into Covent Garden market amongst the other terminal drunks who, Arcimboldo-like, seem clad in "trodden vegetable refuse which is so like their own dress" says the narrator, "that perhaps they take the Market for a great wardrobe" (Dickens 1989, 729), where he is set upon, "as in a gratuitous drama," by a company of barefoot "young savages" with gleeful violence. The elements of carnival grotesque here have been subdued, but the comic structure is still visible, despite the mordant tone. Mr Dolls is a puppet: he has been morally dead for some time, his consciousness having been substituted by temporary injections of alcohol. Taken on a stretcher (personified as a machine called "Stretcher") into an apothecary's shop, perhaps the last things he sees from the inside of the shop-window, are the faces of the crowd outside staring in, a street lamp behind them, suspended and refracted into deformed shapes by the rows of very large coloured bottles in the window:

> Thither he was brought; the window becoming from within a wall of faces, deformed into all kinds of shapes through the agency of globular red bottles, green bottles, blue bottles, and other coloured bottles. A ghastly light shining upon him that he didn't need, the beast so furious but a few minutes gone, was quiet enough now, with a strange mysterious writing on his face, reflected from one of the great bottles, as if Death had marked him "Mine." (731)

He becomes "it":

> It was carried home, and, by reason that the staircase was very narrow, it was put down in the parlour–the little working-bench being set aside to make room for it–and there, in the midst of the dolls with no speculation in their eyes, lay Mr Dolls with no speculation in his. (731)

The narrator echoes the address of Macbeth here to the ghost of the murdered Banquo which has appeared to him at the feast (*Macbeth*, III, iv, 96). But the death of Mr Dolls reverses this archetypally Gothic moment: it has the aspect of a cancelled resurrection. And "speculation" which means consciousness in Shakespeare has become a playful reference to the contemporary Victorian obsession with profit in the mordantly joking insistence of Dickens's narrator. Whether consciously or not,[13] in this final

---

[13] See Dickens's review of Mrs Catherine Crowe's anthology of ghost stories, "The Night-side of Nature; or, Ghosts and Ghost seers," first published in *The Examiner,* 26 February, 1848 (in Dickens 1996). By the late 1840s, on this evidence, he shows himself clearly aware of basic features of the German *Shauer* tradition, including the *Doppelganger*. He could also have read some Hoffmann and others in Carlyle's translations. Jules Barbier, later to become Jacques

cancelling of the "paralytic animation" of Mr Dolls, Dickens seems very close to Hoffmann at this point, and thus very close to Bakhtin's New or Romantic Grotesque.

References

Bakhtin, Mikhail. (1965) 1984. *Rabelais and His World*. Translated by Helene Iswolsky. Bloomington: Indiana University Press.

Carlyle, Thomas. (1838) 1987. *Sartor Resartus*. Edited with an Introduction and Notes by Kerry Sweeney and Peter Sabor. Oxford and New York: Oxford University Press.

Dickens, Charles. (1843-4) 1959. *Martin Chuzzlewit*. London: Oxford University Press.

—. (1843) 1960. *A Christmas Carol*. London: Oxford University Press.

—. (1846) 1998. *Pictures from Italy*. Edited by Kate Flint. London: Penguin.

—. (1850) 1996. "The Amusements of the People." In "Reports, Essays, and Reviews 1834-1851." In *Dent Uniform Edition of Dickens's Journalism,* Vol. 2, 80-91, edited by Michael Slater. London: Dent.

—. (1865) 1989. *Our Mutual Friend*. Edited by Michael Cotsell. London: Oxford World's Classics.

Cohen, Claudia. 1994. *The Fate of the Mammoth: Fossils, Myth and History.* Translated by William Rodamor. Chicago: Chicago University Press.

Goldberg, Michael. 1972. *Carlyle and Dickens*. Athens: University of Georgia Press.

Ledger, Sally. 2011. "Dickens, Natural History and *Our Mutual Friend*." *Partial Answers: Journal of Literature and the History of Ideas*. Vol. 9 (2): 363-98.

Lewes, Georges Henry. (1872) 1961. "Dickens in Relation to Criticism." In *The Dickens Critics,* edited by George H. Ford and Lauriat Lane Jr., 54-76. New York: Cornell University Press.

Maupassant, Guy de. (1881-90) 1989. *The Dark Side, Tales of Terror and the Supernatural.* Translated by A Kellett. New York: Carroll and Graf.

Milner, Max. (1960) 1971. *Le Diable dans la littérature française*. 2 vols. Paris: Jose Corti.

Offenbach's librettist, and Michel Carre, produced a first version of *The Tales of Hoffmann* at the Odeon theatre in Paris in 1851.

Padian, Kevin. 1997. "The Rehabilitation of Sir Richard Owen." *Bioscience.*
Vol. 47 (7): 446-53.

Rupke, Nicholas A. 1994. *Richard Owen: Victorian Naturalist.* New York
and London: Yale University Press.

Sage, Victor. 1999. "Dickens and Professor Owen: Portrait of a
Friendship." In *Le Portrait*, edited by Pierre Arnaud, 87-101. Paris:
Presses Universitaires Paris-Sorbonne.

Slater, Michael. 2009. *Charles Dickens.* New Haven and London: Yale
University Press.

Ulrich, John M. 2006. "Thomas Carlyle, Richard Owen and the
Palaeontological Articulation of the Past." *Journal of Victorian
Studies.* Vol. 11 (1): 30-58.

CHAPTER THIRTEEN

THE GROTESQUE AND DARWIN'S THEORY IN CHARLES DICKENS'S *GREAT EXPECTATIONS* AND WILKIE COLLINS'S *NO NAME*

DELPHINE CADWALLADER-BOURON

> It was the best of times, it was the worst of time, it was the age of wisdom, it was the age of foolishness, it was the epoch of belief, it was the epoch of incredulity, it was the season of Light, it was the season of Darkness, it was the spring of hope, it was the winter of despair. (Dickens 2008, 7)

This extract from *A Tale of Two Cities*, written in 1859, exemplifies what Dickens did throughout his literary career, which was to bring together contraries or contradictions. One aspect of his writing–brought to the fore by Michael Hollington[1]–is the grotesque which permeates the novels from the very outset. Animals and human beings, objects and machines commingle: Magwitch in *Great Expectations* morphs into a dog, Mrs Jellyby in *Bleak House* into an elephant, Mrs Sparsit, spying on Louisa (*Hard Times*), into a smouldering fence. Examples of this kind are legion in Dickens, but this vision of life is not merely Dickensian, it is decidedly Victorian.

Wilkie Collins, who started writing fiction in 1850, was the most famous sensationalist novelist of the period. A prolific writer, Collins, like Dickens, seems to have been somewhat obsessed with the apparent permeability between the different realms of being. His characters are all made up of opposed and supposedly irreconcilable features: his men are surprisingly feminine and his women startlingly masculine; his spies, who have the discretion of mice and the cunning of foxes, are trapped within elephantine bodies, like Fosco in *The Woman in White* (1860). Cats, snakes and toads, as we will soon see, are genetically fused with human

---

[1] See Hollington 1984.

beings, who pounce on their prey or bask in the sun to warm up their cold skin and cool temper in *No Name* (1864). These "startling" ("startling" being one of Collins's favourite words throughout his career) crossings of boundaries between animal, man, woman and object seem to be a vestige of the Romantic imagination which pervades the Victorian vision of the world. Dickens and Collins use the fusion between different realms of existence as a forceful way of conveying the sense that the world and all things therein form a great continuum, an organic, breathing entity in which boundaries are blurred, it is organicist, rather than mechanistic, and holistic rather than dualist.

As early as *Dombey and Son*, Dickens introduces the idea that "things" are in flux, that "nothing," no *thing* is fixed, definable or identifiable for long:

"My dear Louisa must be careful of that cough," remarked Miss Tox.
"It's nothing," returned Mrs Chick. "It's merely change of weather. We must expect change."
"Of weather?" asked Miss Tox, in her simplicity.
"Of everything," returned Mrs Chick. "Of course we must. It's a world of change. Anyone would surprise me very much, Lucretia, and would greatly alter my opinion of their understanding, if they attempted to contradict or evade what is so perfectly evident. Change!" exclaimed Mrs Chick, with severe philosophy. "Why, my gracious me, what is there that does not change! Even the silkworm, who I am sure might be supposed not to trouble itself about such subjects, changes in all sorts of unexpected things continually." (Dickens 2002, 159)

For Dickens, the silkworm and Mrs Chick have the same surprising ability to change, evolve and react to weather or biology. Both partake of nature's unconscious and wonderful gift of life and in this I cannot but recognize–"anticipate" might be more accurate–the revolution that was to shake the Victorian world in 1859, a notion aptly summed up by Thomas Huxley in 1863, and which could be applied to a lot of grotesque characters at least in Collins:

It is a truth of very wide, if not universal, application, that every living creature commences its existence under a form different from, and simpler than, that which it eventually attains. (Huxley 1897, 81)

He is here of course referring to Darwin's theory and echoes the corresponding passage in *The Origin of Species*:

> There is grandeur in this view of life, with its several powers, having been
> originally breathed into a few forms or into one; and that, whilst this planet
> has gone cycling on according to the fixed law of gravity, from so simple a
> beginning endless forms most beautiful and most wonderful have been,
> and are being, evolved. (Darwin 1988, 154)

I readily admit however that using the word "revolution" to describe
the impact of Darwin's theory may be considered somewhat sensationalist.
As a matter of fact, Darwin's theory did not come as much of an
intellectual shock to Dickens or Collins when it was published in 1859.
The notion that man has more than a little of the animal in him was
commonplace in their novels well before 1859, and Darwin's view of life
as constant variation from a model or archetype was very much part of the
Victorian *Weltanshauung*. The idea of a developing, as opposed to a
created, ordered and immutable, universe came as no surprise to George
Eliot for instance, who thus wrote to Barbara Bodichon about her reading
of Darwin's theory:

> We[2] have been reading Darwin's Book on the "Origin of Species" just
> now: it makes an epoch, as the expression of his thorough adhesion, after
> long years of study, to the Doctrine of Development. (Eliot 1985, xx)

Darwin, who reduces all phenomena to community, all knowledge to
unity, might easily have sided with Dickens when he said to Forster: "it is
my infirmity to fancy relations in things that are not apparent" (Forster
1874, 592), thus between wasps and human beings, between moths and
gorillas, between basic cells and complex organisms.

However, even if Darwin's theory came as no shock to Dickens
intellectually speaking, I firmly believe that it was emotionally devastating
to him, as can be guessed from his particular handling of the Grotesque in
his post-Darwinian novel, *Great Expectations* (1861). After 1859, the new
contradictions that Dickens had to face were not, as in the incipit of *A Tale
of Two Cities*, between antagonistic forces at work in society at large, but
his own inner struggle between the warring forces of mind and instinctive
feeling, which he ultimately resolved in favour of a vision of life,
Darwin's, which he however instinctively hated.

I will concentrate on two post-Darwinian novels: *No Name* published
in 1864 by Wilkie Collins, and *Great Expectations*. Even though, on the
surface, they use similar types of commingling, the aesthetics of the

---

[2] Eliot means G.H. Lewes and herself.

Grotesque in these two novels, published within three years of each other, reveals widely differing reactions to Darwin.

Collins and *No Name*

Magdalen's evolution and adaptation to her environment

Magdalen Vanstone is the main character of the novel and, from the very outset, she stands in sharp contrast to her sister Norah: Magdalen is, according to the circumstances, adaptable, supple, ever-changing:

> The whole countenance [...] was rendered additionally striking by its extraordinary mobility. The large, electric, light-grey eyes were hardly ever in repose; all varieties of expression followed each other over the plastic, ever-changing face, with a giddy rapidity which left sober analysis far behind in the race. (Collins 1998, 14)

Norah on the other hand is fixity itself, reliable, constant, but ultimately resigned to her fate. The differences between Norah and her sister, if treated as mere anecdotes at the beginning of the novel, become the core of the plot as the story gets to the death of their parents. Having had no time to marry, the Vanstones leave their daughters penniless, all their fortune going to the father's horrible brother, Noel Vanstone, who won't help them. Having to leave the house in which they were brought up as ladies, Norah accepts her fate dispassionately and becomes a humble governess whereas Magdalen is unable to become what she is not at heart though she tries, like Norah, to be a governess. She thus feels the violence of what is imposed upon her and expresses it physiologically before her departure, as if biologically anticipating the geographical change she knows she will have to endure:

> Something in her expression had altered, subtly and silently; something which made the familiar features suddenly look strange, even to her sister and Miss Garth. (156)

A change however visible to Mr Clare:

> "What is this mask of yours hiding?" he asked, forcing her to bend to him, and looking close into her face. "Which of the extremes of human temperature does your courage start from–the dead cold or the white hot?" (158)

As a matter of fact, both cold and hot blood constitute Magdalen's animal-like biological possibilities, and she has the characteristics of both a cat and a snake at the beginning of the novel:

> The girl's exuberant vitality asserted itself all over her, from head to foot. Her figure [was] taller than her sister's, taller than the average of woman's height; instinct with such a seductive, serpentine suppleness, so lightly and playfully graceful, that its movements suggested, not unnaturally, the movements of a young cat. (14)

Within the snug domestic life her parents offer her, the catlike nature of Magdalen, who purrs when her hair is combed long enough, expresses itself to the full. But at the end of Book I, Magdalen develops her other biological possibility, as the narration is about to unfold what was encapsulated in only two words: her "serpentine suppleness." Magdalen slowly turns into a cold-blooded and manipulative creature in Book II as she enters a universe infested with other reptilians, some far more aggressive than she is, like Mrs Lecount "hissing emphasis on every syllable" (294) as she talks to Magdalen and recognises the snake inside the young woman.

Magdalen's basic nature is so changeable and adaptable that it cannot be contained. She cannot "struggle" (the word is used several times) against her biological necessity. Twice in the novel she tries to live within set limits unsuited to her needs. As she leaps catlike out of domestic life, incapable of becoming a governess in Book I, she is unable to kill herself, her "leaping blood" refusing instinction:

> [...] despair strengthened her with a headlong fury against herself. In one moment, she was back at the table; in another, the poison was once more in her hand.
> She removed the cork, and lifted the bottle to her mouth.
> At the first cold touch of the glass on her lips, her strong young life leapt up in her leaping blood, and fought with the whole frenzy of its loathing against the close terror of Death. (498)

Magdalen is also defined in terms of species, and a developing one at that, throughout the novel. As her environment changes and her nature adapts, she is redefined. First a Vanstone in Book I, she then morphs, in hostile circumstances, into the "Wragge" species (Book II). Wragge is an uncle, "a species of relation" (210) her mother hid from her daughters because he is a swindler, a man who defines himself as such in terms belonging to natural sciences, dividing and subdividing his group, saying his species is "Rogue" and that he belongs to the variety of "Swindlers" or "Moral Agriculturists:"

> "Swindler is nothing but a word of two syllables. S, W, I, N, D–swind; L, E, R–ler; Swindler. Definition: A moral agriculturist; a man who cultivates the field of human sympathy. I am that moral agriculturist, that cultivating man. Narrow-minded mediocrity, envious of my success in my profession, calls me a Swindler. What of that? The same low tone of mind assails men in other professions in a similar manner–calls great writers, scribblers– great generals, butchers–and so on. It entirely depends on the point of view. Adopting your point, I announce myself intelligibly as a Swindler." (211)

Magdalen has inherited the scoundrel potential from her mother's side of the family and it is about to become apparent in her behaviour. However at the end of Book II, Magdalen is a victim of her adaptability and she becomes stronger than Wragge, who then has to let her go, after she marries Vanstone and leads him to his death.

Book III is the last step of her evolution as she is once more destitute, Mrs Lecount having managed to deshinherit her. The whole inheritance goes to Admiral George Bartram and Magdalen becomes a servant in his house, obsessively chasing her father's money. This last transformation, as in Darwin's theory, owes much to chance, as the clothes and figure of a servant perfectly fit a worn-out and much thinner Magdalen, conveniently weakened by all her forced previous adaptations.

Variation

If the idea of development or growth is a keystone of Darwin's theory, that of "variation" mentioned earlier is just as important both to *The Origin* and to *No Name*. Collins uses the image of animals to show that Magdalen is such a wide variation from her own supposed species that she no longer belongs to it and is, all through the novel, in search of her own species, never quite locating it since her species is never quite to be defined. Magdalen is first introduced as a different kind of bird:

> Her hair was of that purely light-brown hue, unmixed with flaxen, or yellow, or red–which is oftener seen on the plumage of a bird than on the head of a human being. (13)

Magdalen seems more akin to the bird species than to her human parents and does not fit in:

By one of those strange caprices of Nature, which science leaves still
unexplained, the youngest of Mr. Vanstone's children presented no
recognizable resemblance to either of her parents. How had she come by
her hair? How had she come by her eyes? Even her father and mother had
asked themselves those questions. (13)

Variation is a fundamental idea in *The Origin*: Darwin shows that
species change over generations but keep enough characteristics to remain
in the confines of their particular species:

As many more individuals of each species are born than can possibly
survive; and as, consequently, there is a frequently recurring struggle for
existence, it follows that any being, if it vary however slightly in any
manner profitable to itself, under the complex and sometimes varying
conditions of life, will have a better chance of surviving, and thus
be *naturally selected*. From the strong principle of inheritance, any selected
variety will tend to propagate its new and modified form. (Darwin 1988,
108)

The question thus raised is what happens when an individual has
undergone such wide variation that it no longer belongs to the group?
Magdalen is typically the overlapping individual, the one who has evolved
beyond the limitations of the Vanstones.

Fusion

The very way Collins generates his animal-human hybrids or
"grotesques" is worth focusing on. He does not use metaphor, nor does he
yield to comparison. He actually never allows any distance between man
and animal. Mrs Lecount and Magdalen are not *like* toads and snakes: their
very essence is reptilian, as if genetically encoded within them. Magdalen
is serpentine, Mrs Lecount hisses. From the very first encounter between
the two varieties of snake Lecount and Magdalen, Collins conditions his
reader to think about reptilians attacking each other every time they meet,
and he does so by forcing the reader to have stereoscopic vision at all
times.

The first confrontation begins with the description of the vivarium in
the background ("there sat solitary, cold as the stone, brown as the stone,
motionless as the stone, a little bright-eyed toad," 274) and ends with the
snake ("the sight of the hideous little reptile sitting placid on his rock
throne, with his bright eyes staring impenetrably into vacancy, irritated
every nerve in her body," 279). The association between toads, snakes and
women is made obvious by sheer location, because the characters in

question are standing next to the vivarium. The essence of the snake has contaminated Lecount's body. Hence, when she enters a room, "her figure [...] glide[s] smoothly over the ground; it flow[s] in sedate undulations when she walk[s]" (276), or she hisses while her "hands [...] smoothly slid[e] one over the other" (277). After this first introduction of the reptilian element, Collins never needs to make direct comparisons with Lecount's creatures. Having assimilated the essence of the snake, she confidently carries its cold indifference with her:

> She was dressed with her customary elegance and propriety; and she was the only one of the party, on that sultry summer's day, who was perfectly cool in the hottest part of the journey. (383)

Dickens and Darwin

Dickens on the other hand uses grotesque metaphors. Men and animals are not fused, in a Collisian manner, in *Great Expectations*; they co-exist and resemble each other. Magwitch often says he would like to be an animal ("I wish I was a frog. Or a eel," Dickens 1999, 12), thus clearly indicating that he is *not*, unlike Mrs Lecount. Pip compares him to a dog: "the man took strong sharp sudden bites, just like the dog" (21) and explains in the same chapter "I now noticed a decided similarity between the dog's way of eating and the man's" (21). In fact, the same process is at work in both examples: the narrative brings man and animal together while stating their irreducible difference and their impossibility to fuse.

There are numerous examples of this technique throughout the novel: Magwitch is compared to a clock "something clicked in his throat as if he had works in him like a clock and was going to strike" (21). Sarah Pocket is compared to a walnut, "a little dry brown corrugated old woman, with a small face that might have been made of walnut shells" (71). In this example again, Dickens keeps the two elements of comparison (human face and walnut) separate by erecting a rhetorical barrier between them ("might have been").

In *Great Expectations* Dickens doesn't use the Darwinian concept of growth either. Miss Havisham does not change, nor does she age throughout the novel. She, like Norah, is fixity itself, not an expression of Darwinian growth. All the clocks have been stopped at twenty to nine, and she is still dressed in bridal clothes, or rather not fully dressed as one shoe–not put on some thirty years before–is missing. She is compared to a vampire, to a ghost, to a spider, all grotesque elements indicating her heartlessness.

Certain characters *do* change in *Great Expectations*. It is a *Bildungsroman* in which the central character is said to undergo some profound change. Dickens however focuses more on the result of growth (Biddie refers to a grown-up Pip), than on the process itself, unlike Collins. At the end of the original ending for instance, Estella says she has changed, and the reader is asked to believe it:

> In her face and in her voice, and in her touch, she gave me the assurance, that suffering had been stronger than Miss Havisham's teaching, and had given her a heart to understand what my heart used to be. (359)

Dickens even seems to go one step further by challenging the very notion of resemblance, which is the prime observation underlying Darwin's work. Charles Darwin and Richard Owen, a paleontologist,[3] both worked on bones and what became known in science as homologies.[4] They both observed that there was a similarity of structure between different-sized organisms: small animals were structured like medium and larger ones; similar metabolic mechanisms were at work in moths and elephants. From the observation of resemblances, Darwin drew the conclusion that these species were related to common ancestors and had evolved from them (through variation, adaptation, growth, natural selection and mating). Owen on the other hand saw evidence of fixity in the record: for him, one archetype (created by God) was reproduced in each species because it was perfect, and various species did not cross the preordained boundaries between them, least of all mating with individuals that did not belong to their species (a most shocking idea which at the time laid the grounds for all the base attacks against Darwin's theory). Resemblance, for Owen, came from the fact that one and the same hand shaped all species ("and God made the beast of the earth after his kind, and cattle after their kind, and every thing that creepeth upon the earth after his kind: and God saw that it was good," Genesis 1:25).

Magdalen is typically a Darwinian character. Through his comparison of Magdalen and Norah, Collins dramatizes two antagonistic theories: evolution against fixity, Darwinism against an Owenian vision of life. Dickens on the other hand creates Owenian characters. From the very beginning, Pip is a very poor reader as he misconstrues resemblances. He

---

[3] Richard Owen, "the only man Darwin ever hated" (Padian, 1997, 5), was a paleontologist and a renowned scientist of the great Victorian mid-period.
[4] Owen worked with Darwin, then a student, on bones and they both observed homologies (i.e. structural similarities between different species). Yet, Owen and Darwin interpreted those homologies in two different ways (see text).

first confuses the shapes of the letters on his parents' tombstones with their physical features:

> The shape of the letters on my father's [tombstone] gave me an odd idea that he was a square, stout, dark man with curly black hair. From the character and turn of the inscription, "*Also Georgiana Wife of the Above*," I drew a childish conclusion that my mother was freckled and sickly. (9)

This section is quite didactic and warns the reader against Pip's childish and mistaken representation and understanding of the world around him. Throughout the novel, each time Pip fuses two elements, he is mistaken, and each time he is mistaken, the reader is informed of that by the fact that Pip feels discomfort, fear or guilt. When Pip first visits Satis House, he is frightened by the sight of Miss Havisham, precisely because he superimposes, fuses, and thus confuses two elements, here Miss Havisham and waxwork or corpses:

> Once, I had been taken to see some ghastly wax-work at the Fair, representing I know not what impossible personage lying in state. Once, I had been taken to one of our old marsh churches to see a skeleton in the ashes of a rich dress, that had been dug out of a vault under the church pavement. Now wax-work and skeleton seemed to have dark eyes that moved and looked at me. I should have cried out, if I could. (50)

The same process is at work when Pip feels terribly guilty about the attack on his sister. As Mr. Wopsle reads *George Barnwell*, a play in which the hero is tried for murder, Mrs Joe is assaulted by Orlick. Pip's imagination conflates the two scenes: "With my head full of George Barnwell, I was at first disposed to believe that *I* must have had some hand in the attack upon my sister" (96). What Dickens points as Pip's mistake is exactly the mental process at work in Darwinian theory: Pip confuses the actual murder and the fictional one, believing that if two elements resemble each other, then they must be biologically linked. The two scenes share the same scenario and occur at the same time, but they belong to two different realms, which do not overlap.

Dickens thus accentuates the power of comparison, which separates or divides much more than it fuses. In Dickens's estimation, fusion may well amount to confusion. The idea that he might prefer Owen's archetypal theory to Darwin's theory of evolution may be found in the non-fictional writings published in *Household Words*, as the very title of Abraham Hart's article ("Nature's Greatness in Small Things") seems to show:

Thus, beyond and above the law of design in creation, stands the law of unity of type, and unity of structure. No function so various, no labours so rude, so elaborate, so dissimilar, but this cell can build up the instrument, and this model prescribes the limits of its shape. Through all creation the microscope detects the handwriting of power and ordnance. It has become the instrument of a new revelation in science, and speaks clearly to the soul as to the mind of man. (Hart 1858, 99)

Hart claims that "the instrument of the revelation of science," the microscope, "speaking clearly to the soul as to the mind of man," has revealed a system of universal harmony and of reassuringly stable archetypes. Darwin's theory may have spoken to Dickens's mind but not, it would appear, to his soul. And yet Dickens, in what was perhaps a painful inner struggle, did accept Darwin's thesis on the origin of species. In this respect, Dickens was–as Levine convincingly argues in *Darwin and the Novelists*–a man of his time, leaning towards modernity rather than the past and having already divined the "Darwinian connection" between all forms of life, all things, as early as *Bleak House* (1852).

Let me conclude with another section from the incipit of *Great Expectations*, in which Dickens has Pip's eyes scan the horizon:

Ours was the marsh country, down by the river, within, as the river wound, twenty miles of the sea. My first most vivid and broad impression of the identity of things, seems to me to have been gained on a memorable raw afternoon towards evening. At such a time I found out for certain, that this bleak place overgrown with nettles was the churchyard; and that Philip Pirrip, late of this parish, and also Georgiana wife of the above, were dead and buried; and that Alexander, Bartholomew, Abraham, Tobias, and Roger, infant children of the aforesaid, were also dead and buried; and that the dark flat wilderness beyond the churchyard, intersected with dikes and mounds and gates, with scattered cattle feeding on it, was the marshes; and that the low leaden line beyond, was the river; and that the distant savage lair from which the wind was rushing, was the sea; and that the small bundle of shivers growing afraid of it all and beginning to cry, was Pip. (Dickens 1999, 9-10)

This is typically the world before Genesis. In Genesis, names pre-exist because "in the beginning," God, the Word, breathed life and order into all things, naming them and assigning them to their allotted roles in Creation. In this incipit, things pre-exist in confusion. Here, syntactically and ontologically, the world is Darwinian: things look frightening, incomprehensible and messy. How can the reader understand, for instance, that "this bleak place overgrown with nettles" is the churchyard, before Pip names it? Dickens witnesses a terrifying, despairing, meaningless and cruel world where the reader is made to feel as dizzy as the narrator changing scales over and over again. The focus shifts from wide to narrow, to wide and then narrow again, across "the dark flat wilderness" before settling at last on a "small bundle of shivers growing afraid of it all." Is Dickens then referring to Pip or to himself?

References

Collins, Wilkie. (1862-3) 1998. *No Name.* Oxford: Oxford World's Classics.

Darwin, Charles. (1859) 1988. *The Origin of Species.* London: W. Pickering.

Dickens, Charles. (1849) 2002. *Dombey and Son.* London: Penguin Classics.

—. (1859) 2008. *A Tale of Two Cities.* Oxford: Oxford University Press.

—. (1861) 1999. *Great Expectations.* New-York: Norton Critical Edition.

Eliot, George. (1860) 1985. *The Mill on the Floss.* London: Penguin Classics.

Forster, John. 1872-4. *The Life of Charles Dickens.* Volume 3. London: Chapman & Hall.

Hart, Abraham. (1857) 1858. "Nature's Greatness in Small Things." In *Littell's Living Age*, edited by E. Littell. 2nd Series, Vol. 20, 97-9. Boston: Littell, Son & Cie.

Hollington, Michael. 1984. *Dickens and the Grotesque.* Beckenham (Kent): Croom Helm.

Huxley, Thomas Henry. (1863) 1897. *Man's Place in Nature, and Other Anthropological Essays.* New-York: Appleton & Company.

Levine, George. 1988. *Darwin and the Novelists: Patterns of Science in Victorian Fiction.* Cambridge, Mass.: Harvard University Press.

Padian, Kevin. 1997. "The Rehabilitation of Sir Richard Owen." *BioScience.* Vol. 47, n°7: 446-53.

CHAPTER FOURTEEN

THE FEMALE GROTESQUE IN DICKENS

MARIANNE CAMUS

The grotesque is a fluctuating concept that has evolved in time. In order to avoid the temptation to digress–and end up with a grotesque essay–Arthur Clayborough's basic definition has been chosen as a particularly relevant starting point. It centres on form and defines the grotesque as "characterized by its rejection of the natural conditions and organization and the combining of heterogeneous forms. Natural physical wholes are disintegrated and the parts fantastically redistributed" (Clayborough 1965, 3). Clayborough also refers to Montaigne who abstains from any moral judgment on the grotesque and writes: "les crotesques (*sic*) […] sont des peintures fantasques n'ayant grace qu'en la variété et estrangeté" (in Clayborough 1965, 3). A grotesque, to start with, is then the representation or the invention of a creature impossible to find in nature. This definition, based on form, must however be considered in the light of the increasingly insistent moral aspects of the grotesque, of which Clayborough himself is aware. This is all the truer when it comes to Dickens, so often perceived as one of the moral voices of his time. I will attempt to argue that Victorian morality or ideology, when it concerns women, is an important element in the construction of nineteenth-century female grotesques.

The first question that arises from this definition is whether the female characters in Dickens (and in many Victorian novels) cannot all be labelled grotesques. Most of them are variants of the prevalent female stereotypes, themselves products of the masculine imagination, and it is obvious that these stereotypes are constructed from elements not only at odds with one another but often irreconcilable. The most obvious example is that of the "Angel in the House" which immediately suggests wings. The crinoline may even be a Victorian version of these wings. The *femme fatale* is another example with her basilisk eyes and long wavy hair as signs of her half-human half-serpent nature. Feminist critics have pointed to the absurd dimension of these constructions, which leads, naturally as it were, to the female grotesque in Victorian fiction in general and in Dickens's novels in particular.

The question is particularly relevant when one considers the stereotype as an imaginary construction breaking the bonds of realism, freeing the imagination and allowing the creation of characters which become even more bizarre with the addition of extravagant traits to the existing stereotypical ones. Female characters might then be considered as doubly grotesque, going from the polite grotesque of the stereotype to the grotesque in full.

It is true that when one looks at Dickens's grotesques the first impression is that there is no difference of treatment between male and female characters. In order to create his grotesques, Dickens used anything and everything at hand, as we know. The animal element produced serpentine Uriah Heep, the vegetal element Sarah Pocket.[1] His favourite technique was the conjunction of the animate and the inanimate: Wemmick, the wooden man, is the exact counterpart of Miss Murdstone, "[the] metallic lady" (Dickens 1990, 47).

But a comparison of Wemmick at the beginning of *Great Expectations* and Mrs. Skewton, the female puppet in *Dombey and Son,* quickly reveals significant differences. Wemmick is a mechanically animated mixture of flesh and blood, wood and metal components (the letter box) while Dickens makes Mrs. Skewton grotesque by adding to her body accessories supposed to be typically feminine: false hair, false teeth, rouge, etc. The grotesque is here constructed by the accumulation of signs of the feminine on a female human being. The narrator makes it clear that it is the gap between the youthful aspect of the accessories and the advanced age of the person that generates absurdity and ridicule. The question is, however, whether the end product is a grotesque or a simple caricature.

The doubt subsists when one considers the change that Mrs. Skewton undergoes when she withdraws to her bedroom, where she is undressed by her maid:

> The painted object shrivelled underneath her hand; the form collapsed, the hair dropped off, the arched dark eyebrows changed to scanty tufts of grey; the pale lips shrunk, the skin became cadaverous and loose; an old, worn,

---

[1] In *Dickens and the Grotesque*, Michael Hollington rightly points out the link between Sarah Pocket and Arcimboldo's portraits (Hollington 1984, 220).

yellow, nodding woman, with red eyes, alone remained in Cleopatra's place. (Dickens 2002, 431)

If the artifices she uses to hide her age turn her into a grotesque, the return to the original human being, the text implies, only induces another form of grotesque. Unlike Wemmick, who becomes less of a machine and more of a man as he gets nearer his private "castle" in the evening, Mrs. Skewton is further objectified, inspiring only feelings of pity or disgust. What is problematic is that the second, private, level of grotesque is based on the work of time on beauty which is nothing if not natural. This seems to suggest that an old woman is grotesque *per se*, whether she tries to hide her age or not.

Gender, then, seems to condemn women to become grotesque in so far as the guiding reference is not their humanity but rather their femininity, as defined by stereotypes. Worth noting too is the fact that Wemmick was born the way he appears to the reader and is therefore an innocent grotesque, while Mrs. Skewton is responsible for her appearance, as to the grotesque of old age, she adds the grotesque of all the objects with which she tries to counter its effects.

She is not the only example in Dickens's fiction of women perceived as grotesque because they do not conform to stereotypes. Ugly young women like Miss Squeers in *Nicholas Nickleby* or Charity Pecksniff in *Dombey and Son* are classified among the grotesques by Michael Slater on the basis of their physical appearance. However if ugliness were enough to create the grotesque, many, if not most, characters (men as well as women) would be considered grotesque.[2] Flora is treated in the same way as Miss Squeers or Charity Pecksniff, and is called by Slater "a grotesque travesty" of past love (Slater 1983, 69). But the description of the character reveals the gap between the construction and the reception of a character:

> Flora, always tall, had grown to be very broad too, and short of breath; but that was not much. Flora, whom he had left a lily, had become a peony; but that was not much. Flora, who had seemed enchanting in all she had said and thought, was diffuse and silly. That was much. Flora, who had been spoiled and artless long ago, was determined to be spoiled and artless now. That was a fatal blow. (Dickens 1985-2, 191-2)

---

[2] Cf. George Eliot's description of the humble beauty of old peasant women, pot-bellied Adonises and waddling Venuses in *Adam Bede*.

Her looks do not make her grotesque in the narrator's eye, as this passage makes clear ("that was not much"). The grotesque seems to originate in the conjunction of a thickened body and a rigidified mind. The process, however, is fundamentally human and does not suggest any extra-human element. The narrator's intention is clearly to create a comic character or even a caricature, but does he intend a grotesque? Or does the reader himself, enmeshed in preconceived ideas and prejudices, produce this vision of the grotesque?

As far as Quilp and Mrs. Gamp are concerned, both perceived by generations of readers as archetypal Dickensian grotesques, the difference in the way they are characterised is even more obvious. There is no doubt about Quilp:

> So low in stature as to be quite a dwarf, though his head and face were large enough for the body of a giant. [...] The few fangs that were yet scattered in his mouth [...] gave him the aspect of a panting dog. (Dickens 1986, 65)

The mixture of animal, fairy-tale figure and human monster fits the definition of the grotesque from the start. Mrs. Gamp, though, is not described in the same way at all:

> She was a fat old woman, this Mrs. Gamp, with a husky voice and a moist eye, which she had a remarkable power of turning up, and only showing the white of it. Having little neck, it cost her some trouble to look over herself, if one may say so, to those to whom she talked. She wore a very rusty black gown, rather the worse for snuff, and a shawl and bonnet to correspond. (Dickens 1984, 378)

Neither being old and fat nor snuffing tobacco goes against human nature. Here the extravagance and heterogeneity of the grotesque are subjoined once again to a satire of those women who do not conform to the graceful ideal dreamt up by man. The question remains: why should the lack of beauty and charm man looks for in a woman turn her into a grotesque? Again, the grotesque is the reader's rather than the writer's construction. We have seen that Dickens's ambiguous stance in the example of Flora leaves the reader to think of the character as he pleases. This is also apparent in his description of Mrs. Todgers: "rather a bony and hard-featured lady, with a row of curls in front of her head, shaped like little barrels of beer; and on the top of it something made of net [...] which looked like a black cobweb" (182). He then qualifies this description by repeating on at least two occasions that Mrs. Todgers's ridiculous appearance hides a compassionate woman's heart. The narrator clearly attempts to alter the reader's immediate perception that a female character is grotesque because she does not fit any feminine stereotype.

The extreme form of this grotesque based on nonconformity to the notion of femininity as defined by stereotypes is that of the virile woman and the archetypal example, of course, is Sally Brass in *The Old Curiosity Shop*:

> Miss Sally Brass, then, was a lady [...] of a gaunt and bony figure, and a resolute bearing. [...] In face she bore a striking resemblance to her brother Sampson–so exact, indeed, was the likeness between them, that had it consorted with Miss Brass's maiden modesty and gentle womanhood to have assumed her brother's clothes in a frolic and sat down beside him, it would have been difficult for the oldest friend of the family to determine which was Sampson and which Sally, especially as the lady carried upon her upper lip certain reddish demonstrations, which if the imagination had been assisted by her attire, might have been mistaken for a beard. (Dickens 1986, 320-1)

Wemmick is half-man half-machine, Quilp half-man half-mythical character, Sally Brass is half-woman half-man, which implies that women belong to another species or another order than men. This confirms that the monstrosity of female characters is constructed on the degree of femininity they present, which is in itself a masculine construction and begs further the question of the quality of female grotesque. It can be seen as doubly removed from humanity, first in so far as fundamental human characteristics are forgotten or ignored, and then in the fact that the deformity or extravagance of the grotesque is developed from one aspect, namely gender, which is itself a major source of fantasy. But here again, Dickens's authorial intention to create a grotesque can be questioned, especially if Miss Trotwood is taken into account. Despite her masculine appearance and manners, the character is spared the status of grotesque by the growing complexity of her personality and the fact that she ends up as the archetype of the wise old woman who has learnt from her mistakes and is therefore fully human.

What in the end is most striking is that all the characters mentioned so far are presented as grotesque from the masculine point of view of what is natural or normal in a woman. Michael Hollington points to this in his book on the grotesque; as does Slater when he argues that the portrayal of Flora is probably revenge against Maria Beadnell; and that of Mrs. Gamp the expression of men's malaise when faced with what they see as feminine power: that is women's intimate connection with life and death.

But this only confirms that the universal quality of this type of grotesque–constructed by and for men who are, after all, only half of humanity–is being questioned.

Another point is that the stereotype is rooted in physical traits as signs of the mental and moral organization of a character. Many female grotesques, if analysed from this perspective, can be said to be based on deviance from what was seen as proper feminine qualities or virtues. This is particularly noticeable when it comes to the figure of the perfect wife and mother which provides the basis for most of Dickens's female grotesques. Mrs. Jellyby, whom Slater calls a "grotesque mother" (Slater 1983, 272), Mrs. Joe Gargery, Mrs. Clennam up to a point and even Mrs. Nickleby, in Slater's opinion, all belong to this category. The first three are grotesque simply because they fail as mothers. They are turned into monsters when they give up their primary function of reproduction and nurture, in favour of so-called masculine interests and ambitions. Mrs. Jellyby prefers the improvement of the world to housekeeping and child-minding, Mrs. Gargery has a definite taste for power and Mrs. Clennam puts business above everything else. They can thus be seen as variants of Sally Brass. They are clearly less grotesque physically but can be seen as more monstrous since they lack maternal feeling, which radically deprives them of humanity, specifically female humanity. On this level, writer and reader seem to share the same perception, the Victorian belief that a woman's primary role was to be a mother.

Mrs. Nickleby's case is not as clear; she is, to quote Slater, "grotesquely self-centred and self-satisfied, with the brain, as Gissing put it, of a 'Somerset ewe'" (16). Stupidity and self-centredness, though, are in fact equally shared by both sexes. Slater seems to accept unreservedly the idea that "butterfly-mindedness, illogicality, vanity, garrulousness, preoccupation with petty things, impracticality, sentimentality, proneness to romantic day-dreaming, exaggerated respect for social rank and conventions, complacent pride in superiority of female intuition" (223) are traits that make her unfit as a mother and therefore grotesque. Mrs. Nickleby is a comic character, the caricature of a woman who is simultaneously brainless and a mother, but nothing more. In addition to Slater's questionable conclusion, the vision of Mrs. Nickleby as a ewe, as stupid as it is stubborn, cannot be perceived in the novel. This view is the perception of a Victorian reader, Gissing, who amplifies the caricature and turns it into a grotesque–thus a masculine Victorian perception which Slater quotes, and simply accepts.

It is in fact their very humanity which draws female characters into the grips of the grotesque. When they remain within the framework of the feminine categories defined by the Victorians–fallen women, *femmes fatales*, pure virgins or "Angels in the House"–the Dickensian narrator does not use the distortion of the grotesque. But as soon as they test the limits of the stereotype they are either represented as grotesque by the narrator or perceived as grotesque by the (masculine) reader.

The influence of stereotyping is not, however, simply visible in the manipulations of supposedly feminine characteristics. It is at work in the writing itself. The novelist seems to allow his characters to take a step beyond the confines of the stereotype but never allows them to work free. This is apparent notably in the vitality and liveliness of characters. In comparing Quilp to Miss Havisham and Mrs. Gamp and their attitude to food–the first index of vitality–this is clear as Quilp's appetite needs no more comment than this:

> He ate hard eggs shell and all, devoured gigantic prawns with the heads and tails on, chewed tobacco and water-cress at the same time and with extraordinary greediness, drank boiling tea without winking, bit his fork and spoon till they bent again. (Dickens 1986, 86)

Even though they share a certain gothic extravagance (if he is a gargoyle, she is a mummy), Miss Havisham has no such appetite. She never eats or at least she is never seen eating. Despite her love of food and alcoholic beverages, Mrs. Gamp's appetite does not compare with Quilp's either. She remains very ladylike when she rejects the hashed mutton provided by her employers, orders with great nicety, as if it were medicine, the quantities of porter essential to her work, and keeps her gin in a teapot.

This appetite literally speaking is an index of the desire and capacity to act on others and on the world. Masculine grotesques, like Quilp or Uriah Heep, are active disturbers ceaselessly pursuing their aim; Quilp displaying frantic agitation; Uriah, slow and devious determination. Again, the contrast with Miss Havisham is telling, her only initiative being the setting up of a macabre charade of which she is the centre, immobile in her rejection of the world.

Lack of action also implies lack of power, which is probably more important in so far as it is a characteristic of both female stereotypes and female grotesques. Quilp destabilises everything and everyone around him, forcing Nell and her grandfather to flee. Uriah takes over Mr. Wickfield's business, his home and even his private life. Miss Havisham's only power is over Pip, and it is very much the power that he gives her as he admits himself.[3] The same is true of the other female characters: Miss Murdstone is simply her brother's aide and will not be able on her own to prevent David's and Dora's marriage. And if Mrs. Gamp rules, it is only over the sick, the dying and women in labour, which is power of very limited scope.[4]

If the passivity and lack of power generally associated with the feminine is the rule, there is, however, one field in which female grotesques are at liberty: they are free to say what they want. If, like that of their masculine counterparts, their speech is often repetitive and mechanical, one cannot help noticing that, in their case, it is also excessive and confused. This excess and confusion constitute the specificity of the female grotesque. This applies to many of the characters whose degree of grotesque has been questioned earlier, Mrs. Gamp being the most obvious example. If physically she is only comic, she becomes grotesque as soon as she speaks. The reader finds her extravagant digressions amusing at first, but these eccentric ravings soon become fatally attractive, drawing the reader into a maze of puzzlement, very much like the viewer who progressively becomes lost amidst the visual inventions of grotesque drawings. Further, the invention of Mrs. Harris, who appears as soon as Mrs. Gamp starts to speak, eventually constructs a sort of two-headed monster whose verbal exchanges spiral away and back, constituting a linguistic version of the original visual grotesque.

Like Mrs. Gamp, Flora enters the realm of the grotesque through the logorrhea that characterizes her, even more than her corpulence. Her discourse, interrupted by repetitions of "Arthur–I mean Mr. Arthur–or I suppose Mr. Clennam would be far more proper–but I am sure I don't know what I'm saying" (Dickens 1985-2, 192-3) goes, in beautiful disorder, from the good old times gone forever to Chinese women and their strange exotic charm, to the fortune Arthur must have made, to the difficulty of the Chinese language, to the weight of tea chests, to her horrid married woman's name, to her father and Mrs. Clennam facing each other like mad bulls, Paul and Virginia, etc. Her (to say the least) idiosyncratic syntax only adds to the absurdity, when she says for example: "I am persuaded you speak like a Native if not better for you were always quick and clever though immensely difficult no doubt" (616). Or when she speaks of the copy of *Paul and Virginia* sent back by Clennam: "if it had

---

[3] Even the power she tries to impose on Estella fails: the young woman refuses the role she has been brought up to play when she marries the worst man she can find, in an act of self-destructive rebellion.

[4] One could also mention Mrs Pipchin's ruling over young, isolated and helpless children.

only come back with a red wafer on the cover I should have known it meant Come to Pekin Nankeen and What's the third place barefoot" (617). The accumulation of phrases and sentences that alternatively entwine and unfurl is, again, the linguistic equivalent of the extravagant excrescences of certain grotesque drawings, by Pierre-Adrien Pâris for example; all the more so as they conceal or cover another order that is only perceptible to whoever can look, or listen.

This succession of apparently incongruous topics also characterises Mrs. Nickleby's speech: in a conversation with Kate she talks first about the disdainful manner in which she listened to her late husband's wooing, then goes on with how a nice summer day always makes her think of roast pork with sage and onion sauce, then mentions her daughter's christening, then the bird belonging to the lady at whose house she ate roast pork; parrot or small bird? And she concludes with: "it's just as well to be correct, particularly on a point of this kind, which is very curious and worth settling while one thinks about it" (Dickens 1985-1, 617). Here again, there is a unifying thread running through the tangle of digressions, the memory of her husband's dislike of pork carcasses at the butcher's because they reminded him of the babies he did not want.

What is striking in Mrs. Skewton's speech is its fantastic profusion, one example being the affectionate terms with which she favours Major Bagstock : "false creature," "perfidious goblin," "bad man," "abomination," "naughty infidel," or "barbarous being" (Dickens 2002, 317-27) to quote only a few collated over a dozen pages. The same profusion characterises her enthusiasm for nature and the spontaneity and sincerity it supposedly relays. This enthusiasm can be summed up in one sentence, in itself a perfect example of language grotesque: "Nature intended me for an Arcadian. [...] Cows are my passion. What I have ever sighed for, has been to retreat to a Swiss farm, and live entirely surrounded by cows–and china" (320).

These female characters' nonsensical speech contrasts with that of Quilp, Uriah Heep, Krook or Wemmick, who conversely always make sense. But if female grotesques reveal the capacity of language, under Dickens's pen at least, to rival with the invention of the original visual grotesque, the fact remains that such speech seems to be based on another aspect of non-conformity to the stereotypes that define women: they should remain silent or at best simply repeat what men say. Or perhaps, it is simply based on the age-old notion that women are irrepressible chatter-boxes. Whatever interpretation one chooses, the question of the validity and of the universality of this type of grotesque is still open.

This brings us back to the idea that a female character may be responsible for her own grotesqueness. For if Wemmick, Quilp, Uriah Heep or even Sally Brass are delineated as grotesque by the narrator, the female characters just mentioned transform themselves into grotesques. It is their imagination or their unnatural (from a feminine point of view) aspirations, transcribed in their behaviour or their language, that make them absurd. Therefore they carry full responsibility for the impression they make on the reader.

Female grotesques, in their differences based on patriarchal ideology and masculine expectations at a given moment, raise fundamental questions. Are they not examples–certainly negative, but examples all the same–of the mythification of women which Simone de Beauvoir and Betty Friedan identified in the twentieth century? A corollary is the question of women's feelings toward these grotesques: how did Victorian women react to them? Did they take them as a warning of what was in store for them if they transgressed the norms? Or were they seen as an encouragement to work at their own mythification? Or did they see them– as do many feminists today–as instances of the grotesque in masculine thinking with its tendency to de-humanise women because of a biological difference which feeds masculine fantasies?

In conclusion the rationale behind Dickens female grotesques needs to be reassessed. The ambiguity of the writing and of the reactions it provokes in readers has been evoked with reference to Mrs. Todgers and Miss Trotwood who, though they undoubtedly embody some aspects of the Victorian female grotesque, gradually become characters which are not only appealing as human beings but empowered or at least influential. Flora and her kindness and patience with her mad aunt can here be alluded to again. But Mrs. Boffin (*Our Mutual Friend*), a generally underestimated character, is of particular interest from this perspective. She is a comic character and the reader becomes aware of this as soon as she makes her appearance in her fashionable half of Boffin's Bower. But from the very beginning she is possessed of those human qualities which Dickens deemed essential, and throughout the novel, she is the one who makes most sense for the reader and, when she speaks, for her husband.

Dickens had recourse to all available means, including the clichés of his time, in order to attract and consolidate a wide readership. But he was above all a complex and sensitive artist, and his characterization of Mrs. Boffin shows that his perception and representation of Mankind, including women, were profound, more subtle and less stereotypical than they might appear to be at first sight.

References

Clayborough, Arthur. 1965. *The Grotesque in English Literature*. Oxford: Clarendon Press.

Dickens, Charles. (1839) 1985. *Nicholas Nickleby*. Harmondsworth: Penguin. [1985-1]

—. (1841) 1986. *The Old Curiosity Shop*. Harmondsworth: Penguin.

—. (1843-4) 1984. *Martin Chuzzlewit*. Harmondsworth: Penguin.

—. (1848) 2002. *Dombey and Son*. London: Penguin Books.

—. (1850) 1990. *David Copperfield*. New-York: Norton.

—. (1857) 1985. *Little Dorrit*. Harmondsworth: Penguin. [1985-2]

—. (1861) 1999. *Great Expectations*. New-York: Norton.

—. (1865) 1997. *Our Mutual Friend*. London: Penguin.

Hollington, Michael. 1984. *Dickens and the Grotesque*. London & Sidney: Croom Helm.

Slater, Michael. *Dickens and Women*. 1983. London: J. M. Dent & Sons Ltd.

CHAPTER FIFTEEN

ZULEIKA DOBSON BY MAX BEERBOHM: THE GROTESQUE OF NOT SUCH A GROSS TEXT

GILBERT PHAM-THANH

The Illustrated Zuleika Dobson is the sole novel by Max Beerbohm, and admittedly, it does not belong to the Canon. However, it still raises interest and remains in circulation, as evidenced by the working edition dating back to 2002. The poetics of this small singular text published in 1911 can be termed grotesque, even if this convenient label must be problematized, as hinted by the chronological discontinuity introduced in the evocation of the Warden of Judas College: "Hitherto the Duke had seen nothing grotesque in him" (Beerbohm 2002, 141). It remains that the Beerbohmian grotesque operates as a principle of heterogeneity which points to otherness inherent in turn-of-the-century England. Thus, it founds a pluriverse which reads in teratological terms subsumed by the hegemonic grand narratives of the time. Accordingly, uncommon objects are considered abnormal forms to be recorded and exhibited. Their monstrous presence is emblematized by the figure of the gargoyle, which is conjured up through a comparison to characterize Noakes, "looking like nothing so much as a gargoyle hewn by a drunken stone-mason for the adornment of a Methodist Chapel in one of the vilest suburbs of Leeds or Wigan" (328). The degenerative principle of degradation, which is typical of the grotesque being, is seen to expand with the text, adding unpalatable excrescences. The character is caught in a cumulative logic resulting in metamorphosis, with enough comically incongruous elements to determine the tone of the whole sequence and the measure of Beerbohm's grotesque. Other strange creatures will come along to fill up the teratological grid of *Zuleika Dobson*'s universe–often defamiliarizing early-twentieth-century British society, sometimes anticipating late-twentieth-century evolutions. They are usually eccentric, but not necessarily anomalous, and occasionally embody new modes of being which are acceptable, possibly desirable, though still inassimilable by all.

In his novel subtitled *An Oxford Love Story*, Beerbohm seeks inspiration in deformed memories of his Oxford student days. Accordingly, he locates Zuleika Dobson and John Dorset's romance in the great British university institution, considered in its capacity to deliver symbolic capital, although he turns this seat of symbolic power into a site of negotiation. At times in a mimetic style underlining the nature of the aesthetic project, *Zuleika Dobson* deploys a grotesque microcosm inhabited by creatures with ridiculously misshapen singularity. Their exaggerated features occasionally qualify them as monsters, in the eye of the reader, the characters and the narrator. Yet, the strategic position that Beerbohm secures on the socio-cultural scene of the turn of the century by resorting to the notion of the grotesque and the use of a parodic, playful poetics, proves to be an unstable one, most interestingly in the axiology of Edwardian heterosexist values, since the novel is dealing with romance. The study posits primarily that in this small text, Beerbohm's main achievement is the minorization–by making it equally grotesque–of the patriarchal grand narrative, which is supported by the realist discourse at the base of the great tradition of the novel. Hence Beerbohm's further opposition to the Realist mode of composition.

Taking in the anachronistic dimension of Oxford, Beerbohm first of all maps out a grotesque world–a dysmorphic place of picturesque oddity where the Law of the Father is not conducive to order. The failure of patriarchy is reported through the iconoclastic description of grotesque statues. They stand as ironical monuments revealing the incapacity of the figures of authority to found what is either good, right, true or beautiful. The busts of Roman emperors may give masculine presence in Oxford a hieratic dimension which mineralizes the patriarchal order. Nevertheless, grotesque focalization aims to underline the discredit of these dominant males by disclosing their quasi bestial, utterly trivial and most of all perfectly laughable personalities: "[…] sweat started from the brows of the Emperors. […] Who were lechers, they are without bodies; who were tyrants, they are crowned never but with crowns of snow" (4-5). The debauchees' animalism shows in the sweat running from their foreheads. Their ontic reduction is rendered by textual accumulation, while the staging of their disempowerment shifts failure from the physical sphere of complacent virility to a scene of symbolic castration. They must in effect have their whole bodies amputated in order to get their busts carved. Once phallic figures, they are now pathetic imitations of their former selves, and the text simply mirrors the destitution of these crownless emperors who can no longer ooze imperial dignity. Despite this humiliation, they remain capable of uncovering the grotesque part in real flesh-and-bone men, who creep in their shadow. Their towering position introduces a vertical axis, with the simple mortals crushed underneath their pedestal, at the bottom of hierarchy. This subordination is also conveyed by the repetition of the phrase "stared down at," which connotes contempt for mankind's fallen nature.[1] Dorset sinks even lower when the narrator summons the gods themselves, who deem his pretention ridiculous: "Shaking with laughter, the gods leaned over the thunder-clouds to watch him" (217).

At times through divine and divinized figures, it is in fact the whole town which proves to be demeaning for individuals, and the narrator has to admit that "Oxford walls have a way of belittling us" (92). He acknowledges this demotion by resorting to an anonymous collective *us* which bundles together a multiplicity of persons viewed as interchangeable and thus unworthy of special attention. And yet, Beerbohmian Oxford ultimately unifies these characters harmoniously, completing a grotesque universe that at most generates disconcerted surprise, puzzled curiosity or amused shock. This is indirectly alluded to by the author-narrator, who warns: "Sensitive reader, start not at the apparition [of Noakes]! Oxford is a nexus of anomalies" (40). The very structure of the metafictional comment–a shift from anecdote to general statement with a comfortably phatic address to the reader to start with–articulates a significant part of Beerbohm's art of the grotesque.

It is true that one comes across weird, grotesque male creatures which fail to match the gentleman's ideal. They are seen almost creeping out of primal mire, and could be confused with human spawn, treated in the bulk, as a mass: "punt-loads of young men were being ferried across to the towing-path young men naked of knee, armed with rattles, post-horns, motor-hooters, gongs, and other instruments of clangour" (104). They constitute an aggregate of wild, noisy hybrids whose beastliness is marked by the exhibition of their bare calves and improbable horns. The fragmentation of the sentence is introduced by a long dash, and amplified with the recurrent use of commas, echoing stylistically the imbalance of this grotesque lot. It blocks the integration of co-existing elements and mirrors the disintegrated core of humanity in the young men, by atomization and grafting of different accretions. Grotesque deformity is found to contaminate the whole Oxford Creation, including pets, among

---

[1] "The high grim busts of the Roman Emperors stared down at the fair stranger in the equipage" (35); "The high grim busts of the Emperors stared down at him" (4).

which this pathetically delusional "skimpy and dingy cat, trying to look like a tiger" (207). It sheds some light on the personality of John Dorset, who scrolls down the list of his qualities and possessions in order to demonstrate that he is the one for Zuleika.[2] This extensive self-display reads like a fantasmatic erection reaching almost fantastic proportions. Although it runs for eight pages, eulogy sinks into comic insignificance, for instance with the mention of the Duke's title of Hereditary Comber of the Queen's Lap-Dogs (57-64). In other words, the form of masculinity founded on the hoarding of supposedly praiseworthy social characteristics is immaterial and droll–and the well-certified hero tellingly dies a single man. The interest he has raised in Zuleika turns into contempt and his self-inflation is deflated into residual persistence when the young girl takes her leave saying "[g]ood-bye, little John–small John" (248). Affection is qualified, owing to an objective formulation rendered more unfeelingly reductive by the succession of the two syntagmas. Dorset remains grotesque, in his either diminutive or expanded form; he is both denied convincing virile attributes and deprived of his very humanity, this time according to Zuleika's uncle, who claims: "he always seemed to me rather […] inhuman…" (341-2).

Admittedly, Beerbohm's universe is ruled by the ideological fable of heterosexual conventions which burdens the collective unconscious and imaginary alike, permeating the literature of the time. Thus, the plot follows the rhythm of romance. However, this generative pattern only brings about desolation and death. Nonetheless, the ghastly does not lapse into the gothic but is reconfigured into the grotesque, for this world remains sufficiently ridiculous to arouse amusement in the reader. Still, even though Dorset does feel for the distant young beauty, he soon draws his inspiration from the romantic tradition by declaring his intention to commit suicide for her love. This decision gives their further meetings a baleful ring and illustrates the failure of the model of heterosexual relationships. On one occasion, the narrator eagerly reports Dorset's very words, which mimetically refer to both the turmoil Zuleika causes in him and the end of their fine romance. His inability to articulate long sentences is so formulaic as to discredit the hero and potentially the heterosexual scenario itself:

---

[2] "I, John, Albert, Edward, Claude, Orde, Angus, Tankerton, Tanville-Tankerton, fourteenth Duke of Dorset, Marquis of Dorset, Earl of Grove, Earl of Chastermaine, Viscount Brewsby, Baron Grove, Baron Petstrap, and Baron Wolock, in the Peerage of England, offer you my hand. […] [T]he family jewels […] are many and marvelous, in their antique settings. […] Baron Llffthwchl am I, and… and… […] I am Hereditary Comber of the Queen's Lap-Dogs" (57-64).

"Your fetters have not galled you yet. *My* wrists, *my* ankles, are excoriated. The iron has entered into my soul. I droop. I stumble. Blood flows from me. I quiver and curse. I writhe. The sun mocks me. The moon titters in my face. I can stand it no longer. I will no more of it. To-morrow I die."

The flushed faces of the diners grew gradually pale. Their eyes lost luster. (136)

The narrative structure precipitates the whole scene into melodramatic artificiality, with the characterization of Dorset's companions based on the adjunction of a triple alliteration–"flushed faces," "grew gradually" and "lost luster." This ternary rhetoric integrates them into the grandiloquent sequence. Participative expansion has them make the same decision to take their own lives, then it spreads to the whole student community–none of them will escape death. Thus, everyone indirectly contributes to publicizing the dominant mode of subjectivation in the heteronormative institution–in the institution of heteronormativity–since they owe their diegetic being to it, but in the process they hilariously point to its tragic, monstrous influence. It reaches a cataclysmic scale in a scene mixing suicide, sublimity and ridicule, cosmic and chaotic perspectives:

From the towing-path [...] leapt figures innumerable through rain to river. [...] The dropped oars rocked and clashed, sank and rebounded, as the men plunged across them onto the swirling stream.

And over all this confusion and concussion of men and man-made things crashed the vaster discords of the heavens; and the waters of the heavens fell ever denser and denser, as though to the aid of waters that could not in themselves envelop so many hundreds of struggling human forms. [...] Any face that rose [from the water] was smiling [...]. (291)

The heterosexual route proves to be neither a long and winding river nor even a walkable existential path, and the narrative of heterosexual bliss is just a fable and a fib–a joke gone sick.

But Oxford is not always presented as a grotesque place *per se*. The occasional insertion–nearly the intrusion–of a subjective narratorial comment, sometimes a mere precision, can also create the sense of the grotesque. In particular, the lyrical transcription of some elements marks a critical disorienting distance. In consequence, they are not mimetically reflected in words but undergo a process of surreal reformulation, like this crowd of students, an unpleasant plebeian image for the narrator:

Young Oxford! Here, in this mass of boyish faces, all fused and obliterated, was the realization of that phrase. Two or three thousands of

human bodies, human souls? Yet the effect of them in the moonlight was
of one great passive monster. (162)

The narrator relies on the performativity of language to build up a
poetic representation of reality, one which is playful and fundamentally
iconoclastic in its rejection of common expectations. His vision
materializes in the readers' minds in the very act of reading, while it
substantiates a plane of reality which in consequence achieves truth value.
Indeed, from the readers' viewpoint, only the narrative can charter the
territory the narrator explores, by the semantic effects it produces.

Ordinary perspectives alter, magnifying some typical traits almost
beyond recognition, in accordance with Beerbohm's metafictional remark
that "the loveliest face in all the world will not please you if you see it
suddenly, eye to eye, at a distance of half an inch from your own. It was
thus that the Duke saw Zuleika's: a monstrous deliquium a-glare" (105).
Exaggeration is a form of stylization that reintroduces the grotesque topic
while hinting at Beerbohm's celebrated caricatures. Here again, the author
mindfully scatters clues to his *ars poetica*, for instance with his reference
to Humphrey's portrait, one exemplifying his differential approach to
reality: "His face was not so oval, nor were his eyes so big, nor his lips so
full, nor his hands so delicate, as they appeared in the mezzotint" (124).
Beerbohm's illustrations, placed opposite, testify to the same technique,
and often seem to be designed to cause amused astonishment in the
readers.

Conversely, the narrator sometimes disparages his subject by recording
trivial features apparently not worth reporting at all. The readers are then
expected to take seriously the heuristic of both drawings and language,
while the grotesque is meant to uncover truths usually kept ideologically
hidden. Hence, Beerbohm develops a critical view of the common
representation of the world by opting for a playful mode of composition.
For example, resorting to bombastic mock-heroism enables his narrator to
bring out the problematic side in Dorset's masculinity–and perhaps in
masculinity itself–using the very terms of patriarchy by tapping into the
semantic field of virility:

> I saw the Duke's eyes *contract*, and the *muscles* of his mouth drawn down,
> and at the same time, a *tense upward movement* of his whole body. Then
> *suddenly*, the *strain* undone: a downward *dart* of the head, a *loud
> percussion*. Thrice the Duke sneezed, with a sound that was as the *bursting*
> of the dams of body and soul together; then sneezed again. (197-8, italics
> added)

The unusual focalization sometimes operates its reduction of reality by paradoxically cluttering the utterance with identifiers. Thus, in the early chapters, Dorset is turned into a mere recipient for heterogeneous particulars forced together:

> He was adroit in the killing of all birds and fishes, stags and foxes. He played polo, cricket, racquets, chess, and billiards as well as such things can be played. He was fluent in all modern languages, had a very real talent in water-colour, and was accounted, by those who had had the privilege of hearing him, the best amateur pianist on this side of the Tweed. (30)

Accumulating qualities–were they hyperbolical ones–only knocks up the fragmentary, grinning portrait of a composite creature not unlike Frankenstein's creation. In fact, grotesque reconfiguration of the dominant conception of reality amounts to iconoclastic deconstruction of masculinity and the patriarchal order, at least obliquely.

At times, finding the right focalization is replaced by seeking in language the proper idiom to word elements deemed aberrant. This more imaginative move is achieved by introducing comparisons which mark an effort to inflect description with perception. A stereoscopic image results from the analogical procedure, in a refusal to adhere to the world as it is usually conceived of, and with the consequence that a parallel is drawn between two planes of reality. This incongruous connection enables the narrator to dodge the so-called stabilized representation that conventional discourse has to offer, while maintaining it in filigree, as the primary site of his intervention. It is between these two planes, or rather within their coalescent reunion, that Beerbohm's grotesque originates. Proliferating comparisons shift, derail or perhaps systematize–and oppose at the same time–the analogical principle of reason, while they invade the sphere of signification, metamorphosing Dorset into a Protean being. Man is animalized, while the novel turns into a fable and offers the hero little more than a part in a farce: "he ran–ran like a hare, and rose like a trout, saw the pavement rise at him, and fell, with a bang" (222). The long dash is once more used to advantage. It graphically opens up a space of otherness where the idiom *ran like a hare* is retrospectively resemanticized in a literal way, and offers the matrix for the alteration logic. It also graphically connects the two segments of the utterance in order to produce the combinatory regime of the grotesque. The shift in viewpoints from the narrator to Dorset ("he [...] saw the pavement rise at him") results in extra defamiliarization, adding to the strangeness of the scene. The paradoxical hero's heroism is challenged by his lack of control over his own body and the surrounding world, but his identity gets even more troubled with the comparison to a hare, a trout and even an ox, a little earlier on (24). The process is bound to make him lose a considerable part of his masculine characteristics, while masculinity is shown to rely on representation.

The narrator's hypothetical-deductive constructions work in a similar demystifying way, in particular with the purple patch of the love scene. To this end, Beerbohm produces a reportedly bathetic image, which is instantly activated in the reader's mind and invalidates any further attempt to build romance: "If she had [her task of clearing the table] to perform after telling her love, and after receiving his gift and his farewell, the bathos would be distressing for them both" (253). This derisive vision is meant to cancel out the ideal design of the meeting and rules out the androcentric organization of what remains the insubordinate real. All this contributes to the emergence of a paradoxical incarnation of masculinity, Dorset "the nonpareil" (137), who regularly comes to be disqualified all the same. For instance, the narrator inserts a speculation that flashes through the narrative: "In another minute he would stand sodden, inglorious, a mock" (287), stealing Dorset's thunder and adding to the ridiculous turn of the scene.

More generally, the characters might appear grotesque, but the contorted tale really reveals the absurdity of patriarchal discourse and in particular of its grotesque expectations from individuals. To expose this situation, Dorset is proved to be perfectly inadequate to the part the heterosexual scenario allotted him. The narrator denies this ritual its claim to lay down men's best behaviour and hopes of happiness in their relationships with women. Their incompatibility is set into relief through a persistent metaphor based on the maudlin, impenetrable character of the so-called fair-sex: "Unaccustomed to love-affairs, the Duke could not sail lightly over a flood of woman's tears" (259). The hyperbole transcribes the monstrous obscenity of such a situation. Ignorance breeds mistrust, sometimes even aggressive apprehension. This is why Dorset uses a war metaphor to evoke the pangs of love. The feeling is compared to a form of alienated surrender incompatible with the glorious inheritance of Britannia, represented in arms, eager to defend her integrity and dignity, while resorting to the interrogative mode conveys a sense of urgent despair and helplessness:

> [...] is it possible that Britannia would have thrown her helmet in the air, shrieking "Slavery for ever"? You, gentlemen, seem to think slavery a pleasant and an honourable state. You have less experience of it than I. I have been enslaved to Miss Dobson since yesterday evening; you, only since this afternoon. (135)

The grotesque chronological end-flourish does not deflect the sharp-edged discourse on the world order, and heteronormativity dooms men's happiness and freedom. Destabilization results from the unexpected viewpoints and categories that narration harnesses, questioning the phallogocentric constitution of a universe that is stabilized only ideologically. In other words, this dominant representation of the world remains fictional in essence, and proves deceitful in its pretension to map out the real.

Oxford has been argued to be now a grotesque place, now a place grotesquely represented, in contrast with what could be termed the mainland, but it can still be assessed positively. The grotesque topic of *Zuleika Dobson* cannot be reduced to a grimacing equivalent of the conventional order of things. It is composed of apparently regressive–possibly reactionary–planes of reality, but it will be shown to foster a form of emancipation based in existential openness. This epistemological break echoes in the sudden reversal of the narrative perspective, for instance when the mock-heroic report of the collective suicide ends up in a eulogy combined with the castigation of public opinion: "To slur and sully, to belittle and drag down–that was what the world always tried to do. But great things were still great, and fair things still fair" (348). The final unquestionable tautology resists the dominant judgment in an attempt to have eccentric forms recognized and appreciated by the many. The self-enclosed formulation points to the existence of a whole universe of harmony. Its grotesque appearance might be blurred in common understanding but it may be rehabilitated after being circumscribed.

Great Tom is the Oxford sister of Big Ben, but contrary to its institutional counterpart, and even if its bellowing makes some people cringe too, it expresses Beerbohm's resistance to contemporary England, creating a site apart that is sonorous, scriptural and possibly mythological. The unrefined, off-key melody of the bell shapes a sphere which stands protected from "the outer world" (25). Against the presentism of modernity, which offers access neither to the past nor to eternity, Great Tom lets out the transcendent message that "[a]ll's as it was, all's as it will be" (312). This is not incompatible with being a hoarse caricature of human voice, and the grotesque symbol of a grotesque city. Indeed, in the narrator's rendering, the paradoxical being of the bell echoes that of Oxford itself. Whereas the prevailing foul atmosphere is only fit for Gothic churchyards and therefore creates an unfavorable impression of the town, it is also a blessing in disguise:

Yes, certainly, it is this mild, miasmal air, not less than the grey beauty and gravity of the buildings, that has helped Oxford to produce, and foster eternally, her peculiar race of artist-scholars, scholar-artists. (189-90)

Beerbohm insists that it is the Colleges which give the exceptional place its structure, and it is little surprising if the portrait of the Ward of Judas College undergoes an inflexion. Both diegesis and illustrations mirror and echo each other's typical regime of caricature, but this is not exclusive of praise:

An ebon pillar of tradition seemed he, in his garb of old-fashioned cleric. Aloft [...] appeared those eyes which hawks, that nose which eagles, had often envied. He supported his years on an ebon stick. He alone was worthy of the background. (1)

The positive adjective *worthy* reorients the description, closing the derogatory two-fold hyperbaton sequence with a transparent, unmarked syntax. This final excrescence restores order, after the somewhat humorous piling up of semantic and syntactical monstrosities. It completes the general picture by passing an appreciative comment upon the Warden and discloses what is best in the Oxford grotesque.

Even though the student residents reportedly lack sublimity, the awe they cause being outbalanced by their ridicule, they still reproduce a model of fulfillment reconciling the fields of knowledge and artistry, for they are "[a] peculiar race of artist-scholars, scholar-artists" (189). They are complex figures that find their identitary formula in the dandyism incarnated by Dorset, who was granted the nickname "Peacock" in recognition for his sartorial gifts, and awarded highly-praised academic prizes.[3] In accordance with the grotesque writing regime, the young dandy happens to be openly mocked, for example through the narrator's insistence on the prosaic reactions of Oxford housewives, who impose their epistemological framework to make sense of his garments: "the velvet of the Duke's mantle could not have cost less than four guineas a yard [...], there must be quite twenty-five yards of it" (281). Beerbohm echoes the utter bafflement of the *hoi polloi*, but responds with a counter-discourse to legitimize dress extravaganza, dwelling on Dorset's flamboyant costume of the Knight of the Garter. The dandy actually resignifies this uniform to stage his most perfect dandiacal temperament

---

[3] "At Eton he had been called 'Peacock,' and this nickname had followed him up to Oxford. It was not wholly apposite, however. For, whereas the peacock is a fool even among birds, the Duke had already taken [...] the Stanhope, the Newdigate, the Lothian, and the Gaisford Prize for Greek Verse." (29)

one last time. The choice of a sumptuary, histrionic outfit borrowed from the cloakroom of Institutions reconciles grotesque eccentricity, historical convention and sartorial expressiveness:

> But you must not imagine that he cared for [...] symbols of achievement and power. The dark blue riband, and the star scintillating to eight points, the heavy mantle of blue velvet, with its lining of taffeta and shoulder-knots of white satin, the crimson surcoat, the great embullioned tassels, and the chain of linked gold, and the plumes of ostrich and heron uprising from the black velvet hat–these things had for him little signification save as [...] a finer setting than the most elaborate smoking-suit, for that perfection of aspect which the gods had given him. (32)

And yet, Beerbohmian dandyism usually resorts to toned down versions of self-assertive difference, in which the care of the self results in cool self-containment. What the treatment of the grotesque operates is the modulation of a representation, gliding from the monstrous to the abnormal, then to the mere eccentric, which is reported to be an alternative model and ultimately a desirable norm–an improvement on dominant standards.

The most radical intervention, though, sets the diegesis in a university town where, at the turn of the century, women have to shoulder their way in. Dorset mentions their breaking into Oxford in religious terms by referring to "sheer violation of sanctuary" (25), staging a reversal of conventional gendered postures turned comic by the connotations of violation applied to male students. This results in the caricatural picture of a community of coy teenagers to be pitied. However, it also identifies masculinity outside the dual system of heteronormativity–"so vulgar peril" (29), disconnected from the genital given.[4] In fact, *Zuleika Dobson* tends to discredit or discard the reference to virile heterosexuality. Rather than a pre-genital regression, which is doomed to be pathologized, this decision can be called an ontological reconfiguration based on a post-genital evolution. Such a refusal to infantilize Dorset is supported by his first intention to unite with Zuleika, "the omnisubjugant" (23), marking his sexual coming of age and reliance on patriarchy to organize his destiny. This orthodox genital phase lends its context to his further unease with women and ulterior determination to do away with romance, even if the tone of the tale does not univocally praise him for it. Whereas the dignity of the prestigious "master-dandy" (269) is first laid down, his subsequent

---

[4] Subsequent research should look into the novel in its polymorphously perverse leaning.

embarrassment with the ladies owes him the ontological status of human
noodle, hence his confession that "he had forgotten to kiss Zuleika [...].
To-day it had been as much as he could do to let poor little Katie kiss his
hand. [...] Still, noodledom was nearer than vulgarity to dandyism" (269-
70). His grotesque clownishness is also a reminder that romance is no
natural locus of his. Conversely, the set gestures of heterosexuality are
exposed for their artificiality and arbitrariness, for Dorset keeps forgetting
them, overlooking the other's erotic charge and shifting his own libidinal
investment. Because generalized derision might blur the ultimate meaning
of the text, Beerbohm alternates speech regimes. He occasionally
verbalizes a straightforward message articulating forceful categories, for
instance when Dorset synthesizes his existential credo, stating that "[t]he
basis of my pet system was [...] celibacy of the soul–egoism, in fact" (50).
It ranks this grotesque little text–not such a gross text after all–with quasi
mythological tales of anthropological interest since it enables the critic to
conceptualize an alternative masculine posture. Despite the shifts in
stylistic registers, Beerbohm's decision to compose within the Oxford
Novel tradition also contributes to the myth of the place. In fact, the
grotesque mode of exposition fashions an eccentric line of thought without
impairing the basic message on eternal Oxford, dandiacal ontology and
sexed / gendered identities, unless the globally hostile context makes it the
only possible regimen of visibility.

References

Beerbohm, Max. (1911) 2002. *The Illustrated Zuleika Dobson; or, An
    Oxford Love Story.* With an introduction by N. John Hall and 80
    illustrations by the author. New Haven & London: Yale University
    Press.

CHAPTER SIXTEEN

THE RETURN OF DICKENS'S GROTESQUES ON SCREEN

FLORENCE BIGO-RENAULT

"Twist" is the appropriate surname of the hero of a novel in which grotesque thieves regularly congregate at a pub named The Three Cripples. Denoting deviousness and slyness, it is a favourite word to indicate physical and moral distortion in Dickens's work. (Hollington 1984, 58)

I wish to start by borrowing from Michael Hollington's remark on the pub found at the end of *Oliver Twist* and called "The Three Cripples," because in television adaptations of Dickens's works–and particularly those dated after 2000–the world, like this pub, is physically and morally distorted. Recent adaptations demonstrate a certain relish in twists and an inflation in deformity which mean that adapted works qualify as entertaining as much as they serve to denounce Victorian defects through the use of gothic or grotesque overtones.[1] I am here specifically concentrating

---

[1] My use of the adjective "Gothic" is based on the definition given by M.H. Abrams in his *Glossary of Literary Terms*: "The term 'Gothic' has also been extended to a type of fiction which lacks the medieval setting but develops a brooding atmosphere of gloom and terror, represents events which are uncanny or macabre or melodramatically violent and often deals with aberrant psychological states." (Abrams 1988, 74-5). Abrams adds that in Dickens, examples of gothic fiction can mostly be found in *Bleak House*, more particularly in Chapters 11, 16 and 47, and in the Miss Havisham episodes of *Great Expectations*. I have also found useful Philip Thomson's historical survey of the uses of the word "Grotesque," in *The Grotesque* (1972). Thomson notably recalls the conclusions of the German critic Wolfgang Kayser on the Grotesque: "The grotesque is the expression of the estranged or alienated world, i.e. the familiar world is seen from a perspective which suddenly renders it strange (and, presumably, this strangeness may be either comic or terrifying, or both). The grotesque is a game with the

on miniseries on air in Britain in recent years, which have successfully rejuvenated the genre of literary adaptations on television, namely *Nicholas Nickleby* (dir: Whittaker, 2001), which although not a BBC but an Acorn for ITV production, actually started the trend, *Bleak House* (dir: J. Chadwick and S. White, 2005), *Oliver Twist* (dir: C. Giedroyc, 2007), *Little Dorrit* (dir: D. Walsh, A. Smith & D. Lawrence, 2008), and finally, *Great Expectations* (dir: B. Kirk, 2011). I will devote a few lines to the analysis of "crippled" settings before turning to the representation of morally crippled characters and that of food and drink in such grotesque contexts.

Crippled Settings

In Christine Edzard's 1988 version of *Little Dorrit*, Mrs Clennam's house is a Calvinist looking upper-class city house, in which walls are covered with very dark wood panels with the aim of giving the interior decor impressive and slightly gothic grandeur. The total absence of ornaments contributes to the impression of an austere and puritan place. In Mrs Clennam's room the only visible object is her Bible, its prodigious dimension a symbol of both her distorted perspective on salvation and the value she confers on the Old Testament passages she once read to her vulnerable son. In the 2008 BBC version, the Bible has found a more ordinary aspect in Mrs Clennam's crippled hands, but what is deformed is the house itself. From the outside for example the window-uprights lean to one side, distorting each window-frame and thus the Clennam house is represented as literally falling to pieces. It seems to have been made of cardboard or other flimsy materials, which prepares the audience for the

---

absurd, in the sense that the grotesque artist plays, half laughingly, half horrified, with the deep absurdities of existence. The grotesque is an attempt to control and exorcise the demonic elements in the world." Philip Thomson adds that "Kayser thus offers not so much a definition of the grotesque as a list of overlapping properties. We may object also to the somewhat melodramatic over-emphasis on the 'demonic,' which removes the fearsome aspect of the grotesque to the realm of the irrational—almost of the supernatural. [...] He was [however] the first to insist that the grotesque can be seen, must be seen if it is to be meaningful as an aesthetic category, as 'a comprehensive structural principle,' which is particularly relevant when one analyses literature on screen. The implication of this, which Kayser himself does not always follow, is that there must be a certain pattern peculiar to the grotesque, a certain fundamental structure which is perceivable in the grotesque work of art and its effect, as there is in parody, say, or to take a more complex example—in irony" (Thomson 1972, Part 2).

destruction scene at the end, filmed like an explosion–in itself of grotesque proportions.

In other recent adaptations one systematically finds the same type of gothic place metonymically expressing its owner's grotesque moral distortion: whether it be Krook's warehouse in *Bleak House*, Fagin's den in *Oliver Twist* or Dotheboys hall in *Nicholas Nickleby*, or even Satis House in *Great Expectations*, the overall impression is the same. The places chosen or set up to shoot the scenes are all rendered both gothic and grotesque through the lack of proper light, the presence of dirt and/or dust and the alternation of high- and low-angle shots which contribute to the viewers' feeling that they might lose their balance–a technique meant to metaphorically illustrate the characters' beclouded judgement. Indeed, the characters evolving in such settings hardly ever suspect the owner's moral distortion: Miss Flite seems unaware of Mr Krook's warped mind and his odd connection with the outside world–"anything to sell?" being his first question to the wards in Jarndyce.

Such settings mean that the main characters–and the audience–enter as outsiders a distorted world where the grotesque has become a norm only *they* are in a position to denounce. The main character is here a vector, and the expression to be seen on his/her face has a metonymic quality, showing as it does the consequence–the shock–for the cause, that is to say the grotesque moral distortion.

The audience thus finds that every element composing the distorted world is in keeping with the grotesque setting. If we consider the example used by Michael Hollington in his analysis of *Oliver Twist*, we realise that the remark made about the novel is also valid for its adaptation, and can be generalized further:

> [Fagin] is a kind of ironic Jewish patriarch presiding over a family idyll which inverts familiar bourgeois values. The work of the family community is mock-work; the education it provides is a mock-education [...] whose graduates are mock-professionals. [...] A topsy-turvy morality prevails. [...] The grotesque is thus a mode of indirection, designed to elicit fresh perception and evaluation of the "normal" world and its values. (Hollington 1984, 62-3)

Michael Hollington's statement can be considered generic as it applies to other distorted worlds in other novels: for instance, in *Bleak House*, Krook's warehouse too functions as a nightmarish deformed "realm of the irrational," to use Thomson's words.[2] In the novel it is described in the following way:

> In one part of the window was a picture of a red paper mill, at which a cart was unloading a quantity of sacks of old rags. In another, was the inscription BONES BOUGHT. In another, KITCHEN-STUFF BOUGHT. In another OLD IRON BOUGHT. In another WASTE PAPER BOUGHT. In another, LADIES' AND GENTLEMEN'S WARDROBES BOUGHT. Everything seemed to be bought, and nothing to be sold there. (Dickens 1977, 48)

In these grotesque settings, only the heroes or newcomers perceive the distortion and find it unsettling: this is made extremely clear in the recent trend of adaptations I am analysing, and the close-ups on Nicholas, who cannot conceal his indignation in front of the Squeerses' outrageous behaviour, are used abundantly to demonstrate it.

Morally Crippled Characters: "An Inflation of Visibility"[3]

For the sake of a quick identification by the viewer, morally distorted characters are made visibly crippled and/or turned into clowns. Such is the case of Mrs Sowerberry in the 2007 version of *Oliver Twist*. She is introduced to the reader of the novel in the following way: "Mrs Sowerberry emerged from a little room behind the shop, and presented the form of a short, thin, squeezed-up woman, with a vixenish countenance" (Dickens 2005, 28). The adaptation has turned her into a twenty-first century fashion-victim with a ravenous passion for oversized hats, so that her self-importance is rendered much more visible than in past versions. Buying new hats is the only occupation that can maintain her high spirits, and the audience is quickly given to understand that the subject of new hats is a frequent source of disagreement between the Sowerberries. Indeed, in the dialogues, Mr Sowerberry makes it clear that if his wife complies with his desire to have Oliver work for him, he will lift the ban on hats. Here is the extract from the script, as Oliver is introduced by the undertaker to his wife, in front of Noah and Charlotte:

---

[2] See note 1.

[3] I here borrow from French philosopher Marie-José Mondzain who establishes that recent television and cinema programs have steadily moved towards an inflation of the visible in terms of violence and sex on screen, an inflation which is also to be established in different sorts of programmes such as miniseries based on nineteenth-century classics (see Mondzain 2002).

Mr Sowerberry: He has a most melancholic countenance, don't you think?

Mrs Sowerberry: We could all be melancholic, Mr Sowerberry, with husbands urging thrift upon their household and spending good money on workhouse strays... If you want melancholy, Mr Sowerberry, look to your poor wife!

Mr Sowerberry: He was a bargain, Madam. He'll be very good for business with a face like that.

Mrs Soweberry: Your poor wife, because of thrift, must attend church with a shameful excuse for a hat! Whispers and looks, Mr Sowerberry, I see them, I hear them, and they sting me like a lasso! I dream of mere melancholy, Mr Sowerberry, I dream of it! Melancholy would be a merciful escape from the deep rot of humiliation and despair your loyal wife finds herself in, from being required by thrift to dress a pauper!

Mr Sowerberry: You have many hats, Madam, forty at the last count...you can only wear one at a time.

Mrs Sowerberry: I endure it all, Sir. The petty counting of hats, the buying of paupers... I endure it all like a marital duty, Sir. I'm but a shadow of my former self, my nerves all shattered, are they not, Charlotte?

Charlotte: Oh yes, Mrs!

Mrs Sowerberry: Yes! What does he care? He cares for nothing but coffins and bargains! Never marry, Charlotte, never! Your heart will be broken, torn to pieces by such cruelty. It's too much for a lady's sensibilities!

Mr Sowerberry: If that would restore Mrs Sowerberry's well-being, I will lift the embargo on hats–for one week only...

Mrs Sowerberry: (with a smile of pleasure) Well... (to Oliver) You sleep here, under the counter. (Giedroyc 2007, script)

Obviously, the fight scene which later takes place between Noah Claypole and Oliver ends in the destruction of Mrs Sowerberry's newest acquisition. This illustrates the fact that nothing but vanity is damaged at the undertaker's by Oliver's angry outburst. The hat has no other function but to visually reinforce the grotesque attached to both Mr and Mrs Sowerberry or–more generally–to the episode at the undertaker's. This grotesque dimension is of course present in the novel, but if we consider only Mrs Sowerberry however, the change entailed by the addition of the hat clearly causes the viewer to laugh at the grotesque and is therefore reminiscent of Charles Baudelaire's reflections in *On the Essence of Laughter* (1855), where the author explains that laughter caused by the grotesque is of another nature than "ordinary laughter":

Fabulous creations, beings whose authority and *raison d'être* cannot be drawn from the code of common sense, often provoke in us an insane and excessive mirth, which expresses itself in interminable paroxysms and

swoons. [...] From the artistic point of view, the comic is an imitation: the
grotesque a creation. (Baudelaire 1956, 144)

The gradation between the two sorts of laughter here defined by
Baudelaire seems to correspond to what exists between Dickens's
creation[4] and her adapted self: the run-of-the-mill comic character of Mrs
Sowerberry is transformed into a much more excessive one on screen. I
would like to add that Marcel Pagnol's observations in *Notes sur le Rire*
(*Notes on Laughter*) are also useful to comment on Mrs Sowerberry, as
they bring a different but complementary note. Pagnol explains that there
are two kinds of laughter, a good-humoured one which he calls positive,
through which the reader or the audience express their superiority
regarding the object.[5] This type of laughter is provoked by dialogues such
as the one quoted above which is not found in Dickens's text, but which
nevertheless pertains to its comic vein. It is also triggered off by the
stimulating confrontation with the appearance on screen of such characters
as Mrs Sowerberry, or Mr Turveydrop in *Bleak House*, or Mr Guppy when
he proposes to Esther for the second time. However the reader or the
audience can also resort to "a type of negative laughter originating in
scorn, a desire of vengeance, vendetta or at least revenge" (Pagnol 1947,
32, my translation). The audience who identifies with Jenny's suffering at
her baby's demise (in *Bleak House*) or with Smike's constant humiliations
(in *Nicholas Nickleby*) derive pleasure from laughing at Mrs Pardiggle's
grotesque interference or at the Squeerses' preposterous lesson of spelling.
This second type also corresponds to the laughter directed at Mrs
Sowerberry, the viewer (who sides with Oliver) being given the
opportunity to have his revenge for the hardships endured by the young
boy. These two forms of laughter recall, I believe, the two forms of
grotesque which Michael Hollington distinguishes in Dickens's works,
particularly in novels written after *Dombey and Son*:

> In the novels that succeed *Dombey and Son*, there is frequently a
> confrontation between two alternative grotesques, one positive, one
> negative, one inherently "true" and "innocent," the other debased, or [...]
> "disgraceful." They tend to stand for two phases of the imagination–on the
> one hand the imagination "in a state of nature," as it were, perceiving the

---

[4] Mrs Sowerberry's grotesque is also hardly apparent in George Cruickshank's
original illustration, where she is simply seen in the background, soberly dressed.
[5] Marcel Pagnol was a popular playwright and not an academic, the first adaptor of
his plays on screen (with director Alexandre Korda) who transformed his own texts
for new and different audiences. His *Notes on Laughter* strike a chord I find in
certain aspects Dickensian (see Pagnol 1947).

grotesque from the perception of a child, or the artist who has retained sufficient childhood powers of vision, and on the other hand, the imagination as it must express itself, in and through monstrous distortion, out of radically diseased social conditions and relations. (Hollington 1984, 197)

It is surely necessary for both the screenwriter and the director to be able to display this "childhood power of vision" Hollington defines, in order to sketch out the inflation of visibility necessary to quicken the viewer's perception of a character's grotesque and potentially comic dimension. For instance, the recent adaptation of *Bleak House* makes visual grotesques of Guppy or Deportment Turveydrop by turning them into tableaux vivants, i.e. faithful copies of the original illustrations. Such grotesques constitute tributes to the visual source material, restore the balance between elements of comedy and more serious passages, and prove inventive when one compares them with older versions of the same work.

Going back to the example of adaptations of *Bleak House*, we should remember that the BBC's 1985 adaptation (dir: Ross Devenish, with a script by Arthur Hopcraft, starring Diana Rigg as Lady Dedlock and Denholm Elliott as Mr Jarndyce) was generally praised, but received criticism for having written out comic characters and grotesques, the Jellybys' absence for example being considered "annoying" (Watt and Lonsdale 2003, 210). In that version indeed, all the subplot concerning both the Jellybys and the Turveydrops had been cut out, undoing the Dickensian balance of comic/serious moments. Their reintroduction in the 2005 version definitely changed the tone and made *Bleak House* a lighter story.

However, certain visually inflated distortions raise more questions than laughter in the viewer's mind: it is the case of Miss Havisham's sick hand. Indeed, in *Great Expectations* (dir: B. Kirk, 2011), Miss Havisham's right hand is repeatedly shown as having a form of skin irritation (or is it just warts or eczema?) exacerbated by constant neurotic scratching. "What's wrong with her hand?"–a question often asked on the net–reveals the viewers' difficulty to identify the distortion as metaphorical. Several grotesque visuals such as Miss Havisham's hand are created in adaptations, and are meant to be understood metaphorically. For instance the character of Dolge Orlick has sores on his face which gradually become worse, as his jealousy and resentment of Pip deepen. In the adaptation of *Bleak House*, Rachel Carroll explains, Esther's small pox marks should also be interpreted metaphorically for what they were meant to stand for in the novel:

[...] in Dickens's novel, Esther conflates the visible traces of her illness with the invisible stigma of her illegitimacy: hence, she refers to "my disfigurement and my inheritance of shame." (Carroll 2012, 692)

The audience of the adaptation does not necessarily understand such skin marks for what they are, i.e. the sign of the character's moral distortion or in Esther's case, the stigma of her lack of social status. The added metaphors are nevertheless "Dickensian" in inspiration and nicely complement the other visual codes. They can be considered a positive addition as they perpetuate a tradition which goes back to Dickens, and even further back, to the influences he received. Indeed, this inflation of visual effects–some of which are purposefully disturbing and repellent– recall Dickens's fondness for caricaturists and artists such as Hogarth. According to Nathalie Vanfasse:

> Alexander Ross remarks that literary critics in Dickens's day compared his writing to the art of David Wilkie, William Hogarth, Clarkson Stanfild and Daniel Maclise [...]. He evokes the recurrent use of terms such as "pictural effects," "graphic quality," "a confident brushwork" or "descriptive painting," in articles about the novelist's works. [...] Dickens's writing belongs to a tradition of graphic satire developed by Hogarth, and then taken up and modified by other satirists such as James Gillray and Thomas Rowlandson, or George Cruickshank, Robert Seymour and Hablôt K. Brown. (Vanfasse 2007, 165-8, my translation)

Interestingly, modern television screenwriting and directing also pay tribute, whenever possible, to the two traditions, the narrative and the pictorial, and enhance visibility with a particular style meant to recall that of the caricaturists mentioned as much as Dickens's own. One can see how the illustrations drawn in 1852-3 by H. K. Browne (Phiz) for *Bleak House* literally come to life in the 2005 miniseries as far as costumes and postures are concerned, notably in the cases of Deportment Turveydrop, Guppy, the Bayham-Badgers, Grandfather Smallweed or even Inspector Bucket. And the occasionally childish playfulness with the visual also recalls Dickens's own influences.

Food and Drink in *Oliver Twist* and *Nicholas Nickleby* on Screen

Nathalie Vanfasse highlights the fact that certain satirical portraits reminiscent of Gillray or Rowlandson also provoke fear or disgust (169). Many may have seen, in several adaptations of *Oliver Twist*, the Board of

Guardians represented during a meal, scandalously overeating while Oliver is reprimanded for asking for more. The recent versions (Polanski's in 2005 as well as the 2007 miniseries) seem to give a more prodigious size to the food on the table, even at the risk of undoing the balance of the picture. Both Polanski's and Giedroyc's versions highlight the grotesque, in what could also be seen as a tribute to past adaptations of the same novel, or of other scenes including deformed impressions of food. Indeed, such exaggerations also recall Eisentein's work on close-ups, particularly in *Potemkine*, a film about which Jean-Claude Bonnet explains that "[...] the close-up on the maggot on the meat indicates it is only fair to rebel. Close-ups insist on the torturing elements and how they impact" (Bonnet 1977, 13, my translation). So the food on the table–a translation on screen of "eight or ten fat gentlemen" (Dickens 2005, 9) justifies the viewer's outrage, induced by the directing choices. The same trope is used in the adaptation of *Nicholas Nickleby* where it corresponds to identical aesthetic options. There is a close-up on a roasted hog's head in a platter of what looks like baked apples, one of which is stuffed in its snout, taking pride of place on the Squeers family dinner-table while in the next room the boarders are woefully undernourished.

The biting irony deriving from such choices recalls David Bindman's observations on Hogarth's *Calais Gate, or the Roast Beef of Old England* (1748), about which he explains:

> Once the attitude of the figure has been caught there is no limit to the expressive details which may be added to complete the effect, nor to the additional elements which may be brought into a composition. [...] the contrast between bulk and thinness in the human figures, which makes an important satirical point, is made much more real. (Bindman 1991, 159-62)

In the Squeerses' outrageous consumption of food, one cannot but see an evocation of James Gillray's works, such as *John Bull Taking a Luncheon, or British Cooks, Cramming Old Grumble-Gizzard with Bonne-Chere* (1798), or *Advantages of Wearing Muslin Dresses* (1802). The characters in the two etchings are obese and nauseatingly voracious, displaying neither table manners nor education, and everything in their behaviour to food calls for the viewers' sentence. They are symbols of degraded morals or of an absence of ethics close to savagery, a decline of civilization also seen in the use of dirt at Dotheboys Hall. The children themselves, falling victims of predators, are thus metaphorically devoured at the Squeers family dinner-table.

One of the most striking episodes corresponds to the scene of the couple's return from a visit to the local pub. Mrs Squeers' drunkenness prevents her from climbing the stairs leading to her room, and her husband calls on Smike for help. The bony teenager is unable to bear his mistress's weight and falls down the flight of stairs, Mrs Squeers' gin bottle being broken to pieces in the fall. There is a barely concealed pastiche reference to *Gin Lane*, the engraving by Hogarth in which the central figure of a woman lets her toddler slip over the railing into the stairwell, the expression on the woman's face betraying the fact that she is not aware of what is happening to the child. As a parallel, Smike is a child whom neglect and suffering have turned into a distorted teenager limping his way through life. In *Gin Lane* the central character, the woman, is wearing a dirty cap while in *Nicholas Nickleby* Dickens offers the following description of Mrs Squeers:

> The lady, who was of a large raw-boned figure, was about half a head taller than Mr Squeers, and was dressed in a dimity night-jacket with her hair in papers; she had also a dirty night-cap on, relieved by a yellow cotton hankerchief which tied it under the chin. (Dickens 1994, 93)

It is indeed a description in which Dickens seems to have verbalised what he saw on Hogarth's engraving, and which has been brought to life on screen in practically the same terms by adaptors in 2001, with its full-blown grotesque dimension. Pam Ferris, who plays the part of Mrs Squeers, was dressed up to look exactly like the woman in *Gin Lane*.

This return of grotesques and cripples on screen better testifies to Dickens's pluri-dimensional work on the one hand, and shows more concern for the question of the reception of Dickens's works on the other, than other adaptations in past decades.[6] These childishly playful, inflated visibilities point to the adaptors' reading as minutely analytical and to their desire to reach new audiences beyond the Sunday-night slot one. This renewed audience may have been less in contact with Dickens's novels than enlightened amateurs; for them it is necessary to spell out the

---

[6] I am particularly thinking of adaptations in the 1980s, when the political dimension of Dickens's novels prevailed over every other. This is especially obvious in Clive Donner's cinematic reading of *Oliver Twist* (1982), which has been interpreted as a Marxist response to early Thatcherism (see Hodges Holt, 2010). It is also clear in the version of *Bleak House* directed by South-African director Ross Devenish in 1985, which was acclaimed by critics but which had quite an oppressive atmosphere. Christine Edzard's 1988 adaptation of *Little Dorrit* showed a deep understanding of Dickens's grotesque–an example of that being her Flora Finching, played by Myriam Margolyes; but it still failed to lighten the atmosphere in a proper Dickensian way.

Dickensian concept of comic relief which Dickens calls "streaky bacon"[7] in the incipit of Chapter 17 of *Oliver Twist*. This is part of a strategy aiming at reencoding Dickens on screen with today's standards on visibility, putting old wine into new wineskins, for a renewed and so far successful transmission of the tradition of adaptation: the table below accounts for the audience rates provided by the press at the time of airing, and demonstrates that with their new series, the BBC takes the lion's share of the audience.

Title	Original run	Viewers (millions)	% in audience share	Time-slot rating
Nicholas Nickleby[8]	April 2001	-	-	-
Bleak House[9]	30 November 2005	6.6 to 7.2	29%	1st
Oliver Twist[10]	18 December 2007	5.8 to 8	25 to 35 %	1st
Little Dorrit[11]	December 2008	2.48 to 4.2	10.3 to 24%	2nd/3rd
Great Expectations[12]	18-20 December 2011	5.9 to 6.6	24%	1st

---

[7] "It is the custom on the stage, in all good murderous melodramas, to present the tragic and the comic scenes, in as regular alternation, as the layers of red and white in a side of streaky bacon. [...] Such changes appear absurd; but they are not so unnatural as they would seem at first sight. The transitions in real life from well-spread boards to death-beds, and from mourning-weeds to holiday garments, are not a whit less startling" (Dickens 2005, 119).

[8] For *Nicholas Nickleby* (2001), little information could be found.

[9] For *Bleak House* (2005)
http://www.nathanielparker.com/cms/index.php/home-mainmenu-122/news-mainmenu-133/274-2005-news/349-bleak-house-ratings

[10] For *Oliver Twist* (2007)
http://www.guardian.co.uk/media/2007/dec/19/tvratings.television
http://www.guardian.co.uk/media/2007/dec/20/tvratings.bbc

[11] For *Little Dorrit* (2008)
http://www.guardian.co.uk/media/2008/dec/12/tv-ratings-little-dorrit
http://www.digitalspy.co.uk/tv/news/a137354/little-dorrit-drops-to-series-low.html
http://www.telegraph.co.uk/news/celebritynews/3330757/Little-Dorrit-loses-1.5-million-viewers-as-audiences-fail-to-find-it.html

[12] For *Great Expectations* (2011)
http://www.digitalspy.co.uk/tv/news/a357753/bbc-one-wins-thursday-night-with-earthflight-great-expectations.html

References

Abrams, M.H.. 1988. *A Glossary of Literary Terms*. Orlando: The Dryden Press.

Baudelaire, Charles. (1855) 1956. "On the Essence of Laughter." In *The Mirror of Art, Critical Studies by Charles Baudelaire*. Translated by Jonathan Mayne, 131-54. New-York: Doubleday Anchor Books.

Bindman, David. 1991. *Hogarth*. London: Thames and Hudson.

Bonnet, Jean-Claude. 1977. "Fonctions du gros plan chez Eisenstein." *Cinématographe* n°24: 11-5.

Carnell Watt, Kate and Kathleen C. Lonsdale. 2003. "Dickens Composed: Film and Television Adaptations 1897-2001." In *Dickens on Screen*, edited by John Glavin, 201-16. Cambridge: Cambridge U. P.

Carroll, Rachel. 2012. "Queer Beauty: Illness, Illegitimacy and Visibility in Dickens's *Bleak House* and its 2005 BBC Adaptation." In *Dickens Adapted*, edited by John Glavin. Farnham: Ashgate.

Dickens, Charles. *Oliver Twist*. (1838) 2005. Bloomsbury: The Nonesuch Press.

—. *Nicholas Nickleby*. (1839) 1994. Harmondsworth: Penguin Books.

—. *Bleak House*. (1853) 1977. New-York: Norton Critical Edition.

—. (1861) 1996. *Great Expectations*. Harmondsworth: Penguin Books.

Hall, Stuart. 1994. "Codage/Décodage." *Réseaux* n°68. CENT.

Hodges Holt, Shari. 2010. "'Please, Sir, I Want Some More': Clive Donner's Marxist Adaptation of *Oliver Twist*." *Literature Film Quarterly*, 38, 254-68.

Hollington, Michael. 1984. *Dickens and the Grotesque*. Beckenham (Kent): Croom Helm.

Mondzain, Marie José. 2002. *L'Image peut-elle tuer ?* Montrouge: Bayard.

Pagnol, Marcel. 1947. *Notes sur le Rire*. Monte-Carlo: Editions Pastorelly.

Thomson, Philip. 1972. *The Grotesque*. London: Methuen Critical Idiom Series.
    http://davidlavery.net/grotesque/major_artists_theorists/theorists/thoms on/thomson.html

Vanfasse, Nathalie. 2007. *Charles Dickens, entre normes et déviance*. Aix en Provence: Presses Universitaires de Provence.

CONCLUSION

REGENERATION AND PERMANENCE
OF THE GROTESQUE

ISABELLE HERVOUET-FARRAR

> Beyond the diversity and contradictions of 19th-century theories, the
> Romantic reflection on the grotesque originates in a shared essential quest.
> The aim is to define modernity and to show how modern art can be
> inscribed in the history of aesthetics, which is therefore redefined. (Rosen
> 1991-2, 28, my translation)

Even though Montaigne called his famous Essays "grotesque,"[1] it was
only in the 19th century, thanks to French Romanticism, that the grotesque
was first considered as a key literary category. Used by French Romantics
to define modern art, as Elisheva Rosen explains, it became closely
connected with literature, thanks to Hugo's and then Baudelaire's
theorizing. The grotesque was given pride of place and defined as "all-
embracing" by Hugo, since for him "there can exist only one counterpart
to the grotesque: the sublime" (Rosen 1991-1, 58, my translation). 19th-
century literary grotesque tended to be all-embracing and wide-ranging,
indeed, since it fed on most of the great aesthetic and literary categories of
the time. In turn generous, expansive and deeply entertaining or moody,
sombre and uncanny, the grotesque thus participated energetically in the
construction of modern European fiction, as exemplified by the variety of
the studies found in the present volume.

---

[1] "As I was considering the way a painter I employ went about his work, I had a
mind to imitate him. He chooses the best spot, the middle of each wall, to put a
picture laboured over with all his skill, and the empty spaces all around it he fills
with grotesques, which are fantastic paintings whose only charm lies in their
variety and strangeness. And what are these things of mine, in truth, but grotesques
and monstrous bodies [...] without definite shape, having no order, sequence, or
proportion other than accidental?" (Montaigne 1976, 135)

Because its specific meaning is so hard to pinpoint, the grotesque's ability to regenerate itself and reappear in a variety of contexts seems limitless. It emerges with every human experience whose significance remains uncertain, or, as Harpham writes, whenever we find ourselves in the "purgatorial state of understanding" (Harpham 1982, 15). Its destiny throughout the 20th century was therefore to overlap many categories and theories, and it notably found itself lastingly associated with psychoanalysis. This should come as no surprise: Ruskin himself established a connection between what he called "debased" grotesque (Ruskin 2009, 148) and dreams:

> The grotesque which comes to all men in a disturbed dream is the most intelligible of this kind,[2] but also the most ignoble; the imagination, in this instance, being entirely deprived of all aid from reason, and incapable of self-government. (151)

With Walter Benjamin's analysis of the word "grotesque," the emphasis is displaced from the motif of the cave to that of concealment: "The enigmatically mysterious character of the effect of the grotesque seems to have been associated with its subterraneanly mysterious origin in buried ruins and catacombs. The word is not derived from *grotta* in the literal sense, but from 'burial' in the sense of concealment–which the cave or grotto expresses" (Benjamin 1977, 171).[3] Such shift in emphasis prepares further for the connection with psychoanalysis, since, both literally and figuratively, "every time we invoke the grotesque we must return to the cave" (Singley 1997, 111) and confront the depths of the mind, in chthonic descent. Paulette Singley explains that if one were to "describe[e] the diverse blossoms nestled in the captivating vines of the grotesque," the list would include "Julia Kristeva's *abjection*, Derrida's *cryptonomy*, Georges Bataille's *informe*, [...] [and] Sigmund Freud's *unheimlich*" (111). Many written accounts of underground discoveries eerily evoke what Freud was to call *das Unheimliche*, since the Freudian uncanny partially unveils "the ancient past suddenly revealed in the form of an awesome enigma" a formula used by Harpham to describe the remains of the *Domus Aurea* (Harpham 1982, 23). The grotesque, the uncanny and dreams share "the ambivalent presence of meaning" (31) in a

---

[2] Ruskin is dealing with the "ungovernableness of imagination," or "the error and wildness of the mental impressions" (Ruskin 2009, 151).
[3] Harpham also writes: "The Latin form of grotto is probably crypta (cf. "crypt") [...]. *Grotesque*, then, gathers into itself suggestions of the underground, of burial, and of secrecy (Harpham 1982, 27).

meaningless form (or scenario) or at least one which yields no directly accessible meaning.

The strength of the bond between the grotesque and literature endured throughout the 20th century, as is evidenced in the works of William Faulkner, Carson Mc Cullers, Flannery O'Connor, Carlos Fuentes, Ian McEwan, Umberto Eco, Angela Carter, Salman Rushdie and many, many more. On this side of the Atlantic Kafka is certainly the master of early 20th-century literary grotesque, whose affinity with Dickens has often been noted.[4] In the first two decades of the 20th century, he managed the synthesis of Bakhtinian bodily grotesque and Kayserian nocturnal grotesque. The father's body in *The Verdict*, for example, is both inflated and unstable, "unfinished" (Bakhtin 1984, 320), and deeply frightening. In an entry of his diary, dated 29 May 1914, Kafka muses on what he calls "confidence in one's ability to write" (Kafka 1976, 274) and then suddenly describes the contortions of his body in carnivalesque, oneiric and disturbing terms:

> As I stand here in my misery, already the huge wagon of my schemes comes driving up behind me, I feel underfoot the first small step up, naked girls, like those on the carnival floats of happier countries, lead me backwards up the steps; I float because the girls float, and raise my hand to command silence. [...] Flowers are strewn before and over me; two trumpeters, as if hewn out of stone, blow fanfares; [...] the bright, empty, open squares become dark, tempestuous, and crowded; I feel myself at the farthest edge of human endeavour, and, high up where I am, with suddenly acquired skill spontaneously execute a trick I had admired in a contortionist years ago–I bend slowly backwards [...], draw my head and trunk through my legs, and gradually stand erect again. Was this the ultimate given to mankind? It would seem so. (275)

Through the famous *Metamorphosis* of Gregor Samsa, Kafka produces textbook grotesque. The image of Gregor Samsa as human-animal hybrid, once again, condenses something which the reader feels must be significant but whose meaning is elusive. The effect is reinforced since Samsa has become a type of insect which apparently does not exist, a

---

[4] Critic Mark Spilka famously compares Kafka and Dickens, contending that the grotesque, in the two novelists' work, emerges from comedy seen from the viewpoint of the lonely child (see Spilka 1969). Kafka does not seem to have had a high opinion of the English novelist, whose work, interestingly enough, he described in terms reminiscent of the grotesque: "There is a heartlessness behind [Dickens's] sentimentally overflowing style; [...] the whole does not make sense" (Kafka 1976, 388).

"horrible vermin," (Kafka 2005, Part I) an "anomalous [one] … [which] stands between the categories of an existing classification system" (Stewart 1979, 61). Kafka thus intensifies the grotesque effect by adding to the hybridity of the metamorphosis the indecision of Gregor Samsa's new species–and a dose of the absurd, with the "catastrophic intrusion" of an "overwhelming counter-world" (Gray et al. 2005, 112).

And yet humour is not absent from Gregor's world, for example when he discovers his new body and tries to get out of bed:

> He would have used his arms and his hands to push himself up; but instead of them he only had all those little legs continuously moving in different directions, and which he was moreover unable to control. If he wanted to bend one of them, then that was the first one that would stretch itself out; and if he finally managed to do what he wanted with that leg, all the others seemed to be set free. (Kafka 2005, Part I)

Because *The Metamorphosis* is centred on Gregor's body, its disgusting ugliness and miserable wounds, Kafka forces deformity and the irrational to collide with the norm while simultaneously strongly tying them together. The uncanny is powerfully coupled to normality, the mimetic to the anti-mimetic, so much so that it is possible to postulate that the grotesque here (as elsewhere) provides the missing link between the real and the fantastic.

The return to literal human-animal hybrids, much more daring than anything the realist novel of the 19th century could attempt, is used also as a pretext to a metatextual questioning of enunciation and narrative vision– a logical move at a time when modernism brought to the fore the necessity to explore new narrative modes. *The Metamorphosis* offers quite a complex narrative system in which internal focalisation shows Gregor-turned-vermin still trying to verbalize human emotions he can no longer quite feel or master, in segments pointing to animality.[5] His deep confusion is felt for example during his mother's only visit to his room:

> Hearing these words from his mother made Gregor realise that the lack of any direct human communication [...] must have made him confused–he could think of no other way of explaining to himself why he had seriously wanted his room emptied out. Had he really wanted to transform his room into a cave, a warm room fitted out with the nice furniture he had inherited? That would have let him crawl around unimpeded in any direction, but it would also have let him quickly forget his past when he

---

[5] For a more detailed analysis, see Burkart 2008.

had still been human. He had come very close to forgetting, and it had only been the voice of his mother, unheard for so long, that had shaken him out of it. Nothing should be removed; everything had to stay; he could not do without the good influence the furniture had on his condition. (Part II)

As early as the beginning of the story the likelihood that such a narrative might be produced seems very doubtful, filtered as it is by the mind of a human-insect hybrid. Grotesque enunciation, constantly verging on the absurd, remains here poised between normality (with the use of classic internal focalisation) and the supernatural. Like Kafkaesque grotesque, it may be seen as the missing link–the missing narrative mode–between realism and the fantastic.

References

Bakhtin, Mikhail. (1965) 1984. *Rabelais and His World.* Translated by Hélène Iswolsky. Bloomington: Indiana University Press.

Benjamin, Walter. (1925) 1977. *The Origin of German Tragic Drama.* Translated by John Osborne. New-York: Verso.

Burkart, Milena. 2008. "De la dislocation au dédoublement: voies de la création grotesque chez Kafka." In *Le Grotesque dans la littérature des XIXe et XXe siècles*, edited by Françoise Susini Anastopoulos, 71-87. Nancy: Presses Universitaires de Nancy.

Gray, Richard T., Gross Ruth V., Goebel Rolf J., Koelb, Clayton. 2005. *A Franz Kafka Encyclopedia.* Wesport: Greenwood Press.

Harpham, Geoffrey Galt. 1982. *On the Grotesque: Strategies of Contradiction in Art and Literature.* Princeton: Princeton University Press.

Kafka, Franz. (1915) 2005. *The Metamorphosis.* Translated by David Wyllie. The Project Gutenberg eBook.
http://www.gutenberg.org/files/5200/5200-h/5200-h.htm

—. (1910-23) 1976. *Diaries.* Translated by Joseph Kresh and Martin Greenberg. New-York: Schocken Books.

Kayser, Wolfgang. (1957) 1966. *The Grotesque in Art and Literature.* Translated by Ulrich Weisstein. New-York: McGraw-Hill.

Montaigne, Michel de. (1580) 1976. "On Friendship." In *The Complete Essays of Montaigne*, translated by Donald M. Frame, 135-44. Stanford: Stanford University Press.

Rosen, Elisheva. 1991. *Sur le grotesque. L'Ancien et le nouveau dans la réflexion esthétique.* Vincennes: Presses Universitaires de Vincennes. [1991-1]

—. 1991. "Grotesque, modernité." *Romantisme*, 74: 23-8. [1991-2]

Ruskin, John. (1853) 2009. *Stones of Venice, Vol. III: The Fall*. The
    Project Gutenberg eBook.
    http://gutenberg.readingroo.ms/3/0/7/5/30756/30756-h/30756-h.htm
Singley, Paulette. 1997. "Devouring Architecture: Ruskin's Insatiable
    Grotesque." *Assemblage* 32: 108-25. The MIT Press.
    Stable URL: http://www.jstor.org/stable/3171411.
Spilka, Mark. 1969. *Dickens and Kafka: A Mutual Interpretation*.
    Gloucester, MA: Peter Smith Pub Inc.
Stewart, Susan. 1979. *Nonsense: Aspects of Intertextuality in Folklore and
    Literature*. Baltimore: The Johns Hopkins University Press.

CONTRIBUTORS

Florence Bigo-Renault has just completed her PhD on recent television adaptations of Charles Dickens's novels, from *Nicholas Nickleby* (2001) to *Bleak House* (2005), *Oliver Twist* (2007), *Little Dorrit* (2008), and *Great Expectations* (2011). Her current research focuses on the historical, aesthetic and sociological aspects of adaptation.

Delphine Cadwallader-Bouron wrote her PhD on the influence of Victorian literature on the new developing science of medicine, with special emphasis on Charles Dickens and Wilkie Collins. She now works on the construction, through history, of the relationship between patients and doctors.

Marianne Camus is Professor Emerita of English Literature at Dijon University. She works on the relationships between aesthetics and ideology (gender and class) in nineteenth-century fiction. She has published a number of articles on the subject and two books, *Women's Voices in the Fiction of Elizabeth Gaskell* (Mellen, 2002) and *Gender and Madness in the Novels of Charles Dickens* (Mellen, 2003). She has opened up her field of research to other forms of art (visual and performance) with regular seminars and has edited five books on women and the creative process (*Création au féminin: I Littérature, II Arts visuels,* EUD, 2006; *Filiations,* EUD, 2008; *Les Humeurs de l'humour,* EUD 2010 and *Les Passeuses,* 2012).

Bérangère Chaumont is *agrégée* in French Literature. She is completing her PhD on "The Representation of Nocturnal Feasts in French Romantic Literature (1820-1855)" at the University of Nantes. Her research focuses on the representation of the night in visual arts and literature.

Florence Clerc is a former student of the *Ecole Normale Supérieure* (Saint-Cloud) and Senior Lecturer at Blaise-Pascal University in Clermont-Ferrand. She wrote her PhD on "Gogol and the Spanish Picaresque Tradition." The focus of her research is Spanish Literature of the 16th- and 17th-centuries and comparative literature (the Picaresque tradition, the birth of the European novel, mutual Russian and Spanish influences).

Jacqueline Fromonot is Senior Lecturer at the University of Paris-8 (France), where she teaches translation. The focus of her research is 19th-century British literature (Charlotte Brontë, Charles Dickens and William Makepeace Thackeray, in particular), and her interests include narratology, pragmatics and stylistics. She is a member of the *Société de Stylistique Anglaise* (SSA).

Thierry Goater is Senior Lecturer at the University of Rennes 2. His research mainly focuses on 19th- and early 20th-century British literature. He has published articles on Jane Austen, Thomas Hardy, D. H. Lawrence, E. M. Forster, a monograph on Thomas Hardy (*Thomas Hardy: Figures de l'aliénation,* Presses Universitaires de Rennes, 2010) and co-edited *L'engagement dans les romans féminins de la Grande-Bretagne des XVIIIe et XIXe siècles,* Presses Universitaires de Rennes, 2012.

Isabelle Hervouet-Farrar is Senior Lecturer in English Literature at Blaise Pascal University in Clermont-Ferrand. She wrote her PhD on the Gothic novel in Britain (1764-1824) and has published several articles on the persistence of the Gothic in the Victorian novel and in the sensation novel. Her research now focuses on several aspects of Dickens's fiction and that of Charlotte Brontë. She is the editor of a volume on the representation of wandering children in 19th-century literature (*Enfance et errance dans la literature européenne du dix-neuvième siècle,* Presses Universitaires Blaise Pascal, 2011).

Michael Hollington is Honorary Research Fellow at the University of Kent, Canterbury. Prior to retirement, he was Professor at the University of New South Wales in Sydney, Australia, and latterly at the University of Toulouse-Le Mirail. He has published widely on Dickens, including books on *Dickens and the Grotesque* (1984), on *David Copperfield* (1996), on *Great Expectations* (1999) and *A Tale of Two Cities* (2012); and a number of edited publications including the four-volume *Charles Dickens: Critical Assessments* and *The Reception of Charles Dickens in Europe* (Bloomsbury, two volumes).

Sylvie Jeanneret is Reader in French Literature at the University of Fribourg (Switzerland). She wrote her PhD on "Music and the Poetics of Modernity in the Works of Etienne Barilier." Her research interests include the literature of French-speaking Switzerland from the second half of the 20th century to the present day, and 19th-century French literature, especially Victor Hugo's novels. She has published several articles on

Victor Hugo, Marguerite Duras and other French-speaking authors. She is currently working on Swiss authors Etienne Barilier, Rose-Marie Pagnard and Ella Maillart.

Dominique Peyrache-Leborgne is Reader in Comparative Literature at the University of Nantes. She is a specialist of aesthetic issues in European Romanticism, and has published books and articles on Romantic and post-Romantic Sublime, Grotesque and Arabesque. She is the author of *Grotesques et arabesques dans le récit romantique. De Jean Paul à Victor Hugo* (Paris, Honoré Champion, 2012). Her research focuses on authors such as Friedrich Schiller, William Wordsworth, the brothers Grimm, Jean Paul, Victor Hugo and Edgar Poe.

Gilbert Pham-Thanh is Senior Lecturer at the University Paris 13. He is currently exploring new aspects of dandyism, manners, elegance and masculinity in 19th-century fiction. He is a member of the *Centre d'Etudes des Nouveaux Espaces Littéraires*, the *Société française d'études anglophones sur les femmes, le sexe et le genre* and the *Société Française d'Etudes Victoriennes et Edouardiennes*.

Anne Rouhette is a Senior Lecturer at Blaise Pascal University in Clermont-Ferrand, where she teaches British Literature and translation. Her research focuses mostly on the novel in the 18th century and the Romantic era. She is the author of several articles on 18th- and 19th-century literature from Frances Burney to Matthew Arnold and of *Correspondences: Frances Burney's* Evelina (Fahrenheit, 2013). She also translated and edited Mary Shelley's *Fortunes of Perkin Warbeck* (*Les Aventures de Perkin Warbeck*, Classiques Garnier, 2014) and is currently working on a translation and edition of the Shelleys' 1817 travel narrative, *A History of a Six Weeks' Tour*.

Victor Sage is an Emeritus Professor of English Literature in the School of Literature, Drama and Creative Writing at the University of East Anglia, Norwich, UK. He has edited Maturin's *Melmoth the Wanderer* and Le Fanu's *Uncle Silas*, for Penguin Classics; and he is the author of *Le Fanu's Gothic: The Rhetoric of Darkness*. Recent work includes essays on Dickens, Ludwig Tieck and German Gothic, Nicola Barker and the Grotesque, J.G. Ballard, Kazuo Ishiguro, Scott, E.T.A Hoffmann and the French "Fantastique," and Scottish Women's Gothic. He is currently working on a book on the transmission of Gothic in Europe.

Max Véga-Ritter is Emeritus Professor at Blaise Pascal University in Clermont-Ferrand. He wrote his PhD on Charles Dickens and W. M. Thackeray. He has edited two issues of *Cahiers Victoriens et Edouardiens* devoted to Charles Dickens's fiction, and co-edited a volume on gender issues in European fiction (*L'un(e) mirroir de l'autre,* Presses Universitaires Blaise Pascal). He has published a number of articles about Charles Dickens, Charlotte Brontë, W. M. Thackeray, George Eliot, Rudyard Kipling, Virginia Woolf, Hanif Kureishi and on Algerian literature from a post-colonial perspective.

Isabel Vila Cabanes studied English Philology at the Universities of Valencia and Ghent. She currently works as a research assistant at Jena University, where she is a PhD candidate. Her most recent publications include "Dickens' Uncommercial Traveller as a *Flâneur*" (2012), co-authored with Wolfgang G. Müller; and "Zwei Dokumente der frühen Flaneur-Tradition. Edition und Kommentar" (2013).

INDEX